Saussure and his Interpreters

Second edition

Roy Harris

Edinburgh University Press

© Roy Harris, 2001, 2003

First edition published 2001 by
Edinburgh University Press

Edinburgh University Press Ltd
22 George Square, Edinburgh

Typeset in 11 on 13 pt Ehrhardt
by Hewer Text Ltd, Edinburgh, and
printed and bound in Spain by
GraphyCems

A CIP record for this book is
available from the British Library

ISBN 0 7486 1783 3 (paperback)

Contents

Preface

Anyone who chooses to write about Saussure in English immediately takes up various self-inflicted burdens. It could be argued that most of Saussure's theoretical distinctions would have taken a rather different form if French had not been the language of his lectures (even though he claimed – on rather dubious grounds – that his definitions were of 'things' not of 'words'). Be that as it may, there soon comes a point at which any commentator must have recourse to citing the French texts available. I have done this wherever it seemed to me that the original wording was important or indispensable for the clarification of a particular issue (which is most of the time). My discussion also assumes that the reader is familiar not only with French but with the Francophone tradition of Saussurean studies, including the monumental critical edition of the *Cours de linguistique générale* by Rudolf Engler, to which everyone now engaged in this field is indebted. (The reason why I did not include a chapter on 'Engler's Saussure' is that Engler's Saussure is already familiar to all serious students of the *CLG*.)

However, discussing Saussure in English is an enterprise fraught with familiar problems of its own, prominent among which is the lamentable tendency of scholars who should know better to translate *langue* just as 'language' (without an article), thus immediately blurring Saussure's distinction between *langue* and *langage*. I hope that readers will find the chapters which follow to be free at least from elementary howlers of this order, even if they object to the kind of intellectual Franglais that they plunge into.

Why not just write about Saussure in French and thus avoid all these metalinguistic problems? Part of the answer lies in the fact that Saussurean studies have become part of an international curriculum; a fact which in itself forces one to recognize that Saussure's ideas have a cultural importance no longer limited by the historical circumstances in which they first gained recognition. (If all commentary on Plato had been in

Greek, how many of us would ever have heard of Socrates?) But perhaps more important is the consideration that discussing Saussure in French runs the very real risk of gliding over the surface of some basic problems of exegesis. Such problems are concealed by the ease with which it is possible in French to slip from a technical to a non-technical register, and back again, in the use of terms such as *langue*, *langage* and *parole*. Having French as one's first (or sole) language can thus be as much a hindrance as a help in focussing on some of the conceptual nuances which are of such importance in trying to come to terms with Saussure's thinking.

In previously published work on Saussure, beginning with my translation of the *CLG* (1983), *Reading Saussure* (1987), *Language, Saussure and Wittgenstein* (1988), and the publication of Constantin's notebooks for Saussure's Third Course (1993), I acknowledged indebtedness to students and colleagues in the UK, France and other countries. Since such debts are cumulative, all those acknowledgments should by rights be reiterated here. But they have over the course of time become too numerous to itemize. All I can say to my many helpers is that I hope they will not be too displeased with the use I have made of what I learnt from them. I would like nevertheless to express special thanks to Eisuke Komatsu and George Wolf, collaboration with whom in the publication of Saussurean material has been an invaluable experience.

A reviewer once wondered why I devoted so much attention to Saussure, a theorist with whom I so obviously disagreed on very basic issues. Anyone interested in an answer must look to my own unSaussurean excursions into linguistic theory. For most of the twentieth century, being a linguistic theorist meant *inter alia* having to take a view of some kind with respect to the teachings of Saussure. That is no bad thing. For exactly how and why one agrees or disagrees with Saussure is sometimes more revealing than anything else in identifying a theoretical position. In this respect, the work of Saussure is still a landmark in the history of linguistic thought and seems likely to remain so for the foreseeable future.

R. H.
Oxford, March 2000

Preface to the Second Edition

An observant reader of the first edition of this book told me that he thought he detected, underlying the various cases discussed, a more general thesis concerning the history of ideas. Not just the history of Saussure's ideas, but the history of ideas in general. He was not mistaken. He was also right in relating that underlying thesis to the author's adoption of an integrationist philosophy of language.

The same inquirer wanted to know why that philosophical allegiance had not been made explicit from the outset. The answer is that I preferred to leave readers to draw their own conclusions, unprompted by theoretical nudges from me. But the time has now come to own up, since new material, published since the first edition of this book appeared, itself raises the question of Saussure's integrationist leanings, irrespective of any views of mine. Those leanings went unnoticed by Saussure's contemporaries and were perhaps, for pedagogic reasons, temporarily suppressed by Saussure himself. But in the logic of Saussurean inquiry they cannot be ignored, because they would undoubtedly have surfaced in the lectures on *linguistique de la parole* that Saussure promised but never delivered. Arguably, indeed, an integrationist perspective is the rational termination of that line of thinking about language which regards signs as determined only by their relationships with other signs.

For my part, I am happier to welcome into the historical spectrum a new 'integrationist' Saussure than an old 'structuralist' Saussure whom I never wholeheartedly trusted. As regards the broader question concerning history of ideas, I confess to believing that, in Saussure's case, as in that of other revolutionary thinkers (from Plato to Marx), what survives and is highlighted is whatever can be integrated into the intellectual agendas of their successors. Whatever proves recalcitrant to any easy form of integration tends to drop out of sight: such is the way of the world. So the process of integration involves a recontextualization. That inevitably reshapes in certain respects perceptions of the original thinking.

Thus every reaching out from the present to grasp the past, for whatever motives, has to be seen not as a reconstruction of that which is no longer present, but as a projection into the future of something that already exists only in hindsight. That, at least, is my understanding of the limits within which it is possible for us to understand Saussure today. Within those limits, and having read a great deal of what Saussure's successors had to say about his work, I feel confident that my discussion does not overlook anything of importance to date. If it does, critics will surely not be slow to point it out. And then it will be up to even smarter critics to show how those omissions alter the Saussure we have been content with hitherto. One can only pave the way for new readings of Saussure, however enlightened or misguided those readings may be.

It would indeed be possible to show how, if various *dicta* of Saussure had been emphasized and others marginalized, the world might by now have quite different received versions of Saussurean ideas about language. But such exploratory investigations are not, as yet, accepted by most Western universities as 'research'. Examiners prefer the less imaginative excavation of archive material, and award doctorates accordingly.

I should like to take this opportunity of thanking Barbara Roth, keeper of manuscripts at the Bibliothèque Publique et Universitaire at Geneva, and her staff, for all their help in the work that has gone into this second edition of *Saussure and his Interpreters*. I should also like to record my gratitude to Rita Harris for keeping a vigilant eye on my text and for making many valuable suggestions.

R. H.
Oxford, April 2003

Abbreviations

CLG	F. de Saussure, *Cours de linguistique générale*, ed. Ch. Bally and A. Sechehaye, 2nd edn, Paris: Payot, 1922.
CLG1	F. de Saussure, *Premier Cours de linguistique générale (1907) d'après les cahiers d'Albert Riedlinger*, ed./tr. E. Komatsu and G. Wolf, Oxford: Pergamon, 1996.
CLG2	F. de Saussure, *Deuxième Cours de linguistique générale (1908–1909) d'après les cahiers d'Albert Riedlinger et Charles Patois*, ed./tr. E. Komatsu and G. Wolf, Oxford: Pergamon, 1997.
CLG3	F. de Saussure, *Troisième Cours de linguistique générale (1910–1911) d'après les cahiers d'Émile Constantin*, ed./tr. E. Komatsu and R. Harris, Oxford: Pergamon, 1993.
Coll.	A. Sechehaye, *Collation*, Bibliothèque Publique et Universitaire de Genève, MS. Cours univ. 432–3. (References are to page numbers of the manuscript. These do not always coincide with those given in Engler).
De Mauro	T. De Mauro, *Édition critique du Cours de Linguistique Générale de F. de Saussure*, tr. L.-J. Calvet, Paris: Payot, 1972.
ELG	S. Bouquet and R. Engler (eds), *Écrits de linguistique générale par Ferdinand de Saussure*, Paris: Gallimard, 2002.
Engler	R. Engler, *Édition critique du Cours de Linguistique Générale de Ferdinand de Saussure*, Wiesbaden: Harrassowitz, 1968. (References in small Roman numerals are to the pages of the Preface, and in Arabic numerals to the sections of the text as numbered by Engler.)
Godel	R. Godel, *Les sources manuscrites du Cours de Linguistique Générale de F. de Saussure*, Geneva: Droz (Paris: Minard), 1957. (References are to page numbers.)

CHAPTER ONE

Interpreting the Interpreters

No one writing about Saussure today needs to take on the task of establishing the historical importance of Saussurean ideas; for that has already been established beyond question and many times over. Saussure's influence, direct and indirect, dominates the twentieth-century development of those academic disciplines devoted to the study of language, languages and the analysis of texts. It has also been widespread in disciplines in which Saussure himself laid no claim to personal expertise: these include anthropology, sociology and psychology. However, whether what pass for Saussurean ideas in these various areas are always authentically Saussure's is another question and a much trickier one.

The distinction between a Saussurean idea and an idea attributable to Saussure may at first sound like academic hair-splitting. If it were, writing a book such as this would have been a waste of time. So it may be as well to begin with a fairly simple illustration of the difference.

Here is an example concerning the notion of linguistic units. We have, on the one hand, what Saussure is on record as actually having said about linguistic units. We know, for example, that he distinguished between synchronic units and diachronic units (Engler: 2724 ff.), between *unités linguistiques* and *unités de la parole* (*CLG3*: 78–9), regarding the syllable as a unit of the latter class and not of the former (*CLG3*: 79), and so on. On the other hand, many questions arise concerning what might reasonably be inferred from these remarks, which are scattered throughout the three Courses. There is, for instance, the question of whether what Saussure says about linguistic units is internally consistent. How far can their apparent implications be taken? To what extent did Saussure intend these implications to be evident? Did he always grasp these implications himself? For instance, does his insistence on the necessity of identifying individual synchronic units by reference to the linguistic system (*langue*) as a whole provide a warrant for concluding that some linguistic units are less well established than others? At least one commentator sees this as validating the notion that there are (linguistic) 'degrees' of class-membership.

> On dirait par exemple que *déjeuner* appartient de façon moins nette que *déplacer* à la série < *défaire, décoller* . . . >. Pour justifier cette affirmation, on noterait que si le couple *jeuner | déjeuner* est analogue à *faire | défaire*, il n'y a pas en revanche de couple *rejeuner | déjeuner* à mettre en face de *refaire | défaire*. On pourrait ainsi souligner que *déjeuner* entre dans une proportion où l'on ne rencontre aucun autre verbe en *dé*, celle qui comprend les couples *déjeuner* (verbe) | *déjeuner* (nom), *dîner* (verbe) | *dîner* (nom), *faire* (verbe) | *faire* (nom) . . . etc. Il devient ainsi possible de donner un sens linguistique précis à l'idée, mathématiquement aberrante, d'une plus ou moins forte appartenance de l'élément à sa classe. Du même coup, on pourrait définir des degrés de segmentation, et admettre par exemple que les éléments de *dé-jeuner* sont moins séparés que ceux de *dé-faire*, ce qui rend assez bien compte du sentiment des utilisateurs de la langue: pour eux l'analyse *dé-jeuner*, sans être franchement inadmissible, ne semble pas néanmoins tout à fait naturelle.
> (Ducrot 1968: 52)

Although the example does not translate into English, it has a rough English parallel in the question of whether the verb *breakfast* should be regarded as composed of the two units *break* and *fast*, breakfast being the occasion on which one supposedly 'breaks one's fast'. (This sounds like a silly question, in which etymology and morphology have become confused; but it is the kind of silly question that has to be taken seriously if we wish to examine what kind of analysis is implicit in Saussure's proclaimed principles.) For present purposes, the point of the example is that although Saussure never – as far as we know – explicitly proposed that the class membership of linguistic units was a matter of degree, this can – at least, on one interpretation – be seen as a 'Saussurean' idea, i.e. as consonant with or even implied by what Saussure is known to have said.

This, however, is a fairly straightforward case, inasmuch as drawing the line between interpretation and evidence is not in dispute. (Ducrot, the commentator quoted above, freely admits that the concept of 'degrees' of class-membership goes beyond 'la lettre de Saussure', while nevertheless maintaining the validity of this interpretation.) The more general problem is that the majority of Saussure's most original contributions to linguistic thought have passed through one or more filters of interpretation. Very little of what Saussure himself put on paper about general linguistics in his Geneva years is extant, and what there is has come down in a fragmentary state. The rest – almost all of what is known of Saussure's courses of lectures on the subject from 1907 to 1911 – is interpretation of one kind or another. So much so that even the name 'Saussure' has come to be used by scholars and critics in at least three different ways.

(1) It is often used for convenience as the name of the putative author of the *Cours de linguistique générale,* even though it is known that the linguist to whom the work is credited did not in fact write it. Attributing a certain view to the Saussure of the *CLG* is in effect little more than saying that this view appears in, or can be inferred from, the text of the *CLG,* as posthumously produced by the editors. (2) 'Saussure' can also be used as the name of the lecturer who actually gave the courses of lectures at Geneva on which the *CLG* was based. Attributing a view to this Saussure requires evidence contained in the lecture notes of his students or the scraps of the lecturer's own notes that survive; for there is no other evidence. Furthermore, such attributions must be treated with caution, since the lecturer elaborated both his views and his terminology from one course of lectures to the next. The best published evidence for this Saussure is contained in Engler's critical edition (cited here as 'Engler') and the Pergamon editions of the students' course notes published by Komatsu and his colleagues (cited here as *CLG1, CLG2* and *CLG3,* which contain material not included in Engler). (3) The third Saussure is the putative theorist 'behind' the Geneva lectures; the theorist for whom the lectures were a way of trying out various ideas about language that he had been pondering for a long time, hoping to be able to put these ideas into a coherent form that would be accessible and useful to his students. To gain insight into the thinking of this third Saussure, it may sometimes be necessary to discount oversimplifications that were intended for the benefit of a student audience, or overinterpretations supplied by zealous editors. But whether this theorist reached a mature, definitive formulation of his linguistic views before his death is open to question. His promised lectures on *linguistique de la parole* were never given, and there is no surviving evidence that they were even drafted.

It is unfortunately the case that commentators often conflate these three Saussures, or proceed as if citing evidence relevant to one of them sufficed to establish a point about another. Given this state of affairs and the limitations on our knowledge of what Saussure taught, the question of Saussure's interpreters assumes particular importance: perhaps greater importance than in the case of any other major figure in the history of ideas in the twentieth century. As with other major figures, however, the interpreters in question fall into two main classes: contemporaries and successors. This is not simply a division of chronological convenience: it corresponds almost inevitably to different perspectives of interpretation.

Contemporaries assess a teacher in the first instance by reference to what other contemporary teaching is fashionable, or at least available. (Does teacher T_1 say anything significantly different from what is said by contemporaries T_2, T_3, . . . ?) In the case of contemporary assessments it is pertinent to inquire what personal relations obtained between the interpreters and the teacher in question, for these will be relevant to any assessment of the interpretations offered. For Saussure, we have evidence supplied by two very different groups of contemporary interpreters: on the one hand, Saussure's own students and, on the other, Saussure's colleagues, who were also his editors. These two groups already introduce very different interpretive perspectives.

In the case of successors, crucial questions will be what distance in time and intellectual inheritance separates each of them from Saussure's generation, as well as what sources of information about Saussure were available to them and what purpose their own intepretation of Saussure was intended to serve. As Saussure's generation recedes ever further into the past, the reassessment of other figures of the past inevitably has repercussions on the view that comes to be taken of Saussure's life and work. It is not so much a question of discovering a new Saussure as of reinterpreting a whole pattern of history.

Thus, to take one obvious example, Saussure has been commonly regarded by later commentators – and this term will recur constantly in the chapters that follow – as a pioneer of 'structuralism'. This perspective on his work was quite unfamiliar to his contemporaries, to whom, as to Saussure himself, the epithet 'structuralist' would have meant little. As the subtitle of Georges Mounin's book (Mounin 1968) puts it epigrammatically, Saussure was a 'structuraliste sans le savoir'. Mounin points out that the term *structure* occurs only three times in the *CLG*, and on none of these occasions is it used in the sense of *système*.

Now if calling Saussure a 'structuralist' were merely a question of giving Saussure a retrospective label he would not have recognized, it might not matter a great deal. But it entails much more than that. It involves putting a particular slant on his teaching and making certain assumptions about the relative importance and purpose of various points, including quite specific passages in the surviving textual sources.

For instance, to return to the example of linguistic units, commentators have disagreed about the account given by Saussure of how native speakers come to identify the basic units of their own language (Engler: 1713 ff.). The relevant passage in the *CLG* reads:

> Celui qui possède une langue en délimite les unités par une méthode fort simple
> – du moins en théorie. Elle consiste à se placer dans la parole, envisagée comme

document de langue, et à la représenter par deux chaînes parallèles, celle des concepts (a) et celle des images acoustiques (b). (*CLG*: 146)

A correct analysis will be one in which the divisions in each of the two parallel chains (a) and (b) coincide all along the line.

According to Ducrot, however, this simplistic picture of an utterance (i.e. as comprising the simultaneous unfolding of a set of acoustic images in parallel with a set of matching concepts) is not to be taken too seriously. It was 'conçue surtout comme une introduction pédagogique et destinée à être ensuite rectifiée' (Ducrot 1968: 49). Unfortunately, Ducrot complains, it suffered 'le sort habituel de ces introductions' and was treated not as an introduction but as a conclusion, at least by 'lecteurs pressés'.

So the claim is that what found its way into the *CLG* text was merely a provisional account of the matter, to be refined or replaced subsequently. If we ask on what evidence the claim is based, it soon becomes clear that there is little to support any such conclusion in the extant manuscripts. But the reason why Ducrot is inclined to dismiss or marginalize this passage on contrastive segmentation is not difficult to see: it does not fit very happily with the historical role assigned to Saussure in Ducrot's book (of which the title is *Le structuralisme en linguistique*). In other words, given Ducrot's view of structuralism, contrastive segmentation is not in fact a particularly 'structuralist' mode of analysis. It harks back to a much less sophisticated view of how language works. It could, in principle, be invoked by linguists whose theoretical positions were far removed from Saussure's. Setting aside this misleading picture of the chain of speech, Ducrot directs his readers' attention instead to the chapter in the *CLG* on the 'mécanisme de la langue'. Here, and not in the section on segmentation, Ducrot detects Saussure's authentic and original contribution to the problem of delimiting linguistic units.

The point is that the key to this interpretation is Ducrot's conception of the way in which the notion of linguistic structure had developed historically. According to him, the traditional view, going back to the Graeco-Roman grammarians, was that every language exhibited an internal system of organization of its own (which it was the grammarian's task to describe in detail). So this idea did not by any means originate with Saussure:

Le rôle de Saussure n'est donc certainement pas d'avoir introduit ce thème, mais de l'avoir retrouvé, et surtout d'avoir pu l'imposer après les succès impressionnants de la grammaire comparée. (Ducrot 1968: 43)

In Ducrot's history of structuralism, the comparative grammarians represent an obstacle to be overcome. Their backward-looking view of linguistic structure led them to envisage it as being constantly eroded by the destructive operations of phonetic change. Thus, at any given point in the history of a language, the linguist was confronted not by a coherent grammatical system but by the ruins of former systems. Saussure, according to Ducrot, fought against this view by attacking the underlying notion of linguistic units. He maintained that the identification of particular linguistic units was not the trivial matter the comparativists had supposed. Forms could *not* be analysed by simple inspection. The identification of linguistic units required a careful investigation which took into consideration the linguistic system as a whole: for the existence of the latter was reflected in the existence of the former.

Dans l'élément présupposer le système, cela constitue, selon nous, l'apport propre de Saussure au structuralisme linguistique. (Ducrot 1968: 44. Italics in the original.)

Seen in this light, the contrastive segmentation described earlier is scarcely viable as a reliable procedure for the identification of linguistic units: for it is, in effect, the lay counterpart of the method relied on by the comparative grammarians. (Thus, for example, the assumed correspondence between the Latin genitive and the Greek genitive was based on identifying word segments – endings in this instance – which had the same or comparable case meanings in both languages.) Saussure, consequently, needs to be seen as rejecting rather than embracing that method if he is to play the role required in Ducrot's scenario. Saussure's 'old-fashioned' account of linear segmentation is thus awkward. Ducrot's solution is to explain it away as no more than a simplistic preliminary formulation introduced for purely pedagogic reasons. The way is then clear to highlight the interlocking of associative series as the 'real' mechanism involved in the identification of linguistic units.

But what, in the end, do we learn from this? Saussure, everyone agrees, commented *both* on contrastive segmentation *and* on associative series as having a bearing on the problem of identifying linguistic units. The question is: what did he see the relationship as being? There are certainly other interpretations available than the one Ducrot proposes. For instance, Saussure might have realized that the interlocking of associative series does not make much sense unless the items in the series are already subject to some form of analysis. Otherwise, on what basis would the various series be set up in the first place? An intuitive capacity for contrastive segmentation could thus appear to be both logically and psychologically necessary as part of any hypothesis about the human *faculté de langage*. But in that case Saussure's remarks on segmentation, far from being no more than a pedagogic *entrée en matière*, actually set out an explanation of how associative series are established.

But whether Ducrot is right is not the issue here. The point of taking this example is that Ducrot's interpretation clearly arises not from an 'internal' study of the textual evidence, but from an 'external' view of how Saussure contributed to the broader development of structuralism as later continued by Hjelmslev, Trubetzkoy and others. It is Saussure's place in that line of descent which makes the remarks on associative series seem important but the remarks on contrastive segmentation something of an embarrassment. In other words, historical hindsight here suggests a different interpretation of Saussure's teaching than might have seemed natural or even plausible to Saussure's contemporaries.

A somewhat more complex example of the same kind is the following. It would never have occurred to Bally and Sechehaye in 1916 to compare Saussure's view of the sign with that of C. S. Peirce (for the very good reason that Peirce's work was unknown in Europe at that time). However, the comparison subsequently occurred to a number of scholars. Such a comparison inevitably leads to a search on the one hand for similarities and on the other hand for differences between the two. This in turn may result in focussing attention on features that might not have seemed particularly significant in the teachings of either thinker if the comparison had not been undertaken in the first place.

According to Umberto Eco, for instance, the essential difference between Saussurean semiology and Peircean semiotics hinges on the notion of communication. For this is basic, in Eco's view, to the whole of Saussurean semiology, but not to Peircean semiotics. For Saussure

> the sign is implicitly regarded as a communicative device taking place between two human beings intentionally aiming to communicate or to express something. It is not by chance that all the examples of semiological systems given by Saussure are without any shade of doubt strictly conventionalized systems of artificial signs, such as military signals, rules of etiquette and visual alphabets. Those who share Saussure's notion of *sémiologie* distinguish sharply between intentional, artificial devices (which they call 'signs') and other natural or unintentional manifestations which do not, strictly speaking, deserve such a name. (Eco 1976: 15)

Peirce, on the other hand, according to Eco, is concerned with a much wider domain of semiosis, in which signs are not necessarily produced by human beings at all. The key roles in Peirce's scheme are filled not by human agents but by 'three abstract semiotic entities, the dialectic between which is not affected by concrete communicative behaviour' (Eco 1976: 15). These three abstract entities are *sign*, *object* and *interpretant*. So, unlike Saussure, Peirce does not reduce everything to 'a theory of communicative acts' (Eco 1976: 16).

Eco's account of Saussure's position appears to be based entirely on the *CLG*. The problem is that Eco's version does not in fact square with what the text of the *CLG* says. There semiology is presented as 'une science qui étudie la vie des signes au sein de la vie sociale' (*CLG*: 33). Nothing in this formulation requires the signs to be intentionally produced or devised by human agents. The requirement that signs play a role in social life does not, *pace* Eco, automatically exclude so-called 'natural' signs (such as medical symptoms and meteorological phenomena). Any type of natural occurrence can presumably function as a sign in social life and have consequences for social behaviour, on condition that it is recognized by the community as significant. Saussure's lack of interest in such cases does not mean that he fails to see or feels obliged to deny their status as signs: it is, rather, that by comparison with words and other 'non-natural' signs, the part they play in social life is relatively unimportant. Furthermore, they throw little or no light on the theoretically more complex and interesting case of the linguistic sign, which is Saussure's main concern.

Eco is also barking up the wrong tree by emphasizing the notion of intention. Nowhere in the *CLG* does reference to communicative intentions enter into the definition of the linguistic sign. That would be to confuse *faits de langue* with *faits de parole*. For Saussure, the system as such (*la langue*) has no intentions: it merely provides resources for those individuals who do have intentions, i.e. its speakers. (Such a mistake would be parallel to supposing that money buys goods and services, when in fact its function is merely to provide resources for those who do wish to buy goods and services.)

This is a clear case where the interpretation of Saussure's position has suffered from being forced into the straitjacket of comparison with the work of another theorist. The effort to establish a radical contrast between Saussure's sign and Peirce's has resulted in placing undue emphasis on features which may have been of little or no weight in Saussure's estimation.

Then again there are cases where Saussure is ushered on as a kind of stage illusionist to perform an amazing theoretical feat. Wellek and Warren in their *Theory of Literature* write:

> Linguists such as Ferdinand de Saussure and the Prague Linguistic Circle carefully
> distinguish between *langue* and *parole*, the system of language and the individual

speech-act; and this distinction corresponds to that between the poem as such and the individual experience of the poem. The system of language (*langue*) is a collection of conventions and norms whose workings and relations we can observe and describe as having a fundamental coherence and identity in spite of very different, imperfect, or incomplete pronouncements of individual speakers. In this respect at least, a literary work of art is in exactly the same position as a system of language. (Wellek and Warren 1962: 152)

Exactly the same position? In order to produce this unexpected Saussurean rabbit out of the conjuror's hat, the authors have to combine several substitutions in quick succession. The audience has to be gullible enough to accept the assimilation of *parole* to 'individual experience of the poem', together with the quite unSaussurean notion that a language is just 'a collection of conventions and norms', the no less unSaussurean notion that the 'workings and relations' involved can simply be 'observed', and finally the dubious logic by which, since *parole* = 'experience of the poem', then the poem = *langue*.

No supporting arguments are provided: that would presumably spoil the conjuring trick. But on the very next page the trick is already taken as a demonstration, and the reader is now expected to accept that there is no problem with seeing that 'the literary work of art' is actually a 'system of norms'. This is Saussurean magic, all done by mirrors.

An apparently much more straightforward deployment of Saussurean doctrine in the service of literature is exemplified by F. W. Bateson. His essay on 'Linguistics and literary criticism' (Bateson 1968) first appeared, ironically enough, in a *Festschrift* for René Wellek. Bateson analyses the Saussurean *circuit de la parole* with scrupulous attention to detail, and constructs on this basis a corresponding 'literary cycle' applied to the communication process of a literary work. Bateson's conclusion is as uncompromising as it is famous: 'linguistics, whether historical or descriptive, can contribute little to the study of literature' (Bateson 1968: 80). Whether that conclusion follows from the comparison as Bateson presents it is another question. The point worth noting here is that it is only when Bateson substitutes his own descriptions of the consecutive stages in the *circuit de la parole* for those that appear in the *CLG* that it begins to dawn on the reader that Bateson has quite a different conception of what is going on in the everyday act of speech. Presumably a reader unfamiliar with the *CLG* would never realize this; or at least take it for granted that Saussure's account is to all intents and purposes identical with Bateson's version of it. This is far from being so.

Bateson's account includes a mysterious process not mentioned in the *CLG* at all. This occurs when, in the speaker's brain, 'the "sound-images" detach themselves from the meaning' (Bateson 1968: 73). According to Bateson, the physical transmission of sound waves is the only stage in the whole sequence that is 'common to them both', i.e. to both speaker and hearer (Bateson 1968: 74). All the other stages belong to the two individuals separately. Again, anyone familiar with the *CLG* will recognize that the French text says nothing of the kind; and Bateson's description is in any case a very peculiar one. It is rather as if one were to describe how tennis is played by insisting that the only part of the game that the two players both share is the trajectory of the ball between one racquet and the other. Worse still, Bateson goes on to observe that 'it is at this physical level that words, in the ordinary sense, are interchanged'; whereas one of the main points of Saussure's analysis, according to most commentators, is to show that at this level nothing *linguistic* is going on at all. The items involved are sound waves, not words: they are physical vibrations and would be transmitted irrespective of whether or not *B* understood the language *A* was speaking. Bateson could hardly have contrived a more misleading commentary on what he nevertheless presents as 'Saussure's' speech circuit.

Then there are the interpreters whose own grasp of linguistics is so obviously shaky as to make it difficult to take anything they say about Saussure seriously. I do not – it hardly seems necessary to say – regard any of the interpreters discussed at length in this book as falling into this category, in spite of the howlers some of them occasionally perpetrate. But I will give just a couple of illustrations of the level of ineptitude I am now referring to. For missing the dartboard altogether, it is difficult to beat the pronouncement that 'Chomsky's transformations are a specific subset of Saussurean transformations' (Hodge and Kress 1988: 33). Or the following passage from Fredric Jameson's book *The Prison-House of Language*, where the author is discussing Saussure's 'image acoustique'. Jameson poses what is, in Saussurean terms, already a very odd question: 'At what point do sounds become acoustical images?' His answer is that it is all a matter of a shift in 'perception'.

> The acoustic image of signifier is made up of a series of differential or distinctive features. Our perception of a given phoneme is a differential perception, which is to say that we cannot identify a word as a singular masculine noun without at the same time apprehending it as *not* being a plural, or a feminine word, or an adjective. (Jameson 1972: 34)

This gives the impression of having been written by someone who had many years ago attended an undergraduate course in linguistics, but sat in the back row and whiled away most of the time doing crossword puzzles instead of taking notes. Unfortunately, it is not a-typical of the level which is often attained nowadays when Saussure is discussed under the rubric of 'critical theory' or 'cultural studies'.

* * *

It is important not to draw any mistaken conclusions from the various examples cited above. There is no question of the interpretations of Saussure's contemporaries always being 'right' and the retrospective interpretations of later generations 'wrong'; or vice versa. Nor should the views of Saussure's intimates necessarily have greater value than the views of those to whom he was always a somewhat remote, albeit respected, figure. These are simply views from different viewpoints, as doubtless Saussure would have been the first to insist. The important thing – he might have added – is not to mix synchrony with diachrony. This does not mean that no judgment can be passed on interpretations of either kind, nor that they can never come into conflict, but simply that the relevant criteria of assessment will be different in the two cases. One must not criticize Saussure's contemporaries for failing to see what would become apparent only later; nor Saussure's successors for pointing out what would not have been apparent in Saussure's day. Nevertheless, the binoculars of historical hindsight can distort and foreshorten, just as the contemporary microscope can sometimes give a close but too restricted view.

Neither binoculars nor microscope, however, can justify the number of times the *CLG* has been misquoted or sloppily paraphrased. There is the curious case of one commentator (Tallis 1988: 56) who discusses at length the implications of Saussure's phrase 'vague, uncharted nebula', without apparently realizing that these adjectives have been supplied by the American translator (Baskin 1959: 112) and do not appear in the *CLG* at all. But even scholars of note have been less than scrupulous in their attributions. It is disconcerting, for instance, to find Guillaume taking Saussure to task for proposing the equation: '*langage = langue + parole*', but then admitting airily that this equation 'ne se rencontre pas dans le livre'. He nevertheless proceeds as if it did, and refers to it as 'la formule de Saussure', objecting that it leaves out of account 'le facteur temps' (Guillaume 1948: 111). This is a quite astonishing objection, in view of the fact that this very point about *temps* and *langue* is made explicitly in the chapter Guillaume appears to be discussing (*CLG*: 112–13). In no less cavalier a fashion Jakobson tries to saddle Saussure with the thesis that *la parole*, unlike *la langue*, lacks homogeneity: 'la parole est à cheval sur différents domaines, étant physiologique d'une part, psychique de l'autre' (Jakobson 1942b: 430). But this is actually a transposed version of what the *CLG* says about *langage*: 'à cheval sur plusieurs domaines, à la fois physique, physiologique et psychique' (*CLG*: 25). Jakobson has conflated the two, thus making nonsense of Saussure's carefully drawn distinction between *langue* and *langage*. Likewise, Benveniste quotes Saussure as claiming: 'Le langage est forme, non substance' (Benveniste 1974: 31); whereas the text of the *CLG* has a quite different proposition: 'la langue est une forme et non une substance' (*CLG*: 169). Derrida cites *CLG*: 45 as 'Langage et écriture sont deux systèmes de signes distincts' (Derrida 1967: 46), where the text has 'Langue et écriture sont deux systèmes de signes distincts': the result is a complete misrepresentation of Saussure's point concerning writing's 'unique raison d'être'. (The same misquotation is perpetuated in Derrida 1972a: 179: an interesting detail in the work of a writer who has had so much to say about texts and repetition.) Wartburg claims: 'Saussure sagt: «Il nous est interdit absolument d'étudier simultanément les rapports dans le temps et les rapports dans le système»' (Wartburg 1939: 4), and proceeds forthwith to query this interdiction. But what he cites is a truncated version of a sentence which appears in the *CLG* as: 'La multiplicité des signes, déjà invoquée pour expliquer la continuité de la langue, nous interdit absolument d'étudier simultanément les rapports dans le temps et les rapports dans le système': a rather different point and a rather different use of the verb *interdire* than Wartburg's decontextualized version seems to imply. Merleau-Ponty, often said to be the most eminent philosopher influenced by Saussure, refers to Saussure's 'fameuse définition du signe' as a unit which is 'diacritique, oppositif et négatif' (Merleau-Ponty 1953: 33). This alleged definition seems to be a garbled account of the units that are described in the *CLG* as 'oppositives, relatives et négatives' (*CLG*: 164). But there the units in question are not signs but *phonèmes*. Signs, as the *CLG* makes clear, are positive elements (*CLG*: 166). Again, it would have been difficult for Merleau-Ponty to make a more complete muddle of Saussure's point.

The sorry list could be extended. These are not just casual or random errors: they illustrate how easy it is for commentators to convince themselves that Saussure said what they wanted him to say, and reconstruct the text of the *CLG* in their own minds accordingly.

*   *   *

The following chapters are not intended to present a comprehensive history of twentieth-century interpretations of Saussure. That would take many volumes and need many contributors. To appreciate the scale required for such an enterprise, it perhaps suffices to consider the extent to which Saussure's world-wide reputation was built on translation. The text of the *CLG* has been translated, in whole or in part, into Japanese, German, Russian, Spanish, English, Polish, Hungarian, Italian and, most recently, Chinese. Each translation is itself an interpretation: every translator is obliged to become an interpreter, for what was said in the *CLG* included things that had never been said before, either in French or in any other language. Furthermore, what was said there about differences between languages (*langues*) should have sufficed to raise serious doubts about the viability of interlingual translation as re-presentation of anyone's ideas. These would be problems that a historian of Saussure's legacy would have to tackle. No attempt will be made to engage with them here.

Nor should the reader assume that each chapter gives a comprehensive account of what Saussure's teaching meant to one particular interpreter (or school of interpreters). There are, for example, many more references to Saussure in the published works of Roland Barthes than have been taken into account (either tacitly or overtly) in my chapter on 'Barthes's Saussure'. If all those references had been given their full due, and corresponding analysis, the result would have been a book, not a chapter. And it would have been a book more about Barthes than about Saussure.

The question of my selection of interpreters is different again. Why, the reader may well ask, does Barthes merit a chapter and not, say, Gustave Guillaume? No one will deny the originality of Guillaume's work as a linguistic theorist. Unfortunately, Guilluame's *psycho-systématique*, although based to some extent on Saussurean principles, made little impact – in my judgment – on mainstream linguistics in the twentieth century and even less on the world of ideas outside. Furthermore, given Guillaume's *a priori* approach to linguistic psychology, it seems as time passes less and less likely to make any significant contribution in the future. Whereas Barthes, although – and perhaps because – a far shallower thinker than Guillaume, managed to project an awareness of Saussure's thinking to a much wider public.

Had more space been available, others who have been mentioned only *en passant* would have deserved chapters to themselves, including at least Meillet, Trubetzkoy, Jespersen, Martinet, Lacan and Merleau-Ponty; and some (including Voloshinov, Bakhtin, Piaget and Gardiner) who have not been mentioned at all. In short, what are picked out for discussion here are only a few landmarks in a complex intellectual landscape. The landmarks do indeed illustrate the range and diversity of interpretation to which Saussure's thinking about language has been subjected. But, even in the cases chosen, attention has been focussed on what I consider to be the most significant aspects of the interpreter's approach. Hence much has been neglected that would need to be mentioned in a well-documented history. Whether such a history will be attempted in the future remains to be seen. In any case, my main aim is not historiographical. Even less is it to set the historical record straight on Saussure's behalf. The questions which prompt my selection of interpreters have more to do with understanding what the fate of Saussure's ideas reveals about modern culture. What elements in Saussure's teaching made it simultaneously so controversial but so canonical? How did Saussure come to acquire this curious dual role as theoretical prophet-cum-scapegoat for the twentieth-century's obsessive concern with language? Why did attention focus in this way on the lectures diffidently – even reluctantly – given to a handful of students in the (then) quiet intellectual backwater of Geneva? What the reader is offered here are not answers to such questions but a rough framework in which to situate them.

CHAPTER TWO

The Students' Saussure

At one point in his notes on Saussure's First Course (*CLG1*: 65), Albert Riedlinger added in pencil: 'Je vois que tout le monde, au cours, avait compris comme moi, même Caille qui sténographiait!' The note confirms what we know from other sources: that Saussure's students were assiduous and conscientious note-takers, often checking with one another after the class, particularly on points where there was any doubt about their understanding of what Saussure had said (Engler: xii).

The point Riedlinger was querying in this instance is particularly significant. Here, for the first time, Saussure gives an explanation of his distinction between *langue* and *parole*. It would be a mistake to suppose that Saussure was merely spelling out pedantically an elementary terminological point that would already have been familiar to any member of his audience. No such distinction had ever been drawn by a French-speaking linguist before. What Saussure said, according to Riedlinger, was:

> Tout ce qui est amené sur les lèvres par les besoins du discours et par une opération particulière: c'est la *parole*.
> Tout ce qui est contenu dans le cerveau de l'individu, le dépôt des formes <entendues et> pratiquées et de leur sens: <c'est> la *langue*. (*CLG1*: 65)

There follows a little sketch (did Saussure draw it on the blackboard?) showing the schematic head of a speaker with a speech 'balloon' issuing forth from the mouth, as in the usual cartoon convention. The top half of the head is labelled '*sphère langue*' and the inside of the balloon '*s. parole*'. The text then continues:

> De ces deux sphères la sphère parole est la plus sociale, l'autre est la plus complètement individuelle. La langue est le réservoir individuel; tout ce qui entre dans la langue, c'est-à-dire dans la tête, est individuel.

We do not know when Riedlinger added his pencilled comment in the notebook, except that it was presumably after he had consulted the other students. What exactly was puzzling him in what Saussure had said, or in what he thought he had heard Saussure say?

Almost certainly it was a point which remained obscure in the Second Course and was not clarified until, in the Third Course, Saussure eventually produced his detailed account of the *circuit de la parole*. The question was: where precisely does the act of speech begin? For this makes a difference to what is included in *parole*, as distinct from what is included in *langue*. At first sight – or on first hearing – it might seem that the distinction can be mapped quite simply, physically and physiologically, by reference to what is internal and what is external. This is indeed the implication of the talking head with its speech 'balloon': the 'sphère parole' lies outside the speaker, the 'sphère langue' within. A moment's reflection, however, suggests that this cannot be quite right. That would limit the domain of *parole* to the audible public utterance. But everyday experience tells us that the activity involved is a process which begins inside the speaker's head, and the audible utterance is only its end-product. The phrase 'tout ce qui est amené sur les lèvres' (not 'tout ce que nous disons') seems implicitly to acknowledge this whole chain of events as belonging to *parole*.

If that is the case, however, the emphasis on the social nature of *parole*, as opposed to the individual nature of *langue*, seems puzzling. Should not all the contributions of the individual belong, by the same token, to *langue*? The three oppositions 'internal' vs. 'external', 'individual' vs. 'social' and '*langue*' vs. '*parole*', all invoked in a single passage of this lecture in the First Course, do not match up in any straightforward or unproblematic way. Saussure was later to revise his account along the lines which his editors incorporated into the 1916 text. There it is clearly stated that the act of *parole* begins in the brain of the individual, is 'un acte individuel de volonté et d'intelligence' and that 'l'individu en est toujours le maître' (*CLG*: 30). This later account in turn is by no means problem-free; but the relevance of Riedlinger's query for our present purposes is that it reveals Saussure's audience not only as scrupulously attentive to details but also as not lacking in critical acumen concerning the explanations put before them. They had straight away spotted a contentious area in the developing network of Saussurean theory.

*   *   *

The question of the value of the students' evidence concerning Saussure's thinking about language and linguistic study has two aspects which must not be confused. One of these is whether the students always understood correctly the points made in the lectures they attended. The other, more complex, is whether what was said in the lectures always provided a reliable indication of Saussure's considered position on the issue in question. This second question itself divides into two. 1. Did Saussure – who seems to have lectured in a fairly informal manner on the basis of rough notes – always express his view *viva voce* with the lucidity and exactitude that he himself would ideally have wished? 2. Did he sometimes deliberately skate over a complex or subtle matter in order to put it in a way that – provisionally at least – his students would more easily be able to grasp? No less an expert exponent of 'difficult' distinctions than Jean-Paul Sartre, when taxed with dumbing down his own views in order to make them acceptable, replied that when you are teaching theory in a philosophy class, you may have to settle for deliberately weakening an idea in order to make it comprehensible (Sartre 1966: 82). (Anyone who has ever lectured to a class of university students will recognize the general point Sartre was making.) The likelihood is that, unless Saussure were an altogether exceptional performer in the classroom, there would have been room for occasional hitches of both kinds, i.e. cases where the lecturer did not succeed in putting his point clearly, and cases where the lecturer purchased clarity at the price of oversimplification.

One of the students' severest critics was Sechehaye, who used their notes in compiling his own *Collation* of the Third Course. Sechehaye does not mince his words. On various occasions he complains that what appears in the notes is 'très confus' (*Coll.*: 144), 'inintelligible' (*Coll.*: 150) or 'mal compris' (*Coll.*: 392). He criticizes Joseph for 'une tendance à exagérer, à formuler des affirmations trop absolues' (*Coll.*: 306). At one point he observes, with evident exasperation, 'Tout ce passage a été 'haché'' par mes preneurs de notes' (*Coll.*: 188) and on another occasion 'j'ai mis une demi-heure à leur trouver un sens' (*Coll.*: 340)

Godel comments on a number of instances where, at least in his view, it is not clear from the students' notes exactly what point Saussure made. These include the example of *tri-polis* (*CLG2*: 56); the final cryptic observation in the lecture of 27 June 1911 concerning the connexion between syntagmatic structure and associative relations (*CLG3*: 132); some comments about Avestan spellings (*CLG3*: 50); the remark about 'valeur' being an 'élément du sens' (*CLG3*: 134); an observation in the Second Course about the two 'valeurs' of the linguistic sign (*CLG2*: 15); the meaning of the statement that 'la langue' is 'la somme des signes évocables' (Engler: 268); and the famous comparison between synchronic and diachronic linguistics and the transversal and longitudinal sections of the stem of a plant (Engler: 1458). But when reviewing these cases in detail – which will not be attempted here, being far too tedious an exercise to repeat in print – it is very difficult to put one's finger on any detail where the obscurity is *indubitably* to be laid at the door of the students. Particular students did occasionally miss out on particular points, as one might expect. But their collective testimony is impressive.

Thus, benefiting from the hindsight of history, one can look back on the work of Saussure's students with an appreciation which almost certainly would have caused them no little surprise. For it is highly unlikely that they regarded themselves as privileged witnesses to the genesis of a text that was to become the Magna Carta of twentieth-century linguistics. Their main concerns were much more immediate and parochial: to make sure that they had grasped – sufficiently well for purposes of the university curriculum – what the lecturer said, and to reconstruct a condensed version of what he said that would serve them adequately for purposes of revision. (In some cases the surviving notebooks contain what are evidently not actual course notes, but 'fair copies' based on revision and consultation.)

*   *   *

These utilitarian objectives put the students' testimony in a perspective which immediately sets it apart from any other source of evidence posterity may have about Saussure's thinking. In the first place, we can see that it would be silly to imagine that the students' interpretation of what Saussure said was not already circumscribed by certain preconceptions about the function and context of the lectures. From the examples the lecturer gives, and from the apparently unproblematic reception of those examples by his audience, we can infer that Saussure's students were expected to be acquainted in some detail not only with the history of French and German but also with the history of Greek and Latin, as well as having at least a passing acquaintance with other Indo-European languages. (By today's standards, that would already mean a background of linguistic knowledge that it would be vain to expect other than at postgraduate level.) And that in turn throws considerable light on what Saussure – and his audience – understood by 'general linguistics' (*linguistique générale*). The 'generality' of the subject was not derived *either* from universal premises about language *or* from everyday observation of linguistic behaviour. On the contrary, in spite of the fact that Saussure would eventually propose two overriding axioms or 'principles' of general linguistics (arbitrariness and linearity), in practice most of the distinctions invoked in his lectures are products of a process of inductive generalization, the basis of which was provided by what was known (or assumed to be known in the early 1900s) by European scholars about the history of the Indo-European languages. Unless such a body of knowledge is taken for granted as available, Saussure's approach to 'general linguistics' can hardly get off the ground.

So the first major contribution that Saussure's students make (albeit unwittingly) to an interpretation of Saussure's thought lies in the way their role as addressees implicitly contextualizes the 'generality' of general linguistics. We are dealing, in the first instance, with extrapolations from a taken-for-granted corpus of information about – in the main – one particular language-family (i.e. Indo-European). Whether this is a limitation that Saussure ideally would have wished remains an open question. In the circumstances, he did not have much choice. As his editors pointed out in 1916 in their Preface to the first edition,

> il est vrai que les nécessités du programme l'obligèrent à consacrer la moitié de chacun d'eux à un exposé relatif aux langues indo-européennes, leur histoire et leur description; la partie essentielle de son sujet s'en trouva singulièrement amoindrie. (*CLG*: 7)

This survey they therefore decided to drop from the published *CLG* text, and all subsequent editors down to the present day have followed suit. Nevertheless, this is the point at which it may be appropriate to raise the question of whether, for Saussure's audience, the survey of the Indo-European material was quite as irrelevant as Bally and Sechehaye eventually decided it was. Certainly a case can be made for saying that, despite the consensus of editorial opinion, it was perhaps more organic to the conception of the lecture series than is generally allowed.

It is interesting to note in this connexion that the place and the space Saussure allotted to the Indo-European survey varied considerably from one year to the next. Bally and Sechehaye oversimplify when they say that 'half of each course' was obligatorily devoted to this component. In fact, for students enrolled in the First Course it occupied a segment which corresponds approximately to only one twentieth of the whole, whereas in the Second Course it dominated everything else, taking up to three fifths of the total (as measured in both cases by Riedlinger's notes: Godel: 53–76; *CLG1*: 105–11; *CLG2*: 95 ff.). Even allowing for Riedlinger's having taken more copious notes in the Second Course, the disproportion is striking.

Did Saussure feel that Indo-European studies had received inadequate attention in his First Course (which did not begin until January 1907)? Did he overcompensate in the Second? Was he just bad at planning his lectures? Whatever the reason, it is not only the quantitative disparity which is conspicuous. There is also a difference in the position which this material occupied in the structure of the two Courses. In the Second Course everything else leads up to this survey, which brought the series of lectures to its close in the summer semester of 1909 (Godel: 75–6); whereas in the First Course the much briefer survey formed a bridge to a detailed discussion of 'la méthode reconstructive', the topic on which the course concluded (*CLG1*: 111 ff.). On the basis of the evidence afforded by the Second Course, Komatsu goes as far as to suggest that 'the courses were not primarily aimed at the theory of linguistics, but at the description of languages' (*CLG2*: vii). This may seem to many scholars to be going too far; but it does highlight the anomalous position of the Second Course in the series, as well as raising the wider question of Saussure's conception of the relationship between general linguistics and comparative philology. This latter is perhaps the most important of the basic Saussurean questions to which the students' notebooks bear witness.

Saussure was evidently not satisfied with what he had given his students in the Second Course either, for in the Third Course he dealt with the Indo-European survey differently again. It formed part of a wider overview of language families (now including, notably, the Semitic languages) which occupied most of the middle part of the course (January to April 1911). This led up to the final very general lectures on 'la langue' given in April, June and July of that year.

Thus when we compare the Second and Third Courses as presented to Saussure's students (at least one of whom attended both), the contrast is striking. Although the Second Course had a section headed 'Aperçu de la linguistique indo-européenne comme introduction à la linguistique générale' (Godel: 74; *CLG2*: 95), this is not the overall impression given by the arrangement of materials. One might almost say that in the Second Course general linguistics is presented as an introduction to comparative philology, whereas in the Third Course it is the other way round.

Did Saussure's conception of the relationship between general linguistics and comparative philology undergo an important revision at this period? Or was this just a question of slotting in already prepared lecture material? Whatever the motives for Saussure's hesitations about how to treat his overall syllabus brief, nothing is gained by dismissing these questions as irrelevant. Furthermore, if decontextualization inevitably falsifies, Saussure's editors might seem to face a formidable indictment on this score. Suppressing an intrinsic part of a course can hardly pass muster as a conventional editorial practice. Here we see another reason why the students' perspective on Saussure's teaching can claim to be unique. They, unlike subsequent readers of the *CLG*, were in a position to relate the ideas on general linguistics to the complementary picture of an established body of linguistic facts that the lecturer took care to present in tandem. Somehow, the two had to be understood as related.

But how, exactly? This is a question that goes to the heart of any philosophy of linguistics, and Saussure as a theorist must have been acutely conscious of it. Did he nevertheless regard it as an issue of no practical importance as far as his students were concerned? In none of the three Courses does he ever address it directly, and this lacuna is one of the most salient in his teaching. All the more so inasmuch as he constantly raises questions concerning the various points of view from which linguistic phenomena may be considered. (The phrase *point de vue* recurs scores of times in the students' notes for all three Courses.)

If the question is considered from the students' *point de vue*, the answer implicit in Saussure's day-to-day pedagogic practice must have seemed clear enough. In other words, as far as they were concerned, general linguistics and comparative philology were complementary: there would have been no clear divide. Saussure himself gave lectures on topics in comparative philology in the very same years that he lectured on general linguistics (Godel: 16–17). Thus, for Saussure's students there could have been no doubt that general linguistics and comparative philology were intimately related, each study feeding the other. But that relationship hardly squares with the portrait that some commentators later painted (on the basis of the 1916 text) of a Saussure reacting strongly against the naive positivism of the nineteenth century, in which 'facts' lay open to (adequately trained) observation. For although Saussure was critical of the *early* comparative philologists and their methods (see further below on the exact thrust of these criticisms), he never – to his students – suggested that the work of nineteenth-century comparative philology needed to be done all over again with new conceptual tools or fresh historical premisses. Nowhere in the three Courses is any suspicion raised that the commonly accepted comparativist story of the Indo-European languages might be fundamentally flawed, or at least require retelling from a quite different 'point de vue'. The basic assumption throughout the three Courses seems to be that scholars now – at last, and fairly incontrovertibly – know 'the truth' about this language-family (even if a few details might not yet be fully elucidated). So 'general linguistics' and its principles would inevitably have been seen by the students as an ongoing intellectual construction built upon this established truth. The building itself might still be in its early stages: but there was no doubt about the site and the foundations.

Therein – precisely – lies the problem as regards any serious apologia for general linguistics as an *independent* academic discipline. In his pedagogic practice, Saussure seems to have used the 'facts' about the Indo-European languages as providing ambivalently, as the occasion demanded, *both* (1) an empirical proof – or at the very least, illustration – of the validity of certain general linguistic claims, *and* (2) conclusions validated by the rigorous application of the right general linguistic principles and methods. (Of these, (2) is pragmatically tautologous, inasmuch as no one would presumably wish to base conclusions on *mistaken* principles and methods. But that does not deflect the charge of trying to make your examples do double duty as constable and witness.)

This ambivalence comes very close to setting up as judge and jury in one's own court, and it is apparent right from the beginning of the First Course. There the first question of *general* linguistics that is raised concerns the nature of linguistic change. Saussure rejects straight away the notion that linguistic change involves 'corruption':

> Il faut distinguer absolument corruption et changement et se défaire de l'idée de corruption, qui n'a pas de place en linguistique. (*CLG1*: 3)

This mistake is one of various 'linguistic errors' that Saussure likened to Bacon's idols of the cave. But instead of presenting a general argument to show that 'corruption' is an invalid or unacceptable notion, all Saussure does is offer various series of Latin forms:

(i)   *honc, oino, ploirumi, deicere*
(ii) *hunc, unum, plurimi, dicere*
(iii) *vinea, cuneum*
(iv) *vinia, cunium*

The replacement of series (i) by series (ii), he points out, is not regarded as an example of 'corruption', unlike the replacement of series (iii) by series (iv). Why not? Because series (ii) and (iii) offer forms characteristic of what is regarded as a 'classical period'. Whereas in fact the two sets of replacements are 'du même ordre: la langue a évolué' (*CLG1*: 4).

The argument will be opaque – to say the very least – not only to someone who knows no Latin, but to anyone whose knowledge of Latin is restricted to the texts of the Classical authors, where the forms represented in series (i) and (iv) do not appear. More than that, however: it has to be assumed that it is in fact the case that the Latin forms in (ii) and (iv) are related to the corresponding items in (i) and (iii) as historical derivatives in the same etymological line of descent. No attempt is made to show this. It is treated by Saussure as given. Nor, thirdly, is any attempt made to show that the changes connecting (i) to (ii) are indeed 'of the same order' as those connecting (iii) to (iv). That too is taken for granted. In short, straight away in the First Course we see general linguistics clinging firmly on to the coat tails of historical philology, rather than being provided with any independent rationale of its own.

There are various questions about this example that need to be distinguished. It would clearly have been possible for Saussure to have dealt with this issue in quite a different way. He could have presented a *general* argument against the equation of linguistic change with 'corruption'. Instead of doing so, he evidently opted for appealing to his students' prior acquaintance with the history of Latin. But why?

Did he think that they were not intellectually capable of following a more abstract line of reasoning? Or did he himself think that the history of Latin provided more compelling evidence than any abstract argument? If the latter, that says a great deal about Saussure's conception (in 1907) of general linguistics.

*   *   *

A second example from the same set of lectures is no less telling. Saussure lost no time in expounding to his students the orthodox (Neogrammarian) doctrine concerning the regularity of phonetic change (*CLG1*: 31). The all-important proviso about regularity is: given that identical conditions obtain in each particular case. But no attempt is made to explain to the students *why* this proviso should be so. The generalization is supported by giving various examples from the history of German, French, English and Latin. These cases are not analysed, but just listed. Thus:

false   halt
fausse   haut

provide the (sole) corroborative evidence for the allegedly 'regular' change from Old French *l* to *u*. This raises a number of questions, since *prima facie* the forms *false* and *halt* do actually appear to be counterexamples to the proviso as stated ('pourvu que les conditions soient identiques').

Neither in the case of these Old French forms nor in any of the others cited in the discussion of the doctrine of 'regularity' (*CLG1*: 31 ff.) does the exemplification take the form logically required to demonstrate the point; i.e. we need comparisons between series of words, showing that when a given condition (C) holds, the phonetic change in question occurs, whereas when C does *not* hold the change does *not* occur. Just citing a couple of examples where the change *does* occur falls a long way short of what is needed, as Saussure must have known. What he must also have known is that it is by no means easy to state exactly the condition (or rather, set of conditions) under which the change *l* > *u* occurs in French (Bourciez 1937: 184–91), but this question was evidently not discussed. Thirdly, there is the more serious general linguistic problem involved in the proviso itself: that is, explaining what makes conditions 'identical' (or not) for the purpose of conditioning a sound change. (For unless this can be done in some plausible manner, the insistence on 'identical conditions' is vacuous and the whole doctrine of phonetic 'regularity' becomes circular.) As far as we know, none of Saussure's students queried this, even though they were bright enough to query his distinction between *langue* and *parole*. The difference is informative.

What passed for uncontroversial in this lecture (one of the earliest in the Course) leaves us with little alternative other than to suppose that – both for Saussure and for his students – these matters did not stand in need of explication. They were already part of the 'established facts' that investigation of the history of various Indo-European languages had revealed, and that linguists could henceforward rely on. Thus examples like French *false* and *halt* in effect function as no more than tokens or reminders of certain *faits accomplis* in historical linguistics.

*   *   *

What one might suspect purely on the basis of Saussure's treatment of historical examples is amply borne out by the detailed critique in the Second Course (*CLG2*: 79 ff., 155 ff.) of the work of the early comparativists. Saussure lists eight errors (*erreurs, défauts*) characteristic of Indo-European linguistics from Bopp to Schleicher (1816–75). (The work done in this period he calls *l'ancienne linguistique*, as distinct from the 'new' linguistics ushered in by the Neogrammarians.) The errors of *l'ancienne linguistique* are worth considering in detail. In the order in which the lecturer discussed them, they are as follows.

(1) The exaggerated importance attributed to Sanskrit. This error took

two forms. The more serious form was the equation of Sanskrit with the original Indo-European tongue. The less serious, but nevertheless deeply misleading, was the belief that Sanskrit was the 'oldest' Indo-European language: hence giving Sanskrit evidence priority over that of other branches of Indo-European. (2) The comparativists' emphasis on 'pure' comparison, i.e. divorcing comparison from the historical context of the items compared. (3) The intrusion of philosophical and other ideas which have no linguistic basis (e.g. Bopp's belief in a scale or hierarchy of vowels, having the vowel *a* at its summit). (4) The failure to distinguish between spoken and written forms ('la linguistique se trompait sur la situation du document vis-à-vis de l'objet à étudier': *CLG2*: 86). (5) Insufficient attention paid to the 'creative' force in language development, i.e. analogy. (6) General lack of method, resulting from absence of any clear idea about the 'nature of the object' under investigation. (7) The tendency to take the oldest attested language in each of the various branches of Indo-European as representative of that branch (e.g. Gothic as representative of Germanic). (8) The assumption that languages of the past provide a great fund of evidence about the peoples who spoke them and their way of life.

Having recited this bleak catalogue of mistakes, Saussure proceeds by contrast to sing the praises of the Neogrammarians (the *junggrammatische Richtung*) and the 'new direction' which they introduced into linguistics from 1875 onwards. He singles out for attention five merits in their approach. (1) Introduction of a historical framework within which to make sense of the results yielded by comparative studies. (2) Recognition that a language did not develop by a natural process, like vegetation, but as a product of the collective mind of its speakers. (3) Recognition of analogy as a force working for the continuous renewal of languages. (4) Recognition of the importance of studying phonetics (leading in turn to emancipation from reliance on written evidence). (5) Demotion of Sanskrit from its previously prestigious position.

When we compare these five points to the eight listed above, it seems clear enough that Saussure wished his students to see the Neogrammarians as having rectified the major mistakes for which the comparativists had been responsible. If the Neogrammarians in turn were guilty of any errors of comparable gravity, their guilt is here passed over in silence. Thus the picture that emerges is one in which progress in linguistics has been achieved by the gradual elimination of false assumptions, rather than by the discovery of any new evidence.

But what is remarkable about this picture is the survival unscathed of the most important of all the comparativists' assumptions, i.e. of the basic

Indo-European hypothesis itself: namely, that the relationship between Sanskrit, Greek, Latin, etc., as shown by comparison between their word forms and grammar, is to be accounted for by descent from a common ancestral language ('which', as Sir William Jones cautiously put it in 1786, 'perhaps, no longer exists'). Whatever details the comparativists may have originally got wrong (Rask at one time refused to admit Celtic as Indo-European) are seemingly minor when contrasted with the monumental scope and implications of what they got right. Thus the story as presented by Saussure is one in which even the combined mistakes of the comparativists do not suffice to undermine the validity of the comparativist enterprise *per se*.

Given this historical scenario, the role assigned to the Indo-European 'survey' in Saussure's Second Course is hardly in doubt. It represents an up-dated sketch-map of the *terra cognita* that students of 'general linguistics' have to be familiar with. It is rather like a lecturer presenting a current version of the 'periodic table' as a summary of what students of physics and chemistry are expected to know about the elements.

*   *   *

However well-established the history of the Indo-European family might have appeared to be by 1908, as the cumulative result of almost a century of research, that by no means entirely disposes of a more serious theoretical question. Was it an adequate basis for the purposes of general linguistics? Saussure was obviously conscious of the problem, for he raised it himself in the Second Course:

> Pourquoi choisir la famille des langues indo-européennes? Ne risque-t-on < pas de > borner sa vue à des caractères trop spéciaux à ces langues et < qui > nous empêcheront d'avoir une vue générale sur la langue? (*CLG2*: 70)

Saussure's answer to his own question, although forthright, does not entirely carry conviction. The first point he makes is parochial: that the Indo-European languages are in any case of most interest because 'our language' (i.e. French) belongs to this family. Next, to take some other language-family, such as Semitic, as a basis for study would require a real apprenticeship ('un véritable apprentissage'); whereas within Indo-European even languages we may not be familiar with 'do not depart from the well-known type of Latin'. (This latter claim is perhaps more dubious than Saussure was willing to admit, as can be seen even by comparing

Latin with Modern French.) These, however, are local and practical rather than theoretical reasons.

For a more robust defence of his position Saussure refers to Whitney, who thirty-five years earlier had championed giving pride of place to the study of Indo-European:

> ce que < dit > Whitney reste parfaitement vrai: il serait vain pour quiconque < d'entreprendre > une linguistique générale sans partir du capital d'expériences acquis par l'étude de l'indo-européen. (*CLG2*: 71)

Any Semiticist who tried to write the history of the Semitic languages without a prior acquaintance with the results of Indo-European linguistics would be 'doomed to certain failure', unless sheer genius were able to 'compensate for ninety years of collective study'. Indo-European takes pride of place ('tient une place prépondérante') as does the study of a 'superior organism' over an 'inferior organism'. This does not mean that Indo-European exemplifies all possible linguistic phenomena, but nevertheless it exemplifies most ('le plus grand nombre').

This is a remarkable piece of special pleading, which contains the seeds of its own invalidation. For it is unclear how anyone could be certain of the 'superiority' of Indo-European unless a thorough investigation had already been conducted of all other known language-families. Failing this, it seems eminently possible that Indo-European might turn out to be linguistically a-typical, or to lack certain features of particular interest from a general linguistic point of view. Furthermore, in 1908 it remained highly likely that not all Indo-European languages had yet come to light. (The discovery of cuneiform Hittite after Saussure's death is a case in point.) New discoveries might conceivably have occasioned a fundamental revision of facts and relationships previously regarded as proven. What Saussure was struggling with here – not very successfully – was a general difficulty put succinctly by Bloomfield for a later generation of linguists:

> Features which we think ought to be universal may be absent from the very next language that becomes accessible. (Bloomfield 1933: 20)

He might have added: 'And features we think *never* occur in languages may, to our surprise, turn up.'

*   *   *

It is worth going back now to the matter raised at the beginning of the present chapter: Riedlinger's surprise in the classroom on hearing Saussure's original account of the distinction between *langue* and *parole*. For the point at which this occurs is immediately preceded by a discussion of one of the phenomena which (as we know from the Second Course) Saussure thought of as having been neglected by the *ancienne linguistique*, but recognized by the Neogrammarians: the analogical creation of new forms.

Now the explanation of analogy that Saussure gave his students was indeed borrowed directly from the Neogrammarians: it is the account commonly called in French *la quatrième proportionnelle* (*a* is to *b* as *c* is to *d*). The classic Neogrammarian exposition is to be found in the chapter 'On Analogy' in Hermann Paul's *Principien der Sprachgeschichte*. At no point does Saussure query – or even probe – this account, much less ask whether, even if valid, it suffices to account for *all* types of analogical formation. In fact, Paul's account is in some respects rather more rigorous than Saussure's.

> Seeing that the new analogical formation is the solution of an equation between proportions, it follows that at least three terms must be present to enable such an equation to be instituted. Each must be capable of being compared in some point with the other – i.e. in this case an agreement must appear, with the one in the material, with the other in the formal element. Thus in Latin such an equation may be instituted as this, – *animus* : *animi* = *senatus* : *x*, but not *animus* : *animi* = *mensa* : *x*. And thus it happens that a word can undergo no analogical influence from other words unless it agrees with these in the formation of one form or of several. (Paul 1891: 106)

Saussure (*CLG1*: 64) illustrates by means of an example from French: the analogical replacement of the Old French first person singular *treuve* by *trouve*. This is due, according to Saussure, to the analogical influence of the verb *pousser*:

poussons : *pousse* = *trouvons* : *trouve* (in place of *treuve*).

The difference between Paul's explanation and Saussure's is that it is precisely at this juncture that Saussure introduces – for the first time – his distinction between *langue* and *parole*. Saussure evidently sees that one of the problems with Paul's account of analogy is that the 'equation' represented by the *quatrième proportionnelle* must have existed long before its 'solution' by the appearance of the new analogical form. So there is, in principle, a need to bridge this gap, not merely historically but psychologically. Saussure's way of coping with the problem is to posit two different orders of facts which come into the picture: *faits de langue* and *faits de parole*. Clearly, the *langue* (i.e. French) could presumably have continued indefinitely under the old regime where *treuve* was the first person singular of the verb *trouver*. So the intervention of some other factor is logically required in order to rationalize the historically attested sequence (*trouvons – treuve* > *trouvons – trouve*). What Saussure subsumes under the term *parole* is simply the minimum required to assure this rationalization. That is to say: it must at some point have happened in the history of French – in circumstances unknown and historically irrecoverable – that a speaker in the process of communication 'improvised' (the verb used is *improviser*) the form *trouve*. And this happened because momentarily the established form *treuve* was forgotten, and the *quatrième proportionnelle* came into operation to help that speaker fulfil spontaneously the immediate needs of discourse.

> Il faut remarquer que la forme engendrée *je trouve* < avant d'être produite est d'abord > voulue pour répondre à une idée précise < que j'ai > dans l'esprit: la première personne du singulier. Les formes < *nous poussons, je pousse* > sont seulement pensées < ou plutôt senties dans une demi-inconscience > ; seule la forme *je trouve* est exécutée par la parole. Il faut donc se mettre en face de l'acte de la parole pour comprendre < une > création analogique. (*CLG1*: 64–5)

Riedlinger's surprise now appears in an altogether different light. For if *this* is the reason for setting up a distinction between *langue* and *parole*, then *parole* must pre-eminently be the domain of individual attempts to cope (not always successfully) with the occasional demands of discourse; whereas *langue* stands opposed to this as the established social norm (*trouvons – treuve*) by reference to which the improvised form *trouve* stands out as an innovation.

*   *   *

If the above reconstruction is on the right lines, a detailed study of the students' notes reveals a far different Saussure from the one that posterity reconstructed from the *CLG* published in 1916. In the classroom at Geneva we find a Saussure who not only (1) taught that the establishment of a 'general linguistics' was impossible without reliance on the results of the nineteenth century's researches into the history and affiliations of the Indo-European languages, but (2) came to his celebrated and fundamental distinction between *langue* and *parole* not through rethinking the concept of *langage* from scratch, but as a result of trying to make sense of the Neogrammarian view of analogical change.

Nothing remotely like this emerges from reading the *CLG*, which is one reason why failure to publish the students' notes verbatim still counts as one of the most serious charges that can be laid against Saussure's editors. In the *CLG*, analogical formations are mentioned as providing historical evidence (*CLG*: 227) for a distinction already established on *a priori* grounds. But this is not how it appears in the First Course. In short, the connexion and – still more important – the operative sequence of ideas which would have been obvious to the students attending Saussure's lectures in the spring of 1907 was lost in the major reorganization that the editors subsequently imposed on the lecture notes. This point alone would have thrown a quite different light on what subsequently became one of the most controversial issues in the interpretation of Saussure's teaching. Today it is still probably true that the majority of scholars who discuss 'Saussure's' distinction between *langue* and *parole* are completely unaware of its original emergence from the doctrine of analogy.

CHAPTER THREE

The Editors' Saussure

Charles Bally and Albert Sechehaye were themselves the first to raise doubts about their own interpretation of Saussure's linguistic theorizing. As colleagues and close associates of Saussure, they were in the best possible position to understand Saussure's views on language. They had not, however, attended in person the three courses on general linguistics that Saussure gave from 1907 to 1911. Some aspects of what they discovered on reading his students' notes evidently took them by surprise or left them puzzled. This tension (between what they might have expected Saussure to say and what – according to his most recent students – Saussure actually had said in the classroom) emerges repeatedly in their editorial work.

In their preface to the *CLG* Bally and Sechehaye mention two possible criticisms of their own 'reconstruction' and 'synthesis' of Saussure's ideas. One was that their version contained too little; the other that it contained too much. Two gaps that particularly concerned them were the absence of any detailed treatment of semantics and the absence of a *linguistique de la parole*. In both cases they pleaded lack of materials. Why these two lacunae should have been picked out for special mention is a question that will be taken up below, since it bears directly upon the editors' own interpretation of the originality of Saussure's most recent thinking. On the other hand they included a great deal – particularly on sound change – that could hardly be reckoned a novel Saussurean contribution to the discipline of linguistics: this they explained as motivated by the need to show how very different Saussure's conception of linguistic studies was from that of his predecessors. Nevertheless, they concluded diffidently:

> Nous sentons toute la responsabilité que nous assumons vis-à-vis de la critique, vis-à-vis de l'auteur lui-même, qui n'aurait peut-être pas autorisé la publication de ces pages.

Cette responsabilité, nous l'acceptons tout entière, et nous voudrions être seuls à la porter. La critique saura-t-elle distinguer entre le maître et ses interprètes? (*CLG*: 11)

An awkward question to raise, and in some respects a futile one, given that the form of publication Bally and Sechehaye had decided on gave their readers no chance of pursuing the answer for themselves. For more than a generation Bally and Sechehaye clung to their self-appointed role as sole 'official' interpreters of Saussure's thought, a role enhanced by the appointment of Bally as Saussure's successor in the chair of general linguistics. Although the manuscript sources they had used were housed in the library at Geneva, they showed no inclination to publish them, thus in effect blocking any critical appraisal of their editorial work. It was not until well after both men were dead that Godel published his painstaking examination of the students' notes. What this revealed to a later generation of scholars was the absence of manuscript authority for many of the formulations in the 1916 text.

Even more curious is the way that both editors subsequently quoted their own words as if they were Saussure's. Thus in the Introduction to his *Linguistique générale et linguistique française*, Bally claims to be adopting the very method

que F. de Saussure a résumée dans la dernière phrase de son *Cours de linguistique générale*: «La linguistique a pour unique et véritable objet la langue envisagée en elle-même et pour elle-même.» (Bally 1965: 17)

But this pronouncement was never Saussure's (as Godel later pointed out). Furthermore placing it as the conclusion to the *CLG* was entirely due to the editors' arrangement of the text. So Bally is in effect citing his own (and Sechehaye's) summary, while nevertheless attributing it ostensibly to Saussure.

Sechehaye does exactly the same thing when, discussing the *CLG* in his article on 'Les trois linguistiques saussuriennes', he refers to 'la célèbre formule qu'on lit en conclusion de l'ouvrage' (Sechehaye 1940: 20). Sechehaye does not tell his readers that he himself – and not Saussure – was one of the authors of this 'célèbre formule'. These are tell-tale indications of the extent to which, in spite of their public disclaimers concerning the validity of their own interpretation, Bally and Sechehaye nevertheless regarded it as authoritative. They clearly thought they were speaking for Saussure, and most of their contemporaries did not question the *CLG* as that cathedratic statement.

That having been said, however, the fact remains that when today one studies in detail almost any page of Engler's critical edition (1968), which sets out comprehensively in parallel columns the 1916 text and the corresponding passages in the students' notes, it is difficult not to admire the adroitness with which Bally and Sechehaye did succeed in transforming awkward, disjointed and sometimes opaque material into smooth, lucid and occasionally striking prose. Perhaps too smooth and too striking in places, it might be added. Some of the more skilful wordcraft tends to conceal problems which stand out starkly in the students' versions. The controversial last sentence of the 1916 text is by no means the only instance where editorial verbal initiative soared beyond what can be regarded as authentically Saussurean. For example, one of the more quotable dicta to be found in the pages of the *CLG* is: 'c'est dans une large mesure la langue qui fait la nation' (*CLG*: 40). As it stands, this is an assertion open to more than one interpretation, and of particular interest in view of Saussure's Swiss nationality. But when one tries to find out exactly in what context Saussure said this, it emerges that Saussure did not say it at all. The epigram is the work of the editors, who conjured it up as a neat way of putting what appears in the students' notes as a (rather different) pedestrian point about the relationship between language and race (Engler: 380).

*   *   *

The editorial process had begun with Sechehaye's collation of the notes. The 1916 text was a complete reorganization and substantial augmentation of this original draft, which still exists in manuscript, but remains unpublished. The *Collation* provides in effect a composite version of the Third Course, with variants from the notes of Dégallier, Joseph and Mme Sechehaye, together with marginal comments by both Sechehaye and Bally. But this, the editors eventually decided, was not good enough as a representation of Saussure's mature view of linguistics.

Nevertheless the *Collation* is of interest on many points of detail, since it reveals editorial doubts and hesitations with remarkable candour. When the notes are difficult to understand, Sechehaye does not hesitate to say so. He will admit, for example: 'toute cette page a été rédigée sur quelques mots très courts et énigmatiques' (*Coll.*: 91). He confesses he cannot understand Saussure's example of *contremarche* as a syntagm (*Coll.*: 426). He is keen to incorporate, wherever possible, the exact words Saussure used, but does not hesitate nevertheless to make corrections in the interests of coherence and consistency.

Only rarely does he decide to override the unanimous testimony of the students. One of these cases involves another much-quoted dictum, where *la langue* is defined as 'un système de signes, où il n'y a d'essentiel que l'union du sens et de l'image acoustique' (*CLG*: 32). But the notes of Joseph and Mme Sechehaye have *son* not *sens*, while Dégallier renders it as *exécution phonatoire*. Sechehaye will have none of this: 'cela ne me paraît avoir aucun sens et je proposerais de remplacer *son* par *sens*' (*Coll.*: 19). This he proceeded to do, and the substitution was retained in the final 1916 text. If he had had Constantin's notes available, he would probably have seen that it is unlikely that the students in the classroom had misheard *sens* as *son*, for Constantin has *son* too; but Constantin's text adds 'avec l'idée' after 'image acoustique'. If this is right, it was not the students' hearing that was to blame. What happened was that some of them merely took it for granted that it did not (by now) need repeating that signs are signs of ideas. Saussure, then, was here referring to the tripartite correspondence between physical event (*son*), mental impression (*image acoustique*) and concept (*idée*). The *CLG* text silently reinforces Sechehaye's interpretation by referring in the latter part of the same sentence to 'les deux parties du signe' (*CLG*: 31). But in fact this phrase does not belong there: it has been transposed from a different lecture (*CLG3*: 71).

Another such case is Sechehaye's refusal to accept that Saussure spoke of the linguistic sign having *two* values, in spite of the fact that the phrase *deux valeurs* occurs in both Dégallier's and Mme Sechehaye's notes (Engler: 1329). Sechehaye protests: 'je remplace *deux* par *des* qui seul a un sens ici: un signe ne peut pas avoir deux valeurs' (*Coll.*: 340). Presumably, again, he thought the students had misheard. However, unknown to Sechehaye, some manuscript notes of Saussure's survive which relate to this passage. There it is quite clear that *deux*, not *des*, is the authentic reading: 'dans l'association constituant le signe il n'y a rien depuis le premier moment que deux valeurs *existant l'une* < *en vertu de* > *l'autre*' (Engler: 1329). Saussure is here, evidently, considering both *signifiant* and *signifié* as having their own value, each nevertheless being generated by the association which unites them as constituents of the sign.

Interesting as the *Collation* is, however, it is to the *CLG* that one must turn in order to assess the editors' overall interpretation of Saussure's teaching. Given their aims of 'reconstruction' and 'synthesis', and allowing for the attitude of ritual reverence that they invariably adopted towards 'le maître', what did they understand Saussure's basic and original contribution to the linguistic theory of his day as being?

*   *   *

Part of the answer is implicit (but has only become apparent since Godel initiated the scholarly study of the manuscripts) in the way Bally and Sechehaye selected and rearranged the materials at their disposal. One aspect of this has already been discussed in the previous chapter; namely, their rejection of Saussure's comparative survey of the Indo-European languages as being extraneous to the Course proper. While it is clear that Saussure had nothing very original to say on this topic, its exclusion by the editors has a more obvious theoretical motivation. The material in the survey concerns *langues* (in the plural): it does not address the question of *la langue*. To this distinction it will be necessary to return below.

The second significant aspect of the editors' work concerns the order of presentation. From the plan of the *CLG* it seems very evident that they attached great importance to Saussure's distinction between synchronic and diachronic perspectives, and to the reversal of (traditional) priorities, whereby studies of linguistic change were henceforth relegated to a subordinate position. Just how revolutionary this might have appeared to them can be judged by reading Sechehaye's own *Programme et méthodes de la linguistique théorique*, published in 1908 and dedicated to Saussure. Sechehaye there distinguished, as Saussure did, between two orders of linguistic inquiry, 'static' (*statique*) and 'evolutionary' (*évolutif*). However, Sechehaye held out no more than the pious hope that one day theoretical linguistics, when established on a sound basis, would be able to play its role as an auxiliary (*auxiliaire*) to historical linguistics (*linguistique historique*). His assumption clearly is that *linguistique historique* holds the key to all linguistic problems and that the answers to 'static' questions have to be sought by interrogating the history of the language in question. This is not far removed from Hermann Paul's Neogrammarian doctrine that linguistics must be based on 'the examination of the essence of historical development' (Paul 1891: xxvii). As if rejecting Saussure's distinction in advance, Paul had written:

> It has been objected that there is another view of language possible besides the historical. I must contradict this. What is explained as an unhistorical and still scientific observation of language is at bottom nothing but one incompletely historical, through defects partly of the observer, partly of the material to be observed. (Paul 1891: xlvi–xlvii)

All this is manifestly at odds with what was to be presented in 1916 as one of the basic tenets of the *CLG*. In this respect, Saussure must have seemed to many of his contemporaries (including his editors) to be denying what nearly all nineteenth-century scholarship, from Darwin onwards, had recognized; namely, that evolution was the indispensable factor in understanding current states of affairs.

Although the intellectual spanner that Saussure had deliberately thrown into the evolutionary works was crude, it was also impossible to ignore. Saussure pointed out the theoretical implications of what linguists, for most of the nineteenth century, had lost sight of: that it is possible – and furthermore normal – to learn, understand, and speak a language without knowing anything at all about its past. The whole concept of Saussurean synchrony is based on this commonsense observation and its ramifications.

Once it is realized that if this holds true for the present generation of speakers, then it holds equally for all previous generations of speakers, the result is a fundamental revision of what is meant by language 'history'. The development of a language over time presents a succession of synchronic states, and in order to understand it one must first identify and study the states in question. Thus, far from explaining a given state of the language by reference to its antecedents, the linguist comes to see that linguistic evolution can be grasped only in terms of the successive states that it links. Thus *diachronique* is not for Saussure a mere synonym of *historique*: it implies a quite specific way of conceptualizing the relationship between past and present.

> La linguistique diachronique étudiera [. . .] les rapports reliants des termes successifs non aperçus par une même conscience collective, et qui se substituent les uns aux autres sans former système entre eux. (*CLG*: 140)

This definition as given by Bally and Sechehaye follows the manuscript sources closely (except that the term there used is *évolutive*, not *diachronique*). Saussure rejects the terms *histoire* and *linguistique historique* as inappropriate (*CLG*: 116; Engler: 1336).

For the editors, however, it was precisely Saussure's insistence on the absolute separation between synchronic and diachronic studies that generated unresolved problems. How, then, were synchronic facts related to diachronic facts? Evidently Saussure thought that linguistic change was initiated in *parole*. But exactly how, and under what conditions? It is here that the editors' worries about the missing *linguistique de la parole* and the lacuna in the treatment of semantics fall into place. The difference between one *état de langue* and its successor automatically implied that in the interim sound changes had occurred and also changes in meaning. But although Saussure's position on sound change seemed clear enough in broad outline, the same could hardly be said of his position with regard to changes of meaning, or indeed with regard to the notion of 'meaning' in general. One crucial point which remained obscure in the students' notes was how, for Saussure, the *signifié* of a sign related to its *valeur*, and both to the communication of messages in *parole*.

*   *   *

The editors seem to have tried to resolve the semantic problem in part by upgrading a distinction between *valeur* and *signification*. Whether Saussure himself intended the latter term to bear the theoretical weight that the editors implied is open to question. The distinction is introduced in Chapter IV of Part 2:

> Quand on parle de la valeur d'un mot, on pense généralement et avant tout à la propriété qu'il a de représenter une idée, et c'est là en effet un des aspects de la valeur linguistique. Mais s'il en est ainsi, en quoi cette valeur diffère-t-elle de ce qu'on appelle la *signification*? Ces deux mots seraient-ils synonymes? Nous ne le croyons pas [. . .] (*CLG*: 158)

Nevertheless, the two are closely related:

> La valeur, prise dans son aspect conceptuel, est sans doute un élément de la signification [. . .] (*CLG*: 158)

This relationship, the text continues, is easily misunderstood: for it seems that, from one point of view, the *signification* of a word is nothing other than the conceptual correlate of the *signifiant*.

> Prenons d'abord la signification telle qu'on se la représente et telle que nous l'avons figurée p. 99. Elle n'est, comme l'indique les flèches de la figure, que la contre-partie de l'image auditive. (*CLG*: 158)

This statement seems to yield straight away a quite unambiguous definition (i.e. *signification* = *signifié*). But this limited perspective, the reader is warned, is inadequate. For it focusses on the individual linguistic sign in isolation. Within any given linguistic system, every word has to be considered in relation to other words which co-exist along with it.

> Sa valeur n'est donc pas fixée tant qu'on se borne à constater qu'il peut être «échangé» contre tel ou tel concept, c'est-à-dire qu'il a telle ou telle signification; il faut encore le comparer avec les valeurs similaires, avec les autres mots qui lui sont opposables. Son contenu n'est vraiment déterminé que par le concours de ce qui

existe en dehors de lui. Faisant partie d'un système, il est revêtu, non seulement d'une signification, mais aussi et surtout d'une valeur, et c'est tout autre chose. (*CLG*: 160)

This initial and very abstract account is already marked by certain hesitations, if not discords. On the one hand, the text says that the *valeur* of a sign (as far as its conceptual aspect is concerned) is only one 'element' of its *signification*; but, on the other hand, that the *valeur* is something quite different that the sign has in addition to its *signification*. But since the linguistic perspective which reveals the *valeur* is evidently more all-embracing than that which merely reveals the *signification* (= *signifié*), it is hard to see how the *valeur* could be only one 'element' of the *signification*. As Françoise Gadet observes, there seem to be two incompatible propositions here: (1) that *valeur* is one element in *signification*, and (2) that *signification* is dependent on *valeur* (Gadet 1987: 67). The first of these raises a further question. What are the other 'elements' of *signification*? We are never told.

In the history of Saussurean exegesis there have been various attempts to solve the puzzle of what *signification* means, some more speculative than others. Tullio De Mauro, in his critical edition of the text, proposed to interpret the Saussurean terms *signifié* and *signification* as marking the same distinction as Frege had established between *Sinn* and *Bedeutung* (De Mauro: 465). In other words, the *signification* of an expression is its referent, while the *signifié* is the manner of presentation. All that needs to be said here is that there appears to be no textual evidence to support any such neo-Fregean reading.

According to Gadet, the solution to the enigma hinges on the fact that Saussure did not regard certain aspects of meaning as falling within the purview of linguistics at all. *Valeur* is simply the term Saussure uses to designate the linguistic component of something more inclusive and in part extra-linguistic, namely *signification* (Gadet 1987: 67).

A more popular proposal is that, for Saussure, the apparently 'missing' elements of *signification* are supplied contextually. For instance, Jonathan Culler in his book *Saussure* (Culler 1986) supposes that we are dealing here with 'the difference between meanings which are properties of utterances only and meanings which are properties of elements of the linguistic system'. Elaborating this observation, Culler writes:

To characterize this distinction Saussure uses the terms *signification* and *valeur* ('value'). Linguistic units have a value within the system, a meaning which is the result of the oppositions which define them; but when these units are used in an utterance they have a signification, a contextual realization or manifestation of meaning. (Culler 1986: 32–3)

In short, Culler proposes that *signification* is a term referring to meaning in *parole*. A similar interpretation is proposed by Holdcroft, commenting on the following example given in the same chapter of the *CLG*.

Le français *mouton* peut avoir la même signification que l'anglais *sheep*, mais non la même valeur, et cela pour plusieurs raisons, en particulier parce qu'en parlant d'une pièce de viande apprêtée et servie sur la table, l'anglais dit *mutton* et non *sheep*. (*CLG*: 160)

Holdcroft writes:

In these cases, though, it is hard to see how it could be a term belonging to *langue*; presumably Saussure's thought is that sometimes when speaking a Frenchman may clearly be speaking about sheep and not mutton, even though the distinction is not marked lexically. But this, if true, is a fact of *parole*. (Holdcroft 1991: 111)

Evidently what perplexes Holdcroft is how *mouton* and *sheep* could have the same *signification* if the equation *signification* = *signifié* were valid. The solution proposed is that – at least on some occasions in the text of the *CLG* – the *signification* must in fact be understood as the meaning that results from the use of a word in *parole*.

This is a brave attempt to make the best of a bad job, as Holdcroft in effect concedes:

the term 'signification' should only be used with the clear recognition that it is parasitic on the term 'value'. As such it is clearly dispensable, though in fact Saussure does not dispense with it. Indeed, there are occasions on which he uses it where it does not seem to be parasitic on the term 'value' [. . .] (Holdcroft 1991: 111)

There follows the *mouton/sheep* example.

Another example commentators have seized on is what the *CLG* says about the Sanskrit plural:

la valeur d'un pluriel français ne recouvre pas celle d'un pluriel sanscrit, bien que la signification soit le plus souvent identique: c'est que le sanscrit possède trois nombres au lieu de deux (*mes yeux, mes oreilles, mes bras, mes jambes*, etc., seraient au duel); il serait inexact d'attribuer la même valeur au pluriel en sanscrit et en français, puisque le sanscrit ne peut pas employer le pluriel dans tous les cas où il est de règle en français [. . .] (*CLG*: 161)

The telling qualification here is contained in the words *le plus souvent*. How can two things be more often identical than not? Only, it is suggested, if we move from the level of *langue* to that of *parole*. In other words, Saussure is construed as treating the Sanskrit plural and the French plural as being identical in *signification* in certain contexts, but not in all contexts.

When we turn to the manuscript sources of the *CLG* we discover that there is a fourth term that comes into the picture beside *valeur*, *significa-tion* and *signifié*. This is the term *sens*. We find, for example, *valeur des termes* contrasted with *sens des mots* (Engler: 1853). In Dégallier's notes there is an explicit heading for one section of the Third Course: *Valeur des termes et sens des mots; en quoi les deux choses se confondent ou restent distinctes*. This is corroborated by Constantin: *Valeur des termes et sens des mots. En quoi les deux choses se confondent et se distinguent*.

As Godel points out (Godel: 236), the wording adopted by Saussure's editors, i.e. 'La valeur [. . .] est sans doute un élément de la signification' (*CLG*: 158) appears to be a cautious reworking of the sentence that occurs in Dégallier's notes: 'La valeur est bien un élément du sens.' However, this latter statement is immediately followed by the qualification 'mais il importe de ne pas prendre le sens, d'abord, autrement que comme une valeur' (Engler: 1856). Which seemingly generates the paradox that *la valeur* is an 'element' of itself (*sens* being in turn a *valeur*).

Godel's solution is that the word *élément* is not to be understood here in the sense of 'constituent part' (*partie composante*) but in the sense of 'factor' (*ce qui produit*) or 'source' (*ce dont procède qqch.*). Saussure, in Godel's view, did not mean to imply that the *sens* contains something extra, i.e. more than the *valeur*. If this is right, then *valeur* must be what underlies *sens*, insofar as the latter can be derived by abstraction from the former, but not vice versa (Godel: 236, fn. 359).

Ingenious as Godel's conjecture may be, it does not in the end solve the problem. For we are still left with values which are factors in their own production, i.e. they somehow generate senses, which are in turn nothing other than values.

Where exactly does that leave *signification*? In the manuscript sources we find a puzzling juxtaposition of *sens* and *signification*. The statement that 'la signification est déterminée par ce qui entoure' occurs alongside the statement that 'le sens d'un terme dépend de présence ou absence d'un terme voisin' (Engler: 1877, 1883).

Sechehaye had already spotted the problem and believed he had solved it. For he wrote in the *Collation*:

Je crois avoir bien interprété cette énigme: *signification* et *sens* sont synonymes et *ce qui entoure* doit vouloir dire l'occasion, le contexte, et non les rapports qui établissent la valeur comme on pourrait le croire. (*Coll.*: 448)

This at least explains why the term *sens* does not appear in the relevant passages of the text published in 1916 (i.e. because the editors regarded it as a superfluous terminological variant and suppressed it in favour of *signification*).

So Sechehaye's conclusion, right from the beginning, was that *signification* is a term which relates to signs as used in *parole*, whereas *valeur* relates to signs as units of *langue*.

Bally's article 'L'arbitraire du signe: valeur et signification' (Bally 1940) supports this reading of the distinction:

C'est seulement dans la parole, dans le discours, que le signe, par contact avec la réalité, a une signification (p.ex. «L'arbre que vous voyez là-bas ne porte pas de fruits»), et c'est seulement dans la langue, à l'état latent, que ce même signe déclenche un faisceau d'associations mémorielles qui constituent sa valeur (p.ex. *arbre : arbuste, arbre : tronc, arbre : sapin, hêtre; arbre : forêt*, etc. etc.). (Bally 1940: 194–5)

Both editors, in short, agreed on this reading of the Saussurean term *signification*. They were followed by Burger in 1961, who gave it a new twist. According to Burger, what Saussure had in mind was the phenomenon of polysemy:

si la langue est un système de valeurs, si c'est de la valeur que dépend le sens, cela signifie que c'est la valeur, entité purement virtuelle, qui permet la manifestation, dans le discours, de significations diverses mais qui toutes dépendent des rapports qu'elle entretient avec les autres valeurs du système. D'une valeur donnée peut découler un nombre indéterminé de significations; c'est l'ensemble des significations qui se manifestent dans le discours qui représentent le signifié. (Burger 1961: 7)

By 1966, having at first proposed a quite different interpretation, Godel came round to Burger's point of view (Godel 1966: 55). Thus in the end the original editors of the *Cours* succeeded in establishing their own view as the standard interpretation, and were followed in this by a long line of subsequent commentators. The question which remains, however, is whether this interpretation is correct, or even plausible.

That seems very doubtful for several reasons. In the first place, because it presupposes that in his use of the term *signification* Saussure was anticipating a theoretical point which actually belonged in the promised – but never delivered – lectures on *linguistique de la parole*. There is no evidence that this was the case. It would have been quite easy for Saussure to point out any such anticipation to those who attended his Third Course, for the distinction between *langue* and *parole* had already been thoroughly grounded in the lectures given in April 1911 before he got round to introducing the notion of *valeur*. Saussure made no such attempt to situate this distinction by reference to a *linguistique de la parole*: or if he did his students curiously paid no attention to it at all – which seems highly unlikely.

In the second place, as George Wolf (p.c.) has pointed out, Sechehaye's understanding of *ce qui entoure* is difficult to reconcile with the explicit comment in Constantin's notes immediately preceding the statement that 'la signification est déterminée par ce qui entoure' (*CLG3*: 137), which says: 'Le système conduit au terme et le terme à la valeur.'

In the third place, the assignment of *signification* to *parole* blatantly contradicts the equation *signification = signifié*. It assumes, rather, that the *signification* stands to the *signifié* as the individual act of phonation stands to the *signifiant*. But then any claim that *mouton* and *sheep* may have the same *signification* would be the exact semantic parallel to claiming that *mouton* and *sheep* may be identically pronounced.

Looking back from almost a hundred years on, what are we to make of this? The problem has its roots in exegetical attempts to reconcile apparent inconsistencies in the manuscript sources. Different students may well have interpreted what Saussure said differently, and Saussure may have expressed himself differently at different times. But when we look at the most reliable set of notes for the Third Course, i.e. those of Constantin, a reasonably clear picture emerges. According to Constantin, Saussure never said several things the 1916 text makes him say. For instance, what Saussure said according to Constantin was simply that *mouton* and *sheep* could not have the same *valeur*. The gratuitous assertion that, nevertheless, these words could have the same *signification* is an addition by the editors.

Likewise, it is the editors who attribute to Saussure the claim that the *signification* of the French plural and the Sanskrit plural is 'le plus souvent identique'. Constantin records a very different comment:

> La valeur d'un pluriel allemand ou latin n'est pas la valeur d'un pluriel sanscrit. Mais la signification, si l'on veut, est la même. (*CLG3*: 136)

Here there is no 'le plus souvent' (which would indeed have suggested that Saussure was thinking of equivalences that might apply in different circumstances of *parole*), but a revealing 'si l'on veut' (which makes it quite clear that this is not Saussure's preferred way of putting the matter).

What we have here is a comment on the metalinguistic term *pluriel* and a warning to be on one's guard against being misled by its apparent semantic implications. What Saussure is pointing out is that when grammarians apply the concept of plurality to different languages there is – 'si l'on veut' – a sense in which they are drawing attention to common features of meaning: but the point of view from which such comparisons are legitimate is quite different from the point of view which validates the establishment of linguistic values. There can be no equivalence of grammatical *valeurs* where there is no equivalence of grammatical structure.

The puzzle over Saussure's use of the term *signification* arises from his editors' (and subsequent commentators') assumption that the word *signification* must be given the status of a technical term in Saussurean metalinguistics. There is no ground for this assumption. If we read Constantin's very full and lucid notes it becomes clear that what Constantin understood Saussure as doing at this juncture in his Third Course of lectures was drawing attention to various ambiguities in the (traditional) notion of '*signification*'. And in this interpretation Constantin seems almost certainly right. *Signification* was a term Saussure had used repeatedly in his (mainly historical) First Course, but without probing its implications (*CLG1*: 161).

Signs signify, as everyone agrees. But the general relation of 'signifying' will not do for purposes of Saussure's synchronic analysis because it is sufficiently broad to encompass not only the vague lay concept of *sens des mots* ('what words mean') but also the grammarian's use of notions like 'plural' (often defined as meaning 'more than one') and the translator's appeal to interlingual correspondences (such as between *mouton* and *sheep*). All of which are, for the synchronic theorist, meretricious.

In other words, what Saussure was saying in his Third Course was (1) that *signification* is for various reasons a potentially misleading term, and (2) that the only valid interpretation of it within the framework of *linguistique de la langue* is to construe it as the conceptual aspect of *valeur*. Everything else then falls into place. What his editors took him as doing, however, was anticipating a distinction between the semantics of *langue* and the semantics of *parole*, which would have been elaborated in due course in his *linguistique de la parole*.

*   *   *

The other lacuna the *linguistique de la parole* would have filled, in the editors' view, concerns the relationships between *synchronie* and *diachro-*

nie. This is clear from what they subsequently wrote on the subject. Of particular interest are Bally's paper 'Synchronie et diachronie', published in 1937, and two articles by Sechehaye, 'Évolution organique et évolution contingentielle' (1939) and 'Les trois linguistiques saussuriennes' (1940). The last of these throws considerable light on the editors' worries. For Sechehaye, the essential role of a *linguistique de la parole* would have been to provide the missing link between *linguistique synchronique* and *linguistique diachronique*. Sechehaye saw that Saussure's insistence on the absolute separation of synchrony from diachrony would leave linguistics in the untenable position of lacking any coherent account of the transition between one *état de langue* and the next.

In the light of this it is worth reconsidering the contentious concluding statement of the 1916 text: '*la linguistique a pour unique et véritable objet la langue envisagée en elle-même et pour elle-même*'(*CLG*: 317). This eminently quotable 'formule radicale' (Gadet 1987: 78) is explicitly claimed by the editors to be 'l'idée fondamentale de ce cours' (*CLG*: 317). But what exactly did they mean by that?

Was it intended to exclude from linguistics 'proper' the study of *parole*? (And, if so, under what discipline or disciplines did the study of *parole* then fall?) Did it, as one commentator proposed, restrict linguistics to 'internal' linguistics (Leroy 1963: 73)? Did it, strictly speaking, exclude the study of linguistic change, inasmuch as change was envisaged as involving relations between items *not* forming a linguistic system (*CLG*: 193)? Whatever the controversial sentence was supposed to summarize, it was clearly a bad summary, since there were so many possible conflicting interpretations.

De Mauro blames this unhappy formulation for the position adopted by later structuralists, who took it as a Saussurean licence to ignore

> les déséquilibres du système, la dynamique synchronique, les conditionnements sociaux, les phénomènes évolutifs, le lien entre ces derniers et les différentes contingences historiques, tout le flot de phénomènes linguistiques dont et grâce auxquels la langue est forme. L'ajout de la dernière phrase est le sceau d'une manipulation éditoriale des notes saussuriennes qui porte en partie la responsabilité de l'attitude exclusiviste du structuralisme, spécialement dans les courants post-bloomfieldiens des U.S.A. (De Mauro: 476)

Instead, De Mauro proposes that the whole heterogeneous range of concerns mentioned in *CLG*: 20–2 would have been included by Saussure as the legitimate *matière* of linguistics, for which *la langue* nevertheless provides the *objet*. Saussure, according to De Mauro, used *objet* in the medieval scholastic sense of *objectum*, or 'finalité d'une activité' (De

Mauro: 415). In the case of a science, this is 'la matière du savoir en tant qu'elle est apprise et connue', a sense attested in Aquinas and Duns Scotus, and still alive in modern philosophy. In support of this De Mauro quotes Dewey on the application of the term *object* to what has been produced and arranged systematically in the course of research. Similarly for Saussure, 'la totalité des faits qualifiables de linguistique est la *matière*, la langue comme système formel est l'*objet*'.

The question is not quite so easily settled, however. For according to Dewey,

> if knowledge is related to inquiry as its warrantably assertable product, and if inquiry is progressive and temporal, then the material inquired into reveals distinctive properties which need to be designated by distinctive names. As *undergoing* inquiry, the material has a different logical import from that which it has as the *outcome* of inquiry. In its first capacity and status, it will be called by the general name *subject-matter*. [. . .] The name *objects* will be reserved for subject-matter so far as it has been produced and ordered in settled form by means of inquiry; proleptically, objects are the *objectives* of inquiry. (Dewey 1938: 118–19)

For Dewey, therefore, *subject-matter* and *object* are two terms for the same thing, but considered from different points of view; whereas that is not how De Mauro is proposing to construe the difference between *matière* and *objet*, since the former includes all the 'masse hétéroclite' that falls under *langage*. And for Saussure, it seems clear, *langue* is certainly not just *langage* under another name or considered from a different perspective.

Whether De Mauro supposes that the editors were also using the term *objet* in that technical sense (= *objectum*) in the final sentence of their 1916 text is less clear. The explanation, in any case, is not without problems. The editors seem to have interpreted Saussure as distinguishing *three* main questions concerning linguistics: (1) what is its *matière*? (2) what is its *tâche*?, and (3) what is its *objet*? The first two are dealt with in Chapter 2 of the Introduction to the *CLG*, which is entitled 'Matière et tâche de la linguistique: ses rapports avec les sciences connexes', while the third is dealt with separately in the following chapter, entitled 'Objet de la linguistique'. The answers, as presented in the *CLG*, are as follows. The *matière* consists of 'toutes les manifestations du langage humain', of all peoples and levels of society, whether civilized or not, and including written texts as well as speech (*CLG*: 20). The *tâche* has three parts: (1) to describe all known languages, their history, the families to which they belong, and to reconstruct wherever possible the ancestral language of each such family, (2) to discover what universal forces are operative in all languages and formulate general laws which will account for all attested linguistic phenomena, and (3) to delimit and define linguistics itself (*CLG*: 20).

The answer to the third question, however, is less straightforward, since – the reader is told – linguistics, unlike other sciences, does not have its *objet* 'given in advance':

> D'autres sciences opèrent sur des objets donnés d'avance, et qu'on peut considérér ensuite à différents points de vue; dans notre domaine, rien de semblable. (*CLG*: 23)

Instead, the linguist finds that words can be considered as sounds, as expressions of ideas, and in other ways as well, depending on the perspective adopted.

> Bien loin que l'objet précède le point de vue, on dirait que c'est le point de vue qui crée l'objet. (*CLG*: 23)

Furthermore, it is not obvious that any one of the various possible perspectives takes priority over the others. Nowhere do we find 'l'objet intégral de la linguistique' emerging of its own accord. What is the solution?

> *il faut se placer de prime abord sur le terrain de la langue et la prendre pour norme de toutes les autres manifestations du langage.* (*CLG*: 25. Italics in the original.)

This somewhat sibylline answer, unfortunately, still leaves the status of the *objet* unclear. It seems, in fact, to be an answer worded in such a way as to avoid saying that *la langue* is this *objet*. Were the editors hesitant to commit Saussure overtly to this identification?

The reader of the 1916 text may well feel uncertain at this point which of two possible conclusions to opt for: (1) linguistics, having no natural *objet* of its own, since the *manifestations du langage* are too diverse, must therefore – unlike other sciences – define itself in another way, i.e. by *stipulating* what it will investigate in such a manner as to distinguish itself from neighbouring disciplines, or (2) only by focussing on *la langue* will linguistics be able, eventually, to discover what its *objet* really is. Either reading might seem to square with the notion that one part of the *tâche* facing linguistics is self-definition. But neither sits very happily with De Mauro's interpretation of *objet* (= *objectum*). It is hard to see how in that sense a science could already start with an *objectum* which could then be considered from various points of view. And it would be particularly odd to have a science in which the 'finalité de l'activité' were in doubt or open to question in the way that is – apparently – the case in linguistics.

Later in the same chapter of the *CLG* 'la langue' is referred to on three occasions not as *the* 'objet' but as *an* 'objet': it is described as 'un objet bien défini dans l'ensemble hétéroclite des faits de langage' (*CLG*: 31), as 'un objet qu'on peut étudier séparément' – i.e. separately from 'la parole' (*CLG*: 31), and as 'un objet de nature concrète' (*CLG*: 32). These three references are also difficult to reconcile with the interpretation of *objet* as *objectum*: they come after the account of the 'circuit de la parole' and the detailed explanation of how *la parole* differs from *la langue*. But nowhere are we told explicitly that the latter is *the* 'objet de la linguistique'. So it is somewhat less than clear whether the term *objet* is being used consistently in the same sense throughout the chapter.

The picture becomes even more complicated when we turn from the *CLG* to the terminology used in the students' notes. For there, instead of a triple distinction between the *matière*, the *tâche* and the *objet* that the editors propose, we find that the latter two of these are amalgamated. In the fullest notes for the Third Course, those of Constantin, the discussion is introduced by a dictionary definition, apparently quoted with approval by Saussure, which defines linguistics as 'étude scientifique des langues'. (The plural is to be noted.) The questions then raised concerning this 'étude scientifique' are: 'Qu'a-t-elle devant soi: 1) comme matière 2) comme objet ou tâche [?]' (*CLG3*: 3).The answer immediately proposed to the first question is: '1) une étude scientifique aura pour matière toute espèce de modification du langage humain' (*CLG3*: 3).

This answer is then elaborated in some detail (*CLG3*: 3–4). However, when attention switches to the second question the term *matière* disconcertingly reappears: '2) La matière, la tâche ou l'objet de l'étude scientifique des langues, ce sera . . . etc.' (*CLG3*: 4). In this reformulation it seems that *matière*, *tâche* and *objet* are no longer distinct, and that conclusion appears to be borne out by the summarizing remark a few lines later: 'Une fois la linguistique ainsi conçue, c'est-à-dire ayant devant elle le langage dans toutes ses manifestations, un objet qui est aussi large que possible . . .' (*CLG3*: 4–5).

What is now referred to as the *objet* is precisely what was identified in reply to the first question as the *matière*. Furthermore, the lecture has begun with a brief historical survey which mentions three ways in which *la langue* may be or has been considered an *objet d'étude* (*CLG3*: 1). Two of these are normative grammar and comparative philology. It hardly needs emphasizing that normative grammarians patently do not have the same *objectum* as comparative philologists. It seems difficult, therefore, not to conclude that what makes such different pursuits describable as having *la langue* as their *objet* is simply that their *matière* overlaps (i.e. comprises various *manifestations du langage*), normative grammarians and comparative philologists being nevertheless interested in that *matière* for quite dissimilar ends. Thus De Mauro's appeal to the *objectum* of scholastic philosophy, although interesting, seems to be a red herring: it complicates the exegesis of Saussure's terminology unnecessarily without actually illuminating it. If Saussure did, in his classroom exposition, trade on subtle philosophical distinctions of this order, he evidently did not make those distinctions very clear to his audience.

The question of the *objet* comes up again for consideration right at the beginning of the second lecture of the Third Course.

> Sans séparer immédiatement les mots de langue et de langage, où trouvons-nous le phénomène concret < complet > , intégral de la langue ou du langage? C'est-à-dire, où trouvons-nous l'objet devant lequel nous avons à nous placer? Avec tous ses caractères provisoirement contenus en lui et non analysés? C'est une difficulté qui n'existe pas dans telle ou telle autre discipline que ne pas avoir devant soi la matière devant laquelle on doit se placer. Ce serait une erreur de croire que c'est en prenant ce qu'il y a de plus général qu'on aura cet objet intégral, complet. (*CLG3*: 6)

This again speaks against any interpretation of *objet* as *objectum*. For here the *objet* is explicitly identified as the unanalysed whole from which the linguist's investigation begins. And again this is equated with *matière*: 'la matière devant laquelle on doit se placer', which is what other disciplines have unproblematically available from the start. The difficulty for general linguistics would seem to be that scientific generalizations presuppose a well-defined, homogeneous domain over which they hold; and *that* is what the heteroclite phenomena of *langage* fail to provide. Because the *matière* offered by the many and diverse *manifestations du language* is so disparate, there is no clearly delimited *objet* for a linguistics of *langage* to investigate. This produces a chicken-and-egg problem. Generalizations are possible only if one adopts methods of analysis predicated on the assumption that there *is* a well-defined *objet*; and this is exactly what the *matière* does not guarantee. The solution, according to one reading of the *CLG*, is to cut the Gordian knot and opt for the study of *la langue*, because that, although only part of *langage*, at least constitutes a coherent, self-contained whole, whereas none of the other *manifestations du langage* does. But the remainder can nevertheless be accommodated eventually by relating them to *la langue* in one way or another. Is this what the editors interpreted Saussure's programmatic message as being? That would make sense of the concluding sentence of their text.

However, it is an interpretation which is difficult to reconcile with some jarring pieces of counter-evidence from the manuscript sources. In his minute examination of the editorial interventions, Godel suggested that the text of their final sentence should have identified 'les langues et la langue' as the 'véritable objet de la linguistique' (Godel: 181). De Mauro follows Godel in pointing out that the students' notes for the Third Course record an important distinction between *la langue* and *les langues*. If this is taken into account, an ambiguity in the term *langue* emerges, which the editors glossed over or failed to see. That is to say, on one reading *la langue* is merely the singular of *les langues*: what the final sentence of the *CLG* therefore says is that the linguistic study of any speech community is the study of its *langue*. This study, undertaken for its own sake, and not for any ulterior purpose, is the linguist's true and sole concern. On the other reading, however, *la langue* is taken as generic. In other words, the 'unique et véritable objet' is something underlying all particular *langues* and manifested collectively in them. This, clearly, cannot be identified or studied simply by focussing on one *langue*, or even several *langues*, since every single *langue* will have its own peculiarities. The latter reading of the text sets a far higher goal than the former, but one which conforms to and emphasizes the second of the three tasks mentioned in *CLG*: 20: 'chercher les forces qui sont en jeu d'une manière permanente et universelle dans toutes les langues [. . .].'

Support for this latter reading comes from the comments made in the Third Course on the distinction between *la langue* and *les langues*. In his lecture of 8 November 1910, according to Constantin's notes, Saussure explained the difference as follows:

> Première partie: Les langues
> Ce titre s'oppose à celui du second chapitre: la langue. Il n'y a pas d'avantage à préciser plus et le sens contenu dans ces deux titres opposés s'offre suffisamment de lui-même. Ainsi, quoi qu'il ne faille pas abuser des comparaisons avec les sciences naturelles, il y aurait un sens qui, de même, serait clair d'emblée à opposer dans une étude d'histoire naturelle «la plante» et «les plantes» (cf. aussi «les insectes» opposé à «l'insecte»). (*CLG3*: 10)

If only a statement as unambiguous as this had survived into the published text of the *CLG*, much misunderstanding and contentious debate might subsequently have been avoided. The passage continues:

> Ces divisions correspondraient assez bien par le contenu même à ce que nous aurons en linguistique en séparant «la langue» et «les langues»; il y a des carrières entières de botanistes ou de naturalistes qui se déroulent dans l'une et l'autre de ces

directions. Il y a des botanistes qui classent des plantes sans s'occuper de la circulation de la sève, etc., c'est-à-dire sans s'occuper de «la plante». (*CLG3*: 10)

This explicit comparison between botany and linguistics is interesting. Does Saussure imply that there are linguists too who spend all their time on «les langues» and ignore «la langue»? It is difficult to escape that conclusion or pay no heed to the veiled criticism it contains. That criticism seems to be directed primarily at his predecessors, the comparative philologists, and fits in with the accusation the lecturer had already levelled two weeks previously against the comparativist school; namely, that their approach was 'dénuée [. . .] d'un point de vue sur la langue' (*CLG3*: 2). These, it would seem, were the linguists who concerned themselves exclusively with «les langues» and ignored the study of «la langue». Seen in this light, Saussure's emphasis on giving priority to a *linguistique de la langue* is not an empty tautology, as it might otherwise appear. A *linguistique de la langue* is by no means to be equated with a *linguistique des langues*: that is Saussure's point. It is a point that would be obscured by Godel's proposed emendation of the controversial final sentence of the *CLG*.

The distinction between *les langues* and *la langue* is re-stated in even clearer terms later in the same section:

> Les langues, c'est l'objet concret qui s'offre sur la surface du globe au linguiste; la langue, c'est le titre qu'on peut donner à ce que le linguiste aura su tirer < de général > de l'ensemble de ses observations à travers le temps et à travers l'espace. (*CLG3*: 11)

We may note here that the 'objet concret' is not *la langue* but *les langues*. Six months later, on 5 May 1911, Saussure returned to the same topic:

> Avant de passer au chapitre [III], il faut réparer une omission. A la fin du premier chapitre, ajoutez ceci: Telle étant notre notion de la langue, il est clair qu'elle ne nous est représentée que par la série des diverses langues. Nous ne pouvons la saisir que sur une langue déterminée quelconque. *La langue*, ce mot au singulier, comment se justifie-t-il? Nous entendons par là une généralisation, ce qui se trouvera vrai pour toute langue déterminée, sans être obligé de préciser. Il ne faut pas croire que ce terme général *la langue* équivaudra à *langage*. (*CLG3*: 78)

The first two sentences of the above passage were also copied by Constantin on to a loose leaf in his notebook (*CLG3*: 73), evidently with a view to inserting the remark in its rightful place. This seems to be a point which Saussure regarded as sufficiently important to invite his students to take it down verbatim from dictation. What underlay his anxiety about this 'omission'? Perhaps the realization that in his lectures he had not been distinguishing carefully enough between the 'terme général' and the singular of *les langues*, and that in consequence some of his pronouncements about linguistics as the study of *la langue* were open to conflicting interpretations (as indeed they were).

The editors were not unaware of the problem. How did they tackle it? It is interesting to note that in Sechehaye's *Collation* the presentation follows the order of topics adopted by Saussure in his Third Course. The general plan is announced as follows:

> Division générale du cours:
>   1. Les langues
>   2. La langue
>   3. La faculté et l'exercice du langage chez les individus.
>
> (*Coll.*: 14)

There follows a 'Chapitre préliminaire' subtitled 'Justification de cette division et de cet ordre'. At this stage in the editorial process, clearly, the programme Saussure had devised for the Third Course was being taken very seriously and followed as closely as possible. That approach was later abandoned by the editors in favour of the quite different arrangement adopted in the 1916 text. One major consequence is that the distinction between *les langues* and *la langue* drops out of sight. This, it seems *prima facie*, is an editorial error of the first magnitude. What accounts for it?

A clue is perhaps provided by the note that Sechehaye appended to the text on p. 24 of his *Collation*:

> Ma rédaction a pour but de bien faire sentir qu'il n'y a pas de contradiction avec ce qui est dit plus haut que la langue est l'objet *concret* de la linguistique. Cette phrase correspond bien d'ailleurs quant au sens avec celle qui suit dans D, si je l'interprète bien. (*Coll.*: 24)

The reference here is to Dégallier's notes for the Third Course, which read:

> Il faut d'abord étudier les langues, une diversité de langues. Par observation de ces langues, on tirera ce qui est universel. Il aura alors devant lui un ensemble d'abstractions: ce sera *la* langue, où nous étudierons ce qui s'observe dans *les* différentes langues. (Engler: 429)

Here we are presumably dealing with advice to the (trainee) linguist. The first requirement is acquaintance with as wide a range of languages as possible. This is confirmed by the corresponding notes taken by Joseph:

Le linguiste est obligé d'étendre son étude à une diversité la plus grande possible de langues. Par l'étude, il pourra tirer des traits généraux. Il y aura alors devant lui un ensemble d'abstractions pour obtenir *la langue*. C'est le résultat de ce que nous pouvons retirer des *différentes langues*. (Engler: 429)

In all these versions the distinction between *les langues* and *la langue* is stressed. But it is obvious that we are here looking at linguistic inquiry from the point of view of the linguist, not from the point of view of the linguistic community or its members. This is what makes sense of the order of priority, i.e. what underwrites the (otherwise puzzling) claim that 'ce qui nous est donné, ce sont les langues' (*CLG*: 44). The *nous* here is the professional fraternity of linguists. And from 'ce qui nous est donné' we linguists proceed to abstract *la langue*.

It is only in this perspective that Sechehaye's worried note, cited above, makes sense. The problem, as he sees it, is how to reconcile (1) *la langue* as an abstraction from *les langues* with (2) *la langue* as the 'objet concret' of linguistic study. It is the opposition between 'abstract' and 'concrete' that generates the tension and, along with it, the potential ambiguity about what the linguist should be aiming to do. Sechehaye's solution ('ma rédaction'), which Engler does not quote, reads as follows:

Par abstraction il [sc. the linguist] tirera de ces langues ce qu'il y a d'universel en elles. Il aura alors devant lui un ensemble d'abstractions par le moyen desquelles il entre en contact, autant que faire se peut, avec la langue; en d'autres termes nous étudierons dans ces abstractions ce qui s'observe de la langue dans les différentes langues.

Il faut donc passer d'abord par l'étude des langues pour arriver à l'étude de la langue. (*Coll.*: 24)

In the 1916 text, unfortunately, all this is watered down into:

ce qui nous est donné, ce sont les langues. Le linguiste est obligé d'en connaître le plus grand nombre possible, pour tirer de leur observation et de leur comparaison ce qu'il y a d'universel en elles. (*CLG*: 44)

In the end, in other words, the editors declined to grasp the bull by the horns. They opted for leaving the exact relationship between *la langue* and *les langues* open to discussion. This could hardly have been because they lacked evidence for ascertaining Saussure's view: as the students' notes reveal, Saussure went out of his way to make his view clear. The motive underlying the editors' caution, one must assume, is that they felt Saussure's view to be problematic or even untenable.

Possible reasons for this can be traced back to Sechehaye's own

Programme et méthodes de la linguistique théorique (Sechehaye 1908). There Sechehaye had adopted Naville's distinction between *sciences des faits* and *sciences des lois*. The former deal with contingent observed particulars, the latter with generalizations and necessary conditions. According to Se-chehaye, a given *science des faits* and a corresponding *science des lois* will have the same 'objet', but each will consider this 'objet' from a different point of view. (Clearly this is not the sense in which *objet* can be construed as equivalent to *objectum*.) If Saussure's distinction between *les langues* and *la langue* is situated in this framework, the former will belong to a *science des faits* and the latter to the corresponding *science des lois*. This throws some light on Sechehaye's note in the *Collation* quoted above, and also on his proposed 'rédaction' of the passage in question. What Saussure had evidently failed to do, in Sechehaye's eyes, was explain this very distinction: instead, Saussure had proposed a hybrid linguistics which was partly *science des faits* (describing all known languages) and partly *science des lois* (discovering universal forces and general laws), as if these two enterprises were on the same footing. For Sechehaye, this was a mistake, or, at the very least, misleading. Hence Sechehaye makes a point in *Coll.*: 24 of insisting that 'il faut donc passer par l'étude des langues pour arriver à l'étude de la langue', as if these two inquiries were serially ordered. Whether that was Saussure's view is certainly questionable: it corre-sponds to nothing we have in the students' notes for the Third Course. Furthermore, it runs up against the objection Saussure himself voices:

L'opération de généralisation suppose justement l'abstraction, suppose qu'on a déjà pénétré dans l'objet à étudier de manière à en tirer ce qu'on déclare être ses traits généraux. (*CLG3*: 6)

The question is how to reconcile this with what Saussure advocates later in the same lecture, when he says of the linguist:

Il doit étudier d'abord les langues, le plus possible de langues, il doit étendre son horizon autant qu'il peut. C'est ainsi que nous procéderons. Par l'étude, l'observa-tion de ces langues, il pourra tirer des traits généraux, il retiendra tout ce qui lui paraît essentiel et universel, pour laisser de côté le particulier et l'accidentel. Il aura devant lui un ensemble d'abstractions qui sera la langue. C'est ce qu'on peut résumer dans cette seconde division: la langue. Dans «la langue» nous résumons ce que nous pouvons observer dans les différentes langues. (*CLG3*: 10)

But how is this way of proceeding viable if the objection raised previously is valid? Given languages as disparate as, say, Latin and Japanese, how does one set about the process of setting aside their 'particular' and 'accidental' features in order to 'abstract' their common essence? More problematic still, how can the weeding out of inessential features be squared with the thesis that each language is a unique system 'dont tous les termes sont solidaires'? These are questions that remain unanswered. And perhaps they are questions that Bally and Sechehaye never could have answered, given the evidence at their disposal.

What emerges from the editorial treatment of these few crucial points throws some light on the 'guardianship' of Saussure's reputation that Bally and Sechehaye took upon themselves after his death, including their reluctance to publish the students' notes. They could hardly have failed to realize that there were passages in the notes that cast doubt on the validity of their own interpretation. At the same time they wished to present a text that unambiguously offered the world that new vision of linguistics which they attributed to Saussure, and which they believed Saussure would eventually have presented himself, once he had resolved certain difficulties. The text they published in 1916 therefore pushes these difficulties into the background, in order to highlight the innovative features, as they saw it, of Saussure's teaching. The compromise was always going to be an awkward one. In striking it, the editors displayed both intellectual and rhetorical skills of a high order. Their aim was to convince a whole generation of linguists not only that their text 'spoke for' Saussure, but that Saussure, thus spoken for, had at last laid the permanent foundations of a modern science of language.

They did not immediately succeed in convincing everyone, even among those close to Saussure. Meillet, for one, immediately voiced serious doubts. His comments on the *CLG* provide an interesting example of how difficult it was for linguists who regarded Saussure's early *Mémoire sur le système primitif des voyelles dans les langues indo-européennes* as his outstanding contribution to linguistics to refocus their perception of him and come to terms with the new Saussure that Bally and Sechehaye had presented.

Meillet's review of the *CLG*, published in the *Bulletin de la Société de Linguistique de Paris* in 1916, is full of reservations. He emphasizes the lacunae in the work and the sketchy nature of the treatment of many topics: it is not 'un exposé complet de la linguistique générale'. It says nothing, for instance, about grammatical categories. What Meillet – bizarrely – singles out for approval are its treatment of the theory of the syllable and the etymology of Latin *dominus*. This damnation with faint praise reflects how completely Meillet failed to grasp, or at least to sympathize with, Saussure's more ambitious programme for synchronic linguistics. Having cited two cases in which Saussure's linguistic examples happen to be factually incorrect, Meillet adds the gratuitous comment that it would not really matter if they were all wrong: the book, being an exposition of general ideas, would lose nothing essential thereby. (The observation has a studied ambivalence: the idea of a general linguistics founded entirely on erroneous examples is curiously barbed.)

Meillet's objections to the 'general ideas' in the *Cours* focus on two topics in particular. One is the priority given to the study of *langue* over the study of *parole*. For, according to Meillet:

> Ce n'est pourtant qu'en étudiant minutieusement la parole que le phonéticien peut arriver à décrire la langue. Le problème, singulièrement difficile, qui consiste à rechercher comment, en observant la parole, on peut définir une langue n'est pas abordé de front. Or, plus les progrès de la phonétique permettent de préciser l'observation de la parole et plus la technique de l'observation des parlers se perfectionne, plus le problème devient embarrassant. (Meillet 1916)

It seems clear from this that Meillet had failed to realize that, in Saussure's view, it was not the phonetician's task to describe *la langue* at all. Phonetics, for Saussure, is not part of linguistics but an ancillary discipline with techniques of its own. However much these techniques improve (sound recording, instrumental analysis, etc.), this will not cause – and cannot cause – increasing embarrassment for the linguist, since *la langue* is always based on a fixed number of phonetic differences anyway. These do not alter. They are already accessible to speakers of the language, who do not have the phonetician's sophisticated instruments at their disposal, and hence they are also available for description by the linguist who is prepared to rely on the testimony of distinctions recognized – or ignored – by the speakers themselves.

Nor, on the other hand, will the phonetician be able, as time goes by, to provide ever greater assistance in the linguist's analytic task. The entire question of 'facilitating/complicating' a description of *langue* is an irrelevance. All that can happen as the result of technical progress in phonetics is that the range of differences serving to distinguish one *signifiant* from another can be described in ever greater detail. But that will be phonetic detail, not linguistic detail.

In short, Meillet (in 1916) had not fully grasped either (1) the theoretical implications of Saussure's distinction between *langue* and *parole,* or – much more fundamental – (2) Saussure's philosophy of science. Which amounts to saying that he was not on Saussure's wavelength at all. Meillet's objection about how to cope with progress in phonetics reveals precisely the kind of empiricist naivety that Saussure had recognized as inimical to the establishment of a soundly based linguistics.

For Meillet 'scientific' advance evidently consists of accumulating ever more copious and accurate information about observable phenomena, and the question he sees Saussure as having failed to address is how to cope with the continually increasing influx. This is the ever-more-embarrassing 'problem', as Meillet sees it.

Saussure's response would doubtless have been: 'Quel problème?' Here we have a classic dialogue of the deaf. The whole point of the axiomatic distinction between *langue* and *parole* is that describing *langue* is no longer to be seen as 'reducing' the myriad facts of *parole* to a simpler or more perspicuous format. That was the positivist view that eventually triumphed in those schools of linguistics where linguistic description was regarded as a mere matter of 'arranging the data'; but it was not Saussure's. There is a world of difference between saying that *parole* involves making (observable) use of one's *langue* (which is not directly observable) and concluding from this that what the linguist needs in order to deal with the unobservable is better evidence about *parole*. This would be like supposing that installing a television camera focussed on the field of play will lead to a better understanding of the game. (It may indeed lead to detecting infringements that the referee or the umpire did not spot, but that is a different matter.) Meillet's tacit assumption, in other words, is that the role of observation in linguistics is exactly as in the natural sciences. He is seemingly oblivious to the fact that this idea has been confronted and rejected in the *CLG*: we are told that a film showing details of all the movements of the mouth and larynx during the execution of a speech sequence would be of no help in determining its subdivision into phonetic units (*CLG*: 64). And more explicitly still:

> quand on a expliqué tous les movements de l'appareil vocal nécessaires pour produire chaque impression acoustique, on n'a éclairé en rien le problème de la langue. (*CLG*: 56)

The other main objection voiced in Meillet's review of 1916 concerns the treatment of linguistic facts. It is all very well, says Meillet, to isolate a *fait de langue* for purposes of study; but one must not suppose that by so doing the linguist has come to grips with linguistic reality.

> Il est légitime d'examiner un fait de langue en lui-même et de constater, par exemple, qu'un ancien *d* est représenté en germanique par un *t* et un ancien *ly* en français moderne par un *y*. Mais il s'agit là de faits historiques qui ne prennent un sens que si l'on cherche les conditions qui ont déterminé ces changements. Un

changement qui résulte de ce que, en adoptant une langue étrangère, une
population a gardé ses anciennnes habitudes articulatoires est tout autre chose
qu'un changement qui résulte d'une série d'adaptations commandées par quelque
tendance, de caractère universel, à articuler de la manière la plus naturelle possible.
En séparant le changement linguistique des conditions extérieures d'où il dépend,
F. de Saussure le prive de réalité; il le réduit à une abstraction, qui est nécessairement inexplicable. (Meillet 1916)

This is a serious charge to level at the Saussure of the *CLG*, who insists
so emphatically that *faits de langue* are not abstractions and gives pride of
place in his theoretical discussions to the identification of *réalités*. Meillet
is either unconvinced by Saussure's distinction between 'internal' and
'external' linguistics or else has completely missed the point of the
extended analogy with the game of chess. For this goes to some lengths
to explain why, from the point of view of *la langue* (= *le jeu*) it makes no
difference *why* a certain move is made. What results is all that counts. And
whatever does result can be described perfectly accurately in terms of the
game without bothering about looking for reasons, which may in any case
never be known.

Meillet criticizes Saussure's account of the causes of sound change
severely:

il n'essaie aucun classement, il n'apporte aucune vue nouvelle, aucun agencement
nouveau des vues émises. Et il semble, à lire ces pages, que le problème soit presque
chimérique. (Meillet 1916)

Almost chimerical? What *would* be chimerical, from Saussure's point of
view, is supposing that being able to identify the reason for the sound
change would explain what happened. Once again, Meillet's objection
reveals his inability either to see or else, having seen, to accept Saussure's
theoretical position. One suspects the former rather than the latter, if only
because Meillet adduces no counterarguments of his own: it is as if he
thought that merely drawing attention to these points were enough to
show his readers that Saussure's position, although provocative and
challenging, is quite untenable. A general linguistics which ignores the
detailed phonetic study of *parole* and cannot explain phonetic change is
clearly deemed to be a non-starter.

By 1921, when he published his *Linguistique générale et linguistique
historique*, Meillet's view had evidently not changed. There Saussure is
given the briefest of mentions. All Meillet will say is that Saussure's
lecture notes, 'edited under the title *Cours de linguistique générale*',
indicate how one might begin to introduce some order; but a great deal

of work remains to be done if linguistic facts are 'to be ordered from the point of view of *la langue* itself' (Meillet 1921: 11). Hardly an overwhelming endorsement. And once again Meillet evidently conceives of the linguist as first assembling a collection of linguistic facts, and only then trying to put them into some kind of order. Nothing further removed from the *CLG* conception of the linguist's task could be imagined.

If Meillet had edited the students' notes, instead of Bally and Sechehaye, what would he have made of them? Almost certainly, he would have restored the Indo-European survey to its proper place. But Meillet, an outstanding scholar on all counts, hailed by one enthusiastic admirer as the '*pater patriae* of French linguistics', never managed to shake off the mind-set inculcated by nineteenth-century historical-comparative linguistics. In this respect he personifies the problem that the reception of Bally and Sechehaye's text faced. Meillet dedicated his *Introduction à l'étude comparative des langues indo-européennes* to 'mon maître M. Ferdinand de Saussure'. But he remains in Saussurean studies the classic example of the seed that fell upon stony ground.

CHAPTER FOUR

Bloomfield's Saussure

Leonard Bloomfield, eventually to become the most influential figure in American linguistics in the first half of the twentieth century, agreed that the *CLG* had 'given us the theoretical basis for a science of human speech'. Evidently, however, he found it rather difficult to detect much originality in Saussure's thinking at all; at least, to judge by the review of the second edition of the *CLG* that he published in the *Modern Language Journal* (Bloomfield 1923). For there he asserts: 'Most of what the author [sc. of the *CLG*] says has long been "in the air"'. Saussure's contribution, according to Bloomfield's review, lay mainly in his systematization of ideas that had previously been 'here and there fragmentarily expressed' (Bloomfield 1923: 63).

Bloomfield's review is so laconic as to invite reading between the lines: and this was an exercise by no means beyond the readership of the *Modern Language Journal*. The background for that reading they would have taken to be the book on general linguistics that Bloomfield himself had written, before even the first edition of the *CLG* appeared, under the title *An Introduction to the Study of Language* (Bloomfield 1914). It throws a great deal of light on what a non-European linguist of the generation after Saussure's assumed to be generally accepted as the basis of 'linguistic science'.

Like the *CLG*, *An Introduction to the Study of Language* gives the reader a brief history of linguistics (six pages) by way of background. Bloomfield includes this – significantly – not as an introduction but as a final chapter. In many respects Bloomfield's historical account is much the better of the two. It draws attention to the cultural importance of the preservation of religious texts. It mentions Panini alongside the Greek and Roman grammarians (Dionysius Thrax, Apollonius Dyscolus, Donatus, Priscian – all names that are missing from the opening chapter of the *CLG*). It points out how linguistic change and diversification itself gave rise at various times to a social need for language teaching and codification (a motivation that the *CLG* passes over in silence). It relates the renewal of interest in language at the beginning of the nineteenth century to the wider cultural phenomenon of Romanticism and European contacts with India and the East. It says something about the development of phonetics – another gap in the *CLG* chapter. Finally, in addition to mentioning the same nineteenth-century pioneers (Bopp, Grimm, Diez, etc.), Bloomfield gives pride of place to the work of a scholar whose name never appears in the *CLG* at all: Wilhelm von Humboldt.

What might be regarded as more revealing still is that when we put these two accounts side by side we see how in the *CLG* the historical narrative is designed to lead up to what Saussure clearly regarded as the turning point in his own lifetime; namely, the emergence of the Neogrammarian school. In Bloomfield's story, by contrast, we find the Neogrammarians conspicuous by their absence (although books by Paul, Brugmann and Delbrück are eventually included in Bloomfield's list of recommended reading for students). This may reflect the fact that most of *An Introduction to the Study of Language* was written before Bloomfield's studies in Germany (1913–14), but that can hardly be the full explanation. The work of the Neogrammarians was already known in British and American universities (Paul's *Principien der Sprachgeschichte* had been translated into English nearly a quarter of a century previously). But the Neogrammarians evidently did not strike Bloomfield as being nearly as important as they became for Saussure, who, having studied in Leipzig as a young man, acquired a respect for their 'scientific' approach, a respect which endured in spite of their hostility to his own work.

It is not difficult to see how, from Bloomfield's transatlantic perspective, Saussure's view of the history of his subject might appear to be focussed rather myopically on the experiences and exigencies of a European academic career. Such an impression would be reinforced by the linguistic examples offered in the body of the *CLG*: Saussure's illustrations are nearly all taken from the Indo-European languages, whereas Bloomfield's book draws on a much wider range, including Chinese, Malay, Turkish, the Bantu languages of Africa and, especially, the Amerindian languages. Saussure shows no evidence of acquaintance with the latter. Thus the 'general linguistics' of the *CLG* looks decidedly Eurocentric, as compared with the genuinely global scope that Bloomfield's book offers.

An Introduction to the Study of Language also has a section on the relation of linguistics to other sciences, which provides a parallel to Chapter II of the *CLG*. Here again Bloomfield's account is manifestly superior. It deals in turn with the relations between linguistics and

(1) philology, (2) literary history and criticism, (3) history, (4) ethnology, (5) psychology, and (6) philosophy. The *CLG*, curiously, says nothing at all about the last of these, whereas Bloomfield pertinently raises a crucial question. To what extent is the discussion of philosophical issues and even logic itself language-dependent? But what strikes the reader most forcibly on comparing the two, apart from the superficiality of the remarks in the *CLG*, is a difference of purpose. Whereas the *CLG* seems mainly concerned to justify reserving a separate place for linguistics within the gamut of intellectual inquiry, Bloomfield's focusses more on what linguistics has to offer the students of neighbouring disciplines. Where the *CLG* is territorial and apologetic, Bloomfield is generous and outward-looking. The final sentence of his book contrasts markedly with that of the *CLG*'s notorious and narrowly programmatic pronouncement about *la langue*. Bloomfield's reads: 'linguistic science is a step in the self-realization of man'. There can be little doubt about which conclusion offers a would-be student the more exciting prospect.

When Bloomfield published *An Introduction to the Study of Language* he was Assistant Professor of Comparative Philology and German at the University of Illinois and in his late twenties. The title of his book echoes that of Whitney's classic *Language and the Study of Language* (1867). In his preface Bloomfield says that his aim is the same as Whitney's. The progress made in linguistics since Whitney's day is adduced as Bloomfield's reason for this new attempt to 'give a summary of what is now known about language'. No such objective is mentioned in the *CLG*. Bloomfield, on the other hand, says nothing that matches the cautionary statement in the *CLG* that 'aujourd'hui encore les problèmes fondamentaux de la linguistique générale attendent une solution' (*CLG*: 19). If Bloomfield thought that there were such problems, he gives no hint of it in *An Introduction to the Study of Language*. He presents modern linguistics very much as an academic *fait accompli*. The queries, hesitations and successive reformulations that are so characteristic of the *CLG* find little or no place in Bloomfield's exposition. Bloomfield says he is writing both for the general reader and also 'to introduce students of philosophy, psychology, ethnology, philology and other related subjects to a juster acquaintance with matters of language' (Bloomfield 1914: vi). To this end he has limited himself to 'a presentation of the accepted doctrine'.

In a few places I have spoken of views that cannot claim more than probability, of hypotheses, and of problems yet to be solved, but I have done this explicitly and only because I think it fitting to indicate the direction in which our study is at present tending. (Bloomfield 1914: vi)

What, then, was – for Bloomfield in 1914 – 'the accepted doctrine'? How, if at all, did it differ from Saussure's?

Let us first consider Saussure's two basic principles: the principle of arbitrariness and the principle of linearity.

On the question of arbitrariness there appears to be no disagreement at all between Saussure and Bloomfield. Bloomfield even goes further than Saussure by discussing why it should be that language is based on forms that have no apparent connexion with their meanings (Bloomfield 1914: 82). He also deals with exactly the same types of possible exception as Saussure, i.e. the case of exclamations (*CLG*: 101–2; Bloomfield 1914: 72–5) and the case of onomatopoeia (*CLG*: 102; Bloomfield 1914: 81). If for no other reason, arbitrariness is 'accepted doctrine' as far as Bloomfield is concerned because it had been clearly stated some forty years earlier by Whitney, and linguistic research in the interim had uncovered no reason for questioning it. Furthermore, Whitney's formulation of the doctrine was as clear as, if not clearer than, any Saussure had provided:

> every word handed down in every human language is an arbitrary and conventional sign: arbitrary, because any one of the thousand other words current among men, or of the tens of thousands which might be fabricated, could have been equally well learned and applied to this particular purpose; conventional, because the reason for the use of this rather than another lies solely in the fact that it is already used in the community to which the speaker belongs. (Whitney 1875: 19)

It would have been difficult for Bloomfield to see Saussure as having improved on this; for Whitney's account distinguishes lucidly between arbitrariness and conventionality, whereas Saussure's fails to do so. What we find in the *CLG* is a rather vague appeal to a negative criterion: the absence of 'natural' connexion between *signifiant* and *signifié*. Between the former and the latter there is said to be 'aucune attache naturelle dans la réalité' (*CLG*: 101). But what exactly is an 'attache naturelle'? It was the opacity of this phrase that was no doubt in part responsible for the controversy that subsequently arose in Europe over Saussure's *arbitraire du signe*.

Is Saussure's principle of linearity likewise given due recognition in *An Introduction to the Study of Language*? *Linearity* is not a term that Bloomfield employs (and *linéarité* was in any case not a particularly happy term for Saussure to have chosen; as, again, subsequent controversy bears witness). However, it is clear both from Bloomfield's chapter on 'The Physical Basis of Language' (Bloomfield 1914: 18–55) and from his chapter on 'Syntax' (Bloomfield 1914: 167–94) that in practice he takes the sequential concatenation of units for granted, both at the level of articulated sounds and at the level of word combination. Nor had Whitney (or any other nineteenth-century linguist) done otherwise. The question for Bloomfield (although he does not go into it in his 1923 review) must have been whether it was worth erecting this into a 'principle' of general linguistics on a par with arbitrariness, as Saussure had.

Saussure's ostensible reasons for doing so must have seemed to Bloomfield naive, to say the least. The only rationale the *CLG* offers is based on the fact that sound is the medium of expression: 'le signifiant, étant de nature auditive, se déroule dans le temps seul et a les caractères qu'il emprunte au temps' (*CLG*: 103). But this will hardly do. There is nothing about time or sound that intrinsically imposes sequential concatenation on audible signals. What limits the possibilities as far as speech is concerned is the human vocal apparatus, its single expiratory tube and the rather restricted mechanisms for modifying the air flow. But in this respect speech is not significantly different from the barking of dogs or the twittering of birds. Can this really be a principle of general linguistics? (One might as well argue that having lungs or upright posture underwrite principles of general linguistics.) There seems, therefore, to be a gross disparity between Saussure's two principles. One (arbitrariness) is quite independent of human physiology: the other (linearity) is tied directly to the mechanism of speech production.

It is interesting to ask in this connexion why, for Saussure, arbitrariness is the 'first' principle and linearity the 'second'. The *CLG* offers no explanation; nor any comment on the disparity mentioned above between one principle and the other. For Bloomfield this theoretical upgrading of 'linearity' must have seemed tantamount to conflating two quite different aspects of the word. A careful reading of *An Introduction to the Study of Language* shows that Bloomfield did not regard the sequential concatenation of sounds as being on the same footing at all as the sequential concatenation of words. Only the first of these is a *physiological* phenomenon. The second is a *mental* phenomenon: this – and this only – has to do with the arbitrary character of the relationship between form and meaning. It is what makes possible the analysis of experience into a *serially articulated* form. What Bloomfield calls 'discursive relations' (Bloomfield 1914: 60 ff., 110 ff.) are not to be confused with mere sequentiality of sounds uttered. The two concatenations have nothing to do with each other, except that they conveniently coincide, or at least do not conflict. (Bloomfield does not explicitly make this point in his book, but doubtless because he took it for granted that the two belong to quite different orders of analysis.) In other words, it would make no difference if evolution had provided human beings with a vocal apparatus capable of uttering two or more words simultaneously. There would still be a conceptual necessity to rank the verbal units in some order of priority.

If the above suggestions are well founded, Bloomfield is showing in 1914 a considerably more sophisticated approach to 'linearity' than Saussure. In Saussure's defence it must be said that what appears in the *CLG* on the topic of linearity has been questioned as an accurate reflection of Saussure's position (De Mauro: 447–8). That is not an issue that can be pursued here. In any case, Bloomfield did not have access to the manuscript sources of the *CLG*, so he would presumably – like all his contemporaries – have taken the published text as authoritative. For our present purposes what matters is that Bloomfield would have seen no reason for crediting Saussure with originality or insight on this point: on the contrary, Bloomfield might well have supposed that Saussure's thinking was – although on the right lines – rather crude.

On both general principles, therefore, Bloomfield would have re-garded Saussure as being roughly correct, but somewhat simplistic. On related issues he would have detected no serious ground for disagreeing either. As regards the 'objet linguistique', the Saussurean linguist is primarily concerned with the investigation of speech, not writing. Writing can, indeed, give a quite misleading representation of the facts of speech (*CLG*: 45 ff.). Bloomfield makes exactly the same point: writing offers an 'imperfect analysis' of speech (Bloomfield 1914: 19 ff.). It lags behind the development of the spoken language. The 'con-servatism of orthography' (Bloomfield 1914: 21) is something the linguist must be aware of. Bloomfield even surpasses Saussure in accounting for why, psychologically, the written form comes to take priority over the spoken in a literate community (Bloomfield 1914: 21–2), whereas the *CLG* falls back on a rather disparate assortment of contributory factors (*CLG*: 46–7).

Again, Bloomfield is at one with Saussure (*CLG*: 104, 112) in insisting on the social nature of the community's language and the inability of the individual to alter it. Bloomfield had written:

> The individual's language [. . .] is not his creation, but consists of habits adopted in his expressive intercourse with other members of the community. The result of this is the individual's inability to use language except in the form in which the community as a whole uses it: he must speak as the others do, or he will not be understood. As a matter of fact he does not, in normal cases, try to speak otherwise, but unquestioningly follows his and his fellow-speakers' habits. The change which occurs in language is thus never a conscious alteration by individuals, but an

unconscious, gradual change in the habits of the entire community. (Bloomfield 1914: 17)

Even more explicitly, Bloomfield states that 'the facts of language are facts of social, not of individual psychology' (Bloomfield 1914: 198). But he agrees with the *CLG* that, nevertheless, linguistic change begins with the individual.

> Could we definitely mark out the speaker who first spoke a given innovation, trace the forces which impelled him to make it to certain features of his mental situation at the time, and similarly lay clear the motives of all the other speakers who propagated the new form, then we should be accomplishing the interpretation of a social development into terms of individual psychology. This, of course, could be done only by an omniscient observer. (Bloomfield 1914: 198–9)

On all these matters there would have been nothing new in the *CLG* for Bloomfield. The *CLG* account of physiological phonetics (*CLG*: 63–95) he would have regarded, rightly, as inferior to his own (Bloomfield 1914: 24–55). He remarks, rather dismissively, that Saussure's phonetics is 'an abstraction from French and Swiss-German that will not stand even the test of an application to English' (Bloomfield 1923: 64). And it is true that the *CLG* does not even give a satisfactory account of what a diphthong is, much less a coherent outline of the phenomena of stress and intonation. But what might have surprised Bloomfield even more is that the *CLG* makes no mention of a rather important distinction to which he had devoted a section of his own chapter on speech sounds: namely, that some variations in pronunciation are 'significant' but others 'automatic'. Since this is the forerunner of what later phonologists called the distinction between 'phonemes' and 'allophones', it is interesting as evidence that by 1914 Bloomfield's thinking about linguistic form was in at least one respect already more 'structuralist' than Saussure's.

Bloomfield held no higher opinion of Saussure's understanding of the mental side of language, in spite of the insistence in the *CLG* that 'tout est psychologique dans la langue' (*CLG*: 21). Saussure, says Bloomfield, seems to have had 'no psychology beyond the crudest popular notions' (Bloomfield 1923: 64). Bloomfield's own notions of linguistic psychology at the time he wrote *An Introduction to the Study of Language* were heavily indebted to the theories of Wilhelm Wundt, a debt that Bloomfield acknowledges in his preface (Bloomfield 1914: vi). Since Wundt was a professor at Leipzig at the very time when Saussure studied there, and was actually lecturing on language in 1876, Bloomfield must have found it almost incredible that Saussure seemed never to have heard of the founder of experimental psychology.

The conclusion that Bloomfield's review drew from Saussure's apparent ignorance of both phonetics and psychology still strikes one today as having a considerable element of tongue-in-cheek in it:

> Thus he [sc. Saussure] exemplifies, in his own person and perhaps unintentionally, what he proves intentionally and in all due form: that psychology and phonetics do not matter at all and are, in principle, irrelevant to the study of language. (Bloomfield 1923: 64)

No one who has read *An Introduction to the Study of Language* can suppose that the author actually believed 'psychology and phonetics' to be 'irrelevant to the study of language'. For that would make nonsense of the book, of which the preface concludes with the words:

> The day is past when students of mental sciences could draw on their own fancy or on 'popular psychology' for their views of mental occurrence. (Bloomfield 1914: vi)

Likewise the chapter on 'The Physical Basis of Language' berates

> the efforts of those who try to describe languages without adequate knowledge of *phonetics*. (Bloomfield 1914: 19. Italics in the original.)

Nowhere in Bloomfield's book of 1914 do we find the slightest suggestion that any serious study of language can dispense with a basic understanding of phonetics: on the contrary, Bloomfield's list of recommended reading includes primers by Sweet, Jespersen, Passy and Sievers. The same list contains the advice: 'If one has not studied psychology, some modern text of it should be read' (Bloomfield 1914: 315).

The remark about the 'irrelevance' of phonetics and psychology in the review of the *CLG* is, to be sure, hedged by the ominous qualification 'in principle'. The question, then, is: what kind of 'principle' is this? As if realizing that an explanation of the puzzle was required, Bloomfield elaborates as follows:

> Needless to say, a person who goes out to write down an unknown language or one who undertakes to teach people a foreign language, must have a knowledge of phonetics, just as he must possess tact, patience and many other virtues; in principle, however, these things are all on a par, and do not form part of linguistic theory. (Bloomfield 1923: 64)

Again it is difficult to tell how seriously this is to be taken. Can Bloomfield have supposed that, for the linguist, tact and patience were 'on a par' with a knowledge of phonetics? All the tact and patience in the world would hardly produce an accurate description of spoken English, as Bloomfield – and readers of the *Modern Language Review* – must have known. So what is Bloomfield getting at here?

The key perhaps lies in the introduction of the term *linguistic theory*. Bloomfield is here invoking the ancient and epistemologically dubious distinction between 'theory' and 'practice'. In the very first sentence of the review he had referred to 'a willingness of the scientific public to face linguistic theory, which at almost every step shocks our preconception of human affairs' (Bloomfield 1923: 63). What virtue there is in upsetting our preconceptions in the name of 'theory' which bears no relation to practicalities we are not told. Perhaps this is Bloomfield's point: for *theory* is a term he himself seems to avoid in *An Introduction to the Study of Language*. Whatever the reason, these remarks do less than justice to Saussure, who nowhere proclaims the 'irrelevance' either of phonetics or of psychology.

Bloomfield's review then turns to the Saussurean distinction between synchronic and diachronic linguistics. It is here that Bloomfield's failure to understand Saussure begins to become apparent. For Bloomfield, who puts the terms *synchronic* and *diachronic* in inverted commas, 'synchronic linguistics' is evidently no more than a neologistic way of referring to what he is accustomed to call 'descriptive linguistics'. Likewise, 'diachronic linguistics' is just another term for 'historical linguistics'. That Saussure's way of defining those terms imposes any new restrictions on the 'descriptive' and the 'historical' facets of the linguist's enterprise is a thought that does not seem to cross Bloomfield's mind. As far as he is concerned, this is another case of *plus ça change, plus c'est la même chose*. In particular, he takes no notice of Saussure's explicit rejection of 'historical grammar' (*CLG*: 185) or the remarkable lengths Saussure goes to, for example, in arguing that, contrary to superficial appearances, the disappearance of the Old French nominative case was a single isolated fact (*CLG*: 132). Blandly Bloomfield's review reassures readers that *linguistique diachronique* is just concerned with sound changes and analogical changes 'such as are recorded in our historical grammars'. The detail that for Saussure 'our historical grammars' are based on a hopeless confusion of synchronic with diachronic facts seems to have escaped Bloomfield's attention.

This blind spot in Bloomfield's reading of the *CLG* is closely linked to another. He evidently fails to appreciate the holistic character of Saussurean synchronicity. Saussure's *langue*, Bloomfield tells us, is a 'rigid system'. But he does not explain what makes the system 'rigid'. There is no mention of the interdependencies among the constituent signs; nor, *a fortiori*, is there any reference to the fact that the identity of each sign depends on the system as a whole, rather than the system being a mere assemblage of independent signs.

Bloomfield even seems to go out of his way to avoid the term *sign*. He describes the language, as seen from the Saussurean synchronic perspective, as 'a system of signals'. But then he says: 'Each signal is made up of one or more units; these units are the "sounds" of the language.' There are two confusions here. If Bloomfield's 'signal' is meant to render the Saussurean term *signe*, then indeed *la langue* is correctly described as a 'system of signals'. But not if 'signal' is intended to translate *signifiant*. However, only on the latter interpretation can it be said that each 'signal' is made up of 'sounds'. In the second place, a *signifiant* is not made up of sounds as that term is understood by the phonetician or the general public. Perhaps Bloomfield's scare quotes are intended to indicate that, but if so they are no substitute for explaining the notion of an *image acoustique*.

Worse, however, is to come. As an illustration of how the Saussurean system works, Bloomfield cites an example of his own: the suffix *s* in English:

> the signal *s* in English is not used alone; added to certain other signals it gives plural meaning (*hats*), added to certain others, it gives the third-person present-tense verb form (*puts*). (Bloomfield 1923: 64)

This is precisely what Saussure would *not* have said. In Saussurean terms, there are two signs here, each with its own *signifié*. The difference in meaning is dependent not simply on the preceding sign in the syntagm but – for Saussure – on the whole network of relations which differentiates each sign from its neighbours in the system. In short, what is missing from Bloomfield's review is not just a clear explanation of the relationship between *signifiant* and *signifié*: it lacks an account of the crucial Saussurean concept of *valeur* altogether.

If this is simply an oversight on Bloomfield's part, or a deliberate omission made in the interests of keeping his review brief, it is none the less revealing. For *valeur* is the last thing that can be omitted if we wish to give an accurate account of Saussurean linguistic theory. Furthermore, it does not take a great deal of complicated exposition (as many later textbook summaries bear witness). Once it is left out, however, the originality of Saussure's approach is lost and the *CLG* begins to sound like a rather simplistic résumé of ideas commonplace in nineteenth-century linguistics. Which is exactly how Bloomfield's review presents it.

The alternative is to suppose that – in 1923, at least – Bloomfield had failed to see what was radical about the message of the *CLG*. This seems to be confirmed by the astonishing remark in the final paragraph of his review:

> In detail, I should differ from de Saussure chiefly in basing my analysis on the sentence rather than on the word; by following the latter custom de Saussure gets a rather complicated result in certain matters of word-composition and syntax. (Bloomfield 1923: 64–5)

Bloomfield evidently thinks that what matters in the end is the simplicity or elegance of the linguist's description; but this plays no part in Saussure's thinking. Saussurean analysis is in any case not based on the word (in the traditional sense): the whole purpose of Saussure's linguistic sign is to provide the analyst with a unit more basic and less vaguely defined than the word. Thirdly, Bloomfield does not seem to understand why, for Saussure, basing analysis on the sentence is not a viable option, i.e. because it is unclear exactly where *la phrase* stands in relation to the distinction between *langue* and *parole* (*CLG*: 172–3). Bloomfield's announced preference for the sentence could perhaps be read as a back-handed way of rejecting Saussure's account of the distinction between *langue* and *parole* altogether; but it seems more likely, given the rest of his review, that he had simply missed this point too.

*   *   *

Four years later, Bloomfield published an article 'On recent work in general linguistics' in the periodical *Modern Philology* (Bloomfield 1927b). In this article he compares Saussure's conception of the linguistic sign favourably with that of Ogden and Richards, who had published a brief but scathing attack on Saussure in their book *The Meaning of Meaning* (Ogden and Richards 1923). There they had written:

> How great is the tyranny of language over those who propose to inquire into its workings is well shown in the speculations of the late F. de Saussure, a writer regarded by perhaps a majority of French and Swiss students as having for the first time placed linguistic upon a scientific basis. (Ogden and Richards 1923: 4)

They go on to observe with heavy sarcasm that:

Such an elaborate construction as *la langue* might, no doubt, be arrived at by some Method of Intensive Distraction analogous to that with which Dr Whitehead's name is associated, but as a guiding principle for a young science it is fantastic. (Ogden and Richards 1923: 5)

Saussure is accused of 'ignorance', 'naivety' and 'inordinate respect for linguistic convention'. But the nub of Ogden and Richards' complaint is that the Saussurean account of the sign – a purely mental phenomenon – takes no account whatsoever of the external world:

this theory of signs, by neglecting entirely the things for which signs stand, was from the beginning cut off from any contact with scientific methods of verification. (Ogden and Richards 1923: 6)

Ogden and Richards forthwith reject the Saussurean bilateral model of the sign in favour of a trilateral model which takes into account not only relations between the thought (or *reference*) and the *symbol*, but also between each of those and the *referent*. They point out that the relationships are different in all three cases. This yields a far richer acccount of signification than any simple association of *signifiant* with *signifié*. The resultant 'triangle of signification' proposed in *The Meaning of Meaning* subsequently became one of the famous landmarks in the history of semiotics in the twentieth century.

Our present concern, however, is with Bloomfield's attitude to Ogden and Richards. Bloomfield's review of the *CLG* was written before his intellectual conversion to behaviourism. This, all available testimony seems to suggest, began with his acquaintance with the psychologist A. P. Weiss when they were colleagues at Ohio State University. Bloomfield acknowledges his newly incurred debt to Weiss in his article in *Modern Philology* in 1927. ('I follow A. P. Weiss, whose psychology takes account of linguistics': Bloomfield 1927b: 113.) In this same article, however, he gives an interestingly different account of Saussure's sign than in his review of four years earlier.

It would be an exaggeration to say that in *Modern Philology* Bloomfield defends Saussure against Ogden and Richards: nevertheless, he does make the extraordinary claim that Saussure's system is 'more complex' than theirs. And whereas one might have expected Bloomfield, in accord with his recent conversion, to praise Ogden and Richards for at least relating the sign to features of the observable world by including the referent in their model, he says that this 'takes us not one step ahead'.

Saussure's model, says Bloomfield in 1927, has four components: '(1) actual object, (2) concept, (3) acoustic image, (4) speech utterance' (Bloomfield 1927b: 114). This seems to be offered as an account of one half of the Saussurean *circuit de la parole*, because Bloomfield then notes: 'the series to be reversed for a hearer', and gives a reference to *CLG*: 28. Even more surprisingly, he goes on immediately to say: 'The totality of this is *le langage*'. One is at a loss to know where in the *CLG* Bloomfield thought he had found warrant for including any 'actual object' in *le langage*, or indeed anywhere in the *circuit de la parole*. There is certainly no representation of an 'actual object' in the diagram given on the page of the *CLG* to which Bloomfield refers, or in the accompanying text either. The most likely explanation is that this comes from an overhasty reading of *CLG*: 97–8, where the notion that the sign links a thing to its name is mentioned but then rejected.

According to Bloomfield, 'the segment formed by the two purely mental terms (2) and (3) is *la langue*, the socially uniform language pattern'. This last phrase is his own interpolation and shows again that he is conflating the speech circuit account (which, as the *CLG* states quite clearly, is concerned with 'l'acte individuel') with the 'fait social'. More remarkably still, Bloomfield then accuses Saussure of making precisely this confusion:

> What he calls 'mental' is exactly what he and all other linguists call 'social'; there is no need for the popular finalistic terms. We shall do better to drop (2) and (3) and speak instead of a socially determined correspondence between certain features of (1) and (4). (Bloomfield 1927b: 114)

It has been suggested that this is Bloomfield's attempt to 'rescue Saussure from the charge of mentalism' and present him as 'a behaviourist *avant la lettre*' (Joseph 1990: 61–2). In that case, it must count as one of the most desperate rescue bids ever attempted.

If Bally and Sechehaye ever saw Bloomfield's bizarre assessment they must have been puzzled to know how a linguistic theorist could ever suppose that Saussure had actually failed to distinguish the mental from the social aspects of language, or mistaken one for the other, to say nothing of wondering what would be left of Saussure's speech circuit if (2) and (3) were just 'dropped'.

Bloomfield concludes this brief Saussurean excursus by drawing a blank cheque on the future of behaviourist semantics: 'The solution of the problem of meaning will doubtless lie in the psychologist's study of substitute stimuli' (Bloomfield 1927b: 115). One can hardly imagine Saussure's ghost adding 'Amen'.

*   *   *

Bloomfield's mid-career conversion to behaviourism eventually resulted in his *magnum opus*, the book *Language*, published in 1933, which, although claimed by its author to be a 'revised version' of his earlier *Introduction to the Study of Language*, is patently nothing of the kind.

Bloomfield's qualified approval of the *CLG*, as shown in the 1923 review, misguided though it may have been, is now replaced by the academic cold shoulder. In the review, for all its reservations, Saussure had been congratulated on having 'mapped out the world in which historical Indo-European grammar (the great achievement of the past century) is merely a single province.' Saussure had 'given us the theoretical basis for a science of human speech'. No mean achievement – even at second hand – one might have thought. But in *Language* – ten years later – Saussure is mentioned only once, as a scholar who had grasped 'the natural relation between descriptive and historical studies' and 'for years expounded this matter in his university lectures' (Bloomfield 1933: 18–19). Nothing is said about any other aspect of Saussure's work. The reason is not difficult to fathom. For Bloomfield the born-again behaviourist, Saussure's linguistic sign was a remnant of a now outmoded 'mentalism' (of which his own earlier book was likewise an example). As the paper in *Modern Philology* already signals, such unobservable items as Saussure's *signifiant* and *signifié* were henceforth to be banished from a 'scientific' linguistics. In this new era, the meaning of the world *salt* was no longer a concept in the speaker's mind, or – more vaguely still – in the collective mind of the speaker's community, but the actual substance sodium chloride (Bloomfield 1933: 139) or examples thereof.

In his later years – more precisely, in 1945, four years before his death – Bloomfield retrospectively denied any rejection of Saussure and claimed that his own *Language* 'reflects his [sc. Saussure's] *Cours* on every page' (Joseph 1990: 54). In that case there must have been quite a few pages missing from Bloomfield's surviving copies of both books. Joseph suggests that Bloomfield's problem in his 1923 review was that he could not 'hail the theoretical advances of the *CLG* without implicitly acknowledging the shortcomings of his own major work [sc. Bloomfield 1914]'. Hence for Joseph 'Bloomfield's agenda' in the review was 'the defence of his own work' (Joseph 1990: 57). This view, like the theory that Bloomfield later contrived hurriedly to resurrect Saussure as a precursor of behaviourism, does not carry immediate conviction. Joseph is doubtless right when he observes that 'Saussure's principle tenets, if correct, could not fail to cut the legs out from under Bloomfield's major study [sc. Bloomfield 1914]' (Joseph 1990: 57). The question is whether Bloomfield realized at the time that his legs were in any danger at all.

* * *

The suspicion that Bloomfield failed, both in 1923 and thereafter, to understand the relationship between Saussure's theoretical position and his own is confirmed by other pieces of evidence, which, although slight individually, add up to impressive testimony. They include the following.

In his review of Sapir's *Language*, which appeared in *The Classical Weekly* in 1922, Bloomfield congratulates the author on his concept of the 'inner' or 'ideal' phonetic system of a language; only to diminish this by adding that the same concept had already been developed previously by other theorists, including Saussure. In a snide parenthesis, Bloomfield then muses aloud 'whether Dr Sapir had at hand' a copy of the *CLG*. (Read: if he didn't, he should have done, and if he did, then he should have acknowledged his debt.) But using Saussure as a handy stick to beat Sapir with shows Bloomfield himself as a poor reader of Saussure. For nowhere in the *CLG* do we find any 'inner' or 'ideal' phonetic system. The furthest the text goes in this direction is to describe each *langue* as operating 'sur un nombre de phonèmes bien différenciés' (*CLG*: 58). But when we turn to the passage in Sapir to which Bloomfield refers (Sapir 1921: 55–6) we find quite a different proposition. Sapir wants to claim that two historically related languages may have the same 'ideal' sound-systems even though they 'may not have a sound in common'. This would certainly have been news to Saussure and an unheralded theorem in Saussurean linguistics.

There are some further remarks about Saussure in Bloomfield's review of Otto Jespersen's book *The Philosophy of Grammar*. This review appeared in the *Journal of English and Germanic Philology* in 1927. Jespersen, as Bloomfield must have been aware, had been among the first European linguists to criticize the distinction between *langue* and *parole* as formulated in the *CLG*. According to Jespersen this was a false dichotomy because 'la langue n'existe que dans et par la parole des individus' (Jespersen 1916: 111). This is exactly the point that Bloomfield begins by addressing in his review of Jespersen:

> For Jespersen language is a mode of expression; its forms express the thoughts and feelings of speakers, and communicate them to hearers, and this process goes on as an immediate part of human life and is, to a great extent, subject to the requirements and vicissitudes of human life. (Bloomfield 1927a: 81)

With this Bloomfield immediately contrasts his own position, which, he claims, is also that of Saussure and (with qualification) Sapir:

> For me, as for de Saussure (*Cours de linguistique générale*, Paris, 1922) and, in a sense, for Sapir (*Language*, New York, 1921), all this, de Saussure's *la parole*, lies beyond the power of our science. We cannot predict whether a certain person will speak at a given moment, or what he will say, or in what words and other linguistic forms he will say it. Our science can deal only with those features of language, de Saussure's *la langue*, which are common to all speakers of a community, – the phonemes, grammatical categories, lexicon and so on. These are abstractions, for they are only (recurrent) partial features of speech-utterances. (Bloomfield 1927a: 81)

There are a number of very odd features in these pronouncements. In the first place, it is difficult to see why Saussure could not have endorsed Jespersen's position as Bloomfield states it. For Saussure, language (i.e. *le langage*) is indeed a mode of expression whereby speakers express what they think and communicate it to hearers. (This is the underlying rationale of the Saussurean *circuit de la parole*.) In order to drive a wedge between Jespersen's position and Saussure's, Bloomfield resorts to implying that Jespersen's view of linguistics entails corollaries that Saussure (in common with Bloomfield) would reject. But when we examine these we find that the criticism is utterly misdirected; for Jespersen had never (any more than Saussure) proposed that it was part of the business of linguistics to make predictions about particular utterances by particular speakers. Second, Saussure had never claimed that a *linguistique de la parole* was impossible. Saussure's editors made clear in their preface why Saussure had never given his promised lectures on this topic: it was certainly not because he thought that it was 'beyond the power of our science' to say anything pertinent concerning *la parole*. Third, nor had Saussure ever identified *la langue* in terms of features of language 'common to all speakers of a community' (or given any other highest-common-factor definition). What the *CLG* says is something rather different: namely, that *la langue* is complete in no individual, but only 'dans la masse' (*CLG*: 30). Fourth, far from regarding linguistic units as 'abstractions' derived from the utterances of *parole*, the *CLG* says quite explicitly:

> Les signes dont la langue est composée ne sont pas des abstractions mais des objets réels. (*CLG*: 144)

On all these counts, unless we are willing to suppose that Bloomfield wilfully distorted the *CLG* in order to lend weight to his own disagreement with Jespersen, it seems that Bloomfield failed to grasp the theoretical subtleties of Saussure's teaching.

Finally, in the article in *Modern Philology* in 1927, Bloomfield had devoted a whole section to the question 'Do phonemes change?' For Bloomfield there are only two possible answers to this question. One is to suppose that all phonemes in all words are subject to a constant and gradual process of change. Then any apparent exceptions have to be explained by analogy or by borrowing.

> The alternative would be to drop the theory of gradual change in phonemes and define sound change instead as a sudden replacement of one phoneme by another. History and dialectal fact forbid this. (Bloomfield 1927b: 120)

Now this occurs in the very same article in which, according to Joseph, Bloomfield is trying to put Saussure on the side of the angels (if behaviourists indeed admit angels and their works as observables). What Bloomfield unaccountably fails to mention is that the alternative forbidden 'by history and dialectal fact' is Saussure's. According to the *CLG*, this is vital to the notion of an *état de langue*:

> l'évolution des sons est incompatible avec la notion d'état; comparer des phonèmes ou des groupes de phonèmes avec ce qu'ils ont été antérieurement, cela revient à établir une diachronie. (*CLG*: 194)

There could be no clearer illustration of Bloomfield's failure to grasp the Saussurean distinction between *synchronie* and *diachronie* (or, alternatively, Bloomfield's deliberate duplicity in misrepresenting Saussure's view). Again, whichever possibility we opt for, it does not redound to Bloomfield's credit as an interpreter of Saussure.

In the end we are left with two equally awkward alternatives, or some *ad hoc* compromise between the two. One is a Bloomfield who manufactured a 'Saussure' whom he could manipulate for his own purposes, and did so knowing that the *CLG* was a book that very few American linguists would have read in the original, much less studied in detail as part of a linguistics syllabus. The other is a Bloomfield who, whether through a cursory reading of the *CLG* or a lack of intellectual penetration, or both, never succeeded in getting to grips with the originality and subtlety of Saussure's thinking, and merely read his own theoretical assumptions into the text.

CHAPTER FIVE

Hjelmslev's Saussure

Hjelmslev's theory of glossematics, developed during the mid 1930s with H. J. Uldall, has been described as 'de Saussure taken to his logical conclusions' (Dinneen 1967: 326). To what extent that involved pressing Saussurean ideas beyond the point to which Saussure himself would have taken them, had he lived to put his own linguistic theorizing in a definitive published form, remains a contentious issue. Just how contentious is best illustrated by examining Hjelmslev's interpretation – or reinterpretation – of Saussure's distinction between *langue* and *parole*.

This distinction, according to Hjelmslev, represents Saussure's teaching 'ramenée à son essence absolue' (Hjelmslev 1942: 29). Furthermore: 'L'ensemble de la théorie se déduit logiquement de cette thèse primordiale' (Hjelmslev 1942: 29). Saussure's great achievement was the discovery, or rather rediscovery, of *la langue*, which had been neglected by a linguistics preoccupied with *la parole*. 'Les termes dans lesquels se posait tout problème de la linguistique présaussurienne était ceux de l'acte individuel' (Hjelmslev 1942: 30). Saussure's theoretical initiative, while not neglecting this aspect of language, opened up a quite different perspective for linguistics:

> tout en admettant l'importance de l'acte individuel et son rôle décisif pour le changement, et en faisant de la sorte ample concession aux recherches traditionnelles, F. de Saussure arrive à établir quelque chose qui en diffère radicalement: une linguistique structurale, une *Gestaltlinguistik* destinée à supplanter ou du moins à compléter la linguistique purement associative de jadis. (Hjelmslev 1942: 30)

Here, then, we see Saussure overtly hailed thirty years after his death as the founder of structuralism in linguistics. That retrospective judgment was to become one of the commonplaces of popular accounts of structuralism in the second half of the twentieth century (Piaget 1968; Ducrot

1968; Robey 1973; Sturrock 1979). It is perhaps worth noting that Hjelmslev did not, apparently, read the *CLG* until 1925 (Fischer-Jørgensen 1966: 2) and that before glossematics had been formulated as a linguistic theory the phonologists of the Prague school had already developed a 'Saussurean' concept of phonological structure in their own way. (Hjelmslev thought they had misunderstood Saussure's concept of the phoneme: Siertsema 1965: 2. Glossematics offered a structuralism that was in part intended to correct this misunderstanding.)

Hjelmslev's programme for a structural linguistics is perhaps best summed up in his own words:

> Puisqu'une structure est par définition un tissu de dépendances ou de fonctions (dans l'acception logico-mathématique de ce terme), une tâche principale de la linguistique structurale consistera à étudier les fonctions et leurs espèces. Il s'agira de faire un relevé des espèces de rapports nécessaires et suffisants pour pouvoir décrire de la façon à la fois la plus simple et la plus complète toute structure sémiologique. Cette tâche précède logiquement toutes les autres. (Hjelmslev 1942: 31)

It hardly needs pointing out that this first and allegedly essential task does not feature at all among those proposed in the text of the *CLG* (*CLG*: 20). Far from beginning with the investigation and documentation of *les langues*, the approach advocated by Hjelmslev starts (1) in the realm of semiology and (2) in the most abstract reaches of that realm. Although, arguably, this is not incompatible with Saussure's view of the ultimate relationship between linguistics and semiology, in practice it involves a complete reversal of the approach previously familiar to linguists.

Hjelmslev's answer to the question of how and where to begin this completely abstract analysis of semiological relations rests on the acceptance of four basic concepts: (1) 'bilateral dependence' or 'interdependence', (2) 'unilateral dependence' or 'determination', (3) 'commutation' and (4) 'substitution'. Where these concepts come from Hjelmslev never explains very clearly: his implied epistemology appears to take for granted the existence of a logic of relations which is somehow totally independent of language. (Whether this epistemology would have been congenial to Saussure is a question he does not broach.)

Armed with this intellectual equipment, Hjelmslev sets out to tackle 'le problème de savoir quelle est l'espèce de fonction qui existe entre langue et parole'. In his view, the trouble is that the Saussurean distinction between *langue* and *parole* is ambiguous, since both terms can be interpreted in more ways than one. It is possible to interpret *langue* in three ways: (1) as 'forme pure', (2) as 'forme matérielle' or (3) as an 'ensemble d'habitudes' (Hjelmslev 1942: 32). In the first of these, *langue* is defined 'indépendamment de sa réalisation sociale et de sa manifestation matérielle'. On interpretation (2), *langue* is defined 'par une réalisation sociale donnée mais indépendamment encore du détail de la manifestation'. On interpretation (3), *langue* is defined as a set of habits 'adoptées dans une société donnée, et définies par les manifestations observées'. For these three possible interpretations of *langue* Hjelmslev proposes the terms (1) *schéma*, (2) *norme*, and (3) *usage*. As will be seen below, Hjelmslev's own explanation of these distinctions is not entirely perspicuous. However, it needs to be followed in some detail in order to address the question that is here of primary concern, i.e. Hjelmslev's interpretation of Saussure.

By way of illustration (the only one offered in Hjelmslev 1942), Hjelmslev takes 'l'*r* français'. As 'forme pure', says Hjelmslev, French *r* may be defined by reference to four features: (1) being a consonant as opposed to a vowel (these two categories in turn being defined in terms of the unilateral dependence of the former on the latter), (2) being a consonant that can occur in initial as well as final position, e.g. *rue*, *partir*, (3) being a consonant 'avoisinant la voyelle', as in *trappe* as opposed to **rtappe*, and (4) entering into a relationship of commutation with certain other consonants belonging to the aforementioned sets of sub-categories, e.g. French *l*. These four features suffice to establish 'son rôle dans le mécanisme interne (réseau de rapports syntagmatiques et para-digmatiques) de la langue considérée comme *schéma*' (Hjelmslev 1942: 33).

This Hjelmslev evidently regards as an eminently 'Saussurean' ana-lysis. Echoing the words of the *CLG*, he claims:

> L'*r* français est ainsi défini comme une entité oppositive, relative et négative; la définition donnée ne lui attribue aucune qualité positive, quelle que ce soit. (Hjelmslev 1942: 34)

At the level of *norme*, however, 'positive' features of pronunciation are taken into account. Here French *r* is defined as 'une vibrante, admettant comme variante libre la prononciation de constrictive postérieure' (Hjelmslev 1942: 34–5).

> Cette définition de l'*r* français suffit en effet pour fixer son rôle dans la langue considérée comme *norme*. Elle oppose l'*r* aux autres éléments du même ordre, mais, cette fois, ce qui le distingue de ces autres éléments n'est pas quelque chose de purement négatif; l'*r* français se définit maintenant comme entité oppositive et relative il est vrai, mais munie d'une qualité positive: c'est par ses vibrations qu'il

s'oppose aux non-vibrantes; c'est par son articulation postérieure qu'il s'oppose aux constrictives; c'est par sa prononciation constrictive qu'il s'oppose aux occlusives. La définition présuppose une manifestation phonique donnée produite au moyen des organes vocaux. (Hjelmslev 1942: 35)

It should also be noted that this definition of French *r* makes no appeal to its positions of occurrence in the *signifiants* of French. So it would seem that the difference between *r* as *schéma* and *r* as *norme* in effect amounts to replacing the formal and partly syntagmatic criteria of the *schéma* by criteria drawn from the usual classification of sounds employed by phoneticians, plus the somewhat contentious relationship of 'variation'. But what exactly is the connexion between the two apparently quite different sets of criteria? Is it merely fortuitous that they both happen to fit French *r*? Hjelmslev does not tell us. Are the two pronunciations Hjelmslev identifies actually in free variation, as he claims? If they are in free variation for some speakers, but not for others, does this mean we are dealing with two different *normes*, i.e. two different varieties of French? Hjelmslev seems to imply as much, for he observes that his definition

n'implique aucune précision quant au lieu d'articulation. Même si la prononciation habituelle du français changeait à l'intérieure des limites prescrites par la définition, la langue, considérée comme norme, resterait la même. (Hjelmslev 1942: 35)

From this it would seem to follow that any speakers for whom the two pronunciations of *r* are *not* in free variation are already speaking a different *langue*, irrespective of what other features of French they happen to share or not to share with the rest of the community. And if this is the case the move from *schéma* to *norme* has already brought with it a remarkably narrow concept of *langue*, where communicational considerations (e.g. whether or not a difference in pronunciation impedes the comprehension of one speaker by another) have been left out of account. Hjelmslev does point out, however, that:

Selon cette acception du terme *langue*, il y aurait autant de langues qu'il y aurait de manifestations possibles rendant nécessaire une définition différente: le français écrit serait une autre langue que le français parlé, le français exécuté au moyen de l'alphabet morse serait une autre langue que le français exécuté au moyen de l'alphabet latin, et ainsi de suite. (Hjelmslev 1942: 35)

Finally, French *r* is defined at the level of *usage* as 'une vibrante sonore roulée alvéolaire ou comme constrictive sonore uvulaire' (Hjelmslev 1942: 35). This is evidently a more precise description than the preceding one, but now it is purely phonetic. Exactly how to interpret the conjunction 'ou' is a problem, for here there is no appeal to free variation. So it would seem that at the level of *usage*, one is still speaking the same *langue* irrespective of whether one rolls the *r* or not. All Hjelmslev tells us is:

> Cette définition comprendrait toutes les qualités trouvées dans la prononciation habituelle de l'*r* français, et le fixerait ainsi comme élément de la langue considérée comme *usage*. La définition n'est ni oppositive ni relative ni négative; elle épuise les qualités positives caractéristiques de l'usage, mais d'autre part elle s'y arrête: elle laisse à l'improvisation occasionnelle la possibilité de varier la prononciation à l'intérieur des limites prescrites par la définition. Même si la prononciation occasionnelle varie à l'intérieur de ces limites, la langue, considérée comme usage, reste la même. D'autre part, tout changement de la définition donnée entraînerait un changement de langue, et le français prononcé avec un *r* différent, mettons par exemple rétroflexe, pharyngal, chuintant, serait une autre langue que le français que nous connaissons. (Hjelmslev 1942: 35–6)

But this addendum, rather than clarifying the definition, adds to the difficulty of interpreting it. It is unclear why, for example, a retroflex *r* cannot be counted as falling within the range of permissible variation. In spite of Hjelmslev's disclaimer, therefore, it would seem that negative criteria have been tacitly incorporated into the classification, i.e. there is an underlying assumption that certain phonetic characterizations are incompatible.

*   *   *

Having distinguished between *schéma*, *norme* and *usage* as interpretations of *langue*, Hjelmslev investigates their interrelationship in terms of dependence, and the relationship of each to *parole*.

The *norme*, he considers, determines (i.e. presupposes) both *usage* and the act of *parole*:

> l'acte et l'usage précèdent logiquement et pratiquement la norme; la norme est née de l'usage et de l'acte, mais non inversement. (Hjelmslev 1942: 38)

The relationship between *usage* and *parole* is different. This is a case of interdependence: 'ils se présupposent mutuellement'. Commenting on *CLG*: 37, which claims that *langue* and *parole* are interdependent, Hjelmslev maintains that *langue* here has to be understood in the sense of *usage* and points out that this is where the text mentions 'habitudes linguistiques'. So there is no contradiction with the claim that *langue* also (i.e. in the sense of *norme*) determines *parole*. (Here we encounter

Hjelmslev the theoretician at his most subtle: one wonders how many academic linguists of the time – or since – would have appreciated subtleties of this order.)

Thirdly, *schéma* is determined (= presupposed) by *parole*, *usage* and *norme*, but not vice versa.

Thus we see, according to Hjelmslev, that by drawing these distinctions it is possible to reconstruct a Saussurean account that removes any apparent inconsistencies in the *CLG* and leaves intact a coherent concept of *langue* for the linguist to work with.

Hjelmslev's next theoretical move, however, is more difficult to follow. It involves reducing this neat schematization by eliminating both *norme* and *parole*. The reasons Hjelmslev gives for this are as follows.

> Norme, usage et acte sont d'autre part intimement liés ensemble et se ramènent naturellement à ne constituer qu'un seul objet véritable: l'usage, par rapport auquel la norme est une abstraction et l'acte une concrétisation. C'est l'usage seul qui fait l'objet de la théorie de l'exécution; la norme n'est en réalité qu'une construction artificielle, et l'acte d'autre part n'est qu'un document passager. (Hjelmslev 1942: 42)

By a grating piece of special pleading, he counters the objection that this elimination of *parole* suppresses all consideration of the linguistic role of the individual speaker:

> On répondra que dans ces conditions on ne tiendrait pas suffisamment compte du caractère libre et spontané, du rôle créateur de l'acte; mais ce serait une erreur, puisque l'usage ne saurait être qu'un ensemble de possibilités entre lesquelles tout acte aurait libre choix; en décrivant l'usage il convient de tenir compte de la latitude de variation qu'il admet, et cette latitude, pourvu qu'elle soit enregistrée de façon exacte, ne serait jamais dépassée par l'acte; du moment où elle le serait apparemment, la description de l'usage serait à remanier. Il paraît donc que par définition il ne peut rien y avoir dans l'acte qui ne soit pas prévu par l'usage. (Hjelmslev 1942: 42–3)

More theoretical subtleties, but this time less convincing. Via this somewhat tortuous path Hjelmslev reaches the conclusion that the distinction between *schéma* and *usage* is 'la seule subdivision essentielle qui s'impose à la sémiologie' and should replace Saussure's distinction between *langue* and *parole*. For the latter 'n'en constitue qu'une première approximation, historiquement importante, mais théoriquement imparfaite' (Hjelmslev 1942: 44).

*　　*　　*

This conclusion opens a Pandora's box of problems which cannot be pursued here. However, it is important to see where Hjelmslev's argument was leading before returning to the question that is relevant for our present purposes. How 'Saussurean' is Hjelmslev's account of the three different concepts of *langue*? Hjelmslev himself leaves us in no doubt as to his own view. His claim is that it is the concept of *langue* as *schéma* that 'le *Cours de linguistique générale* vise surtout à soutenir' (Hjelmslev 1942: 36). This way of putting the matter seems deliberately designed to postpone or sidestep the issue of how far the editors had succeeded in presenting Saussure's own thinking in the published text. In support of his reading, Hjelmslev refers to specific passages in the *CLG* where we are told that sound is not an essential feature of the linguistic sign (*CLG*: 21, 36, 56, 164) and that the distinction between *langue* and *parole* separates the essential from the accidental (*CLG*: 30). Furthermore, according to Hjelmslev, it is only the concept of *langue* as *schéma* that makes sense of Saussure's most famous analogies: the game of chess (*CLG*: 43, 153 f.) and the coin (*CLG*: 159 f., 164). It is the same concept that lies behind what Hjelmslev describes as 'la maxime fondamentale' of the *CLG*: that 'la langue est une *forme*, non une *substance*' (*CLG*: 157, 169).

On the other hand, the *CLG* also, according to Hjelmslev, appeals to the notion of *langue* as *norme*. For example, the notion of *image acoustique* does not make sense unless we suppose that it is the image of a certain sound: 'elle attache donc la langue à une matière donnée et l'assimile à la *norme*' (Hjelmslev 1942: 37). Finally, the *CLG* also tells us that *la langue* is a certain 'ensemble des habitudes linguistiques' (*CLG*: 112), from which it seems to be 'rien qu'un usage' (Hjelmslev 1942: 37). Therefore all three concepts are introduced at different points in the exposition. From this Hjelmslev concludes that

> la définition de la langue n'est ni dans l'une ni dans l'autre des trois acceptions que nous avons distinguées, et que la seule définition universellement applicable consiste à déterminer la langue, dans l'acception saussurienne, comme un *système de signes*. (Hjelmslev 1942: 37)

This, it seems, suffices in Hjelmslev's view to establish Saussurean linguistics as 'structuralist'. The conclusion is surprising. For it is difficult to see that the rather vague notion of a 'sign system', without further qualification, gives any distinctive structuralist character to Saussure's linguistic theorizing at all. (A nomenclature could also be regarded as a system of signs; but this is a conception of *langue* that is explicitly rejected in the *CLG*.) Hjelmslev is also on questionable ground in supposing that the notion of a 'sign system' is common to all the various ways in which a reader of the *CLG* is invited to consider *la langue*. Thus while we are told in one place that *la langue* is 'un système de signes où il n'y a d'essentiel que l'union du sens et de l'image acoustique' (*CLG*: 32), we are also told in another place that *la langue* is 'un système de pures valeurs' (*CLG*: 116). This difference, which presumably for Hjelmslev reflects the concepts of *norme* and *schéma* respectively, actually goes further than Hjelmslev admits. For it is possible to think of a system of values as being even more abstract than a system of signs (as the phrase 'pures valeurs' seems to suggest): one could, for instance, describe a system of mathematical values without even mentioning the mathematical symbols that are used, or might possibly be used, for making calculations on the basis of values in question. So if we are ranking such notions in order of abstraction, 'values' seem to rank above 'signs'.

However, that is by no means the most crucial objection to Hjelmslev's analysis of the notion *langue* in the *CLG*. Anyone other than a committed glossematician is bound to ask whether Hjelmslev's definition of French *r* at the level of *schéma* succeeds in defining anything at all. It tells us, indeed, what French *r* is not; but does being told *what something is not* count as a definition? Could Saussure have believed or even implied this? Were it not for the po-faced solemnity of Hjelmslev's account, one might suppose it was intended as a *reductio ad absurdum* of Saussurean linguistics.

That is only the beginning of the theoretical problem for glossematics. However seriously such a definition may be taken, it is difficult to give it any satisfactory content without assuming that (as a matter of fact) the investigator is already acquainted with French and knows what a French *r* actually sounds like. Feigning ignorance appears to stand linguistic inquiry (and intellectual inquiry in general) on its head. But this, as Siertsema points out, is exactly what Hjelmslev believed to be necessary. She quotes from Hjelmslev's article 'Structural analysis of language', published in 1947:

> Linguistics describes the relational pattern of language without knowing what the relata are but only by means of describing the relations between their parts and parts of their parts. (Siertsema 1965: 3)

Whether this is a coherent theoretical position is obviously questionable. Siertsema evidently thinks not:

> If linguistics did not know 'what the relata are', its description of the relational pattern in a linguistic sense would become utterly meaningless. (Siertsema 1965: 4)

This abrupt dismissal requires rather more argumentative support than Siertsema provides. For, as Quine points out, it is perfectly possible to describe observed relationships quite accurately while remaining in ignorance of what the items under observation actually are. Quine's example is ancient astronomy. The movements of the planets were well known long before the astronomers who studied their movements knew what the planets were (Quine 1953: 47). Is something similar possible or desirable in linguistics? At least the ancient astronomers knew that they were dealing with moving points of light in the night sky. The question is whether items like 'French *r*' are objectively observable phenomena.

The case against Hjelmslev's position is that, far from being a plain empirical datum, 'French *r*' is quite a sophisticated metalinguistic concept. Moreover, it is one which – as Saussure might well have pointed out – is presumably derived by a process of abstraction from acquaintance with innumerable facts of French *parole* (and very probably influenced by familiarity with written French as well). If this is so, it is hard to see how linguistics can plausibly profess indifference to knowing 'what the relata are'. For linguistic processes are already at work in the identification of such items.

This difficulty emerges at every stage in Hjelmslev's exposition of the case of French *r*, which perversely proceeds from the general to the particular. The actual epistemological order of priority is the reverse. The reader cannot, for example, make sense of condition (4) in the *schéma* account – the commutative relationship between *r* and *l* – without already having some idea of what an *l* sounds like. For under all the previous conditions (1–3) nothing distinguishes an *r* from an *l* at all. But what a French *l* is Hjelmslev never explains: at this point his *schéma* account of *r* peters out. Nothing demonstrates more clearly that the so-called general categories (consonant vs. vowel) are not based on the higher-order logical distinctions invoked by Hjelmslev, but are extrapolations from acquaintance with the pronunciation of French (and other languages). Whereas Saussure at least shows some sensitivity to the question of abstraction, Hjelmslev brashly stands the problem on its head and presents the upturned version as a solution.

Not content with this, Hjelmslev asserts paradoxically that his purely formal definition of French *r* 'implique qu'il est un réalisable, non qu'il soit un réalisé' (Hjelmslev 1942: 34). So it would be valid even if there were no such consonant in French. In short, what has been defined at the level of *schéma* is only a 'possible' French consonant. But if this is equally true of French *l*, and of *p*, *m*, *s* . . . etc., what has been described at this level of abstraction is presumably not an actual language at all, but only a 'possible' language. Why, in that case, it should be called 'French', or be of any interest to linguists engaged in analysing the language currently spoken in Paris or other parts of France, Hjelmslev never explains.

But there are even more surprises to come. This definition of a possible French *r*, as proposed by Hjelmslev, need not be construed as relating to any sound uttered at all.

> Elle laisse ouverte n'importe quelle manifestation: qu'il prenne corps dans une matière phonique ou graphique, dans un langage par gestes (soit dans l'alphabet dactylologique des sourds-muets) ou dans un système de signaux par pavillons, qu'il se manifeste par tel ou tel phonème ou par telle ou telle lettre d'un alphabet (soit l'alphabet latin ou l'alphabet morse), tout cela n'affecterait en rien la définition de notre élément. (Hjelmslev 1942: 34)

So presumably we could have a French *r* produced not only by the familiar mechanisms of speech and writing but also, for instance, by a certain gesture, or a certain wavelength of light, or a variation of temperature, or a combination of any of these. French *r* might be a banana. (It is difficult to get to the bottom of Hjelmslev's thinking without appearing to caricature it; but that is not the present intention.) Taking glossematics seriously seems to require us to make that imaginative effort. The French language (as *schéma*) embraces *all* conceivable material manifestations of its elements and of the relations between those elements.

> Avec les autres éléments définis de façon analogue, l'*r* français constituerait la langue française considérée comme schéma, et, de ce point de vue, quelle qu'en soit la manifestation, la langue française reste identique à elle-même [. . .]. Même si la prononciation habituelle du français changeait du tout au tout, la langue, considérée comme schéma, resterait la même, pourvu que les distinctions et les identités préconisées par elle soient sauvegardées. (Hjelmslev 1942: 34)

Nothing could be more forthright than that. But its very forthrightness invites us to ponder whether this is not a case of 'structuralism' straying beyond the bounds of theoretical coherence. Let us suppose, following Hjelmslev's suggestion, that changes in pronunciation led to a state of affairs where what had once been pronounced as *r* was now pronounced as *l*, and vice versa. And let us furthermore suppose that similar switches had been effected among other pairs of consonants and vowels. If that had taken place, French as currently pronounced would no longer be comprehensible to future generations unaccustomed to the 'old' pronunciation. Yet the internal structural oppositions would *ex hypothesi* be preserved in every case.

If Hjelmslev is to be taken at his word, then in spite of these changes the French language would still be 'identique à elle-même'. But no one can suppose this without conceding that at this point – if not before – we have parted company with the idea of the French language as a means of communication internal to any one community of speakers. Or, to put the point another way, we have crossed the Saussurean boundary between synchronic and diachronic linguistics. Hjelmslev does not seem to realize this. Theoretically, his concept of *langue* as *schéma* allows the possibility that French and Latin are actually one and the same language. And this – even theoretically – Saussure could scarcely have allowed. For it means something tantamount to claiming that *causa* could be then 'the same word' (*identique à elle-même*) as *chose*. To spell the point out in boring detail: suppose that all the sound-elements of Latin *causa* (whatever they were) had been regularly transformed into corresponding consonants and vowels of French, and suppose the sequence of such elements in the individual lexical items had been preserved, and suppose there had been no additions to the lexicon and no losses either, and suppose there had been no changes in the patterns of syntagmatic combination of signs (other than those entailed by the sound changes already mentioned), and suppose there had been no new ideas to express in the language, nor any old ideas to discard, and suppose there had been no borrowings from foreign languages . . . then – and only then – would *causa* be structurally 'identique à' *chose*. But that would not alter the fact that *causa* is not – as it happens – even a dialectal 'variant' of *chose*. It is not a form that French speakers use at all (unless they are speaking or quoting Latin).

A defender of Hjelmslev might perhaps protest at this point that the objection is based on substituting the criteria of *norme* for those of *schéma*. But the protest would be idle. For the objection is, precisely, that Hjelmslev's account of *schéma* is incoherent. It borrows whatever superficial plausiblity it may have from our prior acquaintance with how the French language actually operates in everyday situations (i.e. our acquaintance with French *parole*). What Hjelmslev proposes as a clarification of Saussure's idea of *la langue* as 'form' is, in short, an extravagant piece of pseudo-Saussurean nonsense. It does not even throw light – as it purports to do – on the Saussurean concept of a sign. For French *r*, whatever else it may be, is *not* a sign according to the *CLG*. It has no meaning, no *signifié*. Hjelmslev's prime example of 'forme pure' could scarcely have been more maladroit.

*   *   *

To the reader of the *CLG* it might seem that an even more unSaussurean consequence of accepting Hjelmslev's interpretation of *langue* as *schéma* is that writing thereby gains theoretical parity of status with speech. This follows from the premiss that linguistic units, at the level of *schéma*, are independent of their expression in any material form (Siertsema 1965: 111 ff.), a conclusion that Hjelmslev regarded as following in turn from Saussure's thesis that a language is a form, not a substance.

> Thus the system is independent of the specific substance in which it is expressed; a given system may be equally well expressed in any one of several substances, e.g. in writing as well as in sounds. [. . .] The fact that articulated sound is the most common means of expression is not a consequence of any particularity inherent in the system, but is due to the anatomic-physiological constitution of man. (Siertsema 1965: 111–12)

Similar views are voiced by other glossematicians. According to Uldall, for example,

> it is only through the concept of a difference between form and substance that we can explain the possibility of speech and writing existing at the same time as expressions of one and the same language. If either of these two substances, the stream of air or the stream of ink, were an integral part of the language itself, it would not be possible to go from one to the other without changing the language. [. . .] ink may be substituted for air without any change in the language [. . .]. When we write a phonetic or a phonemic transcription we substitute ink for air, but the form remains the same, because the functions of each component form have not been changed. (Uldall 1944: 11)

It is difficult to reconcile this with the position stated in the *CLG*, where it seems quite clear that anything qualifying as a *langue* must be a system of articulated speech.

> Langue et écriture sont deux systèmes de signes distincts; l'unique raison d'être du second est de représenter le premier; l'objet linguistique n'est pas défini par la combinaison du mot écrit et du mot parlé; ce dernier constitue à lui seul cet objet. (*CLG*: 45)

It would be pointless to object that here we are dealing with *langue* as *norme* and not as *schéma*. For in that case, clearly, one must conclude that Saussurean linguistics is concerned with the former, not the latter; and since for Hjelmslev (1942: 43) *norme* is in the final analysis only 'une fiction' (as distinct from *schéma* and *usage*, which are 'réalités') this would in effect condemn Saussure as having – like so many of his predecessors –

mistaken the true 'objet' of his discipline. For the glossematician, on the other hand, it is legitimate to regard *la langue* as an entirely abstract system, which can be manifested in *any* appropriate material form. This again is borne out by Uldall, who claims:

> The system of speech and the system of writing are [. . .] only two realisations out of an infinite number of possible systems, of which no one can be said to be more fundamental than any other. (Uldall 1944: 16)

One objection that has been raised to the glossematic position is that – as Saussure himself emphasized – the written language rarely corresponds exactly to the spoken language: so it becomes implausible to treat both as equivalent manifestations of exactly the same underlying abstract system. There are often, for instance, words that are spelled alike but pronounced differently. Hjelmslev acknowledges that 'not all orthographies are "phonetic"' (Hjelmslev 1961: 104). But he claims that this is irrelevant: 'it does not alter the general fact that a linguistic form is manifested in the given substance' (Hjelmslev 1961: 105). He goes on to add that

> the task of the linguistic theoretician is not merely that of describing the actually present expression system, but of calculating what expression systems in general are possible as expression for a given content system, *and vice versa*. (Hjelmslev 1961: 105)

It is difficult to find anything in the *CLG* that suggests that Saussure saw the task of the linguistic theoretican in this light. Moreover, it seems that Hjelmslev is in any case confusing two issues. The issue on which he is right (at least, within the constraints of his own theoretical framework) is whether, in principle, it is possible for a given abstract sign system to have materially different but exactly equivalent manifestations, involving, for example, quite different sensory modalities. There seems no good reason to deny this, given the glossematic theoretical framework. For instance, suppose we have a waiting room in which a light flashes when it is time for the next person in the queue to go in to an inner room and be attended to. An exactly equivalent system could replace the light by a buzzer, thus substituting an auditory for a visual signal. Furthermore, there might be a significant distinction between the light flashing once and the light flashing twice. Perhaps it flashes once for the next man in the queue and twice for the next woman in the queue, because men and women are attended to separately. Again, this could be replaced by a distinction between one and two buzzes on the buzzer. And in general, for any number of such distinctions, the buzzer will do as well as the light. This would be a paradigm case to illustrate the glossematic thesis that the same abstract system can be manifested in exactly equivalent ways, although in substantially different signals.

So far, so good. Hjelmslev, on the other hand, is wrong, even in terms of his own theoretical framework, to deny the relevance of the fact that orthographies do not always match differences in pronunciation. He seems not to realize the force of the objection. The objection is that a single written unit may correspond to two different spoken units, as in the case of the noun *refuse* and the verb *refuse*, but this orthographic identity does not automatically obliterate any difference of meaning. All that happens in such cases is that those familiar with written English learn – to put it in traditional terms – that there are quite different usages, grammatical constructions and pronunciations associated with a single written form. However, according to Hjelmslev, the fact that some orthographies are not phonetic shows that 'different systems of expression can correspond to one and the same system of content' (Hjelmslev 1961: 105). The problem is that if cases like *refuse* are admitted as actual examples of this state of affairs, it becomes theoretically possible to imagine writing systems which economize on their inventory of ortho-graphically distinct words by allowing homographs to proliferate. The *reductio ad absurdum* would be a writing system which had only one word.

Even Hjelmslev, presumably, would have regarded a single polysemous homograph as inadequate to manifest in ink the abstract linguistic system of English, whatever that might be. But he offers no rule to determine the limit beyond which the deployment of homographs corresponding to phonetically or semantically distinct units will introduce a non-equiva-lence between the spoken language and the written language.

The difficulty is compounded by Uldall, who claims:

> If we keep the units of content constant, we shall have the same language whatever system is used to make up the corresponding units of expression. [. . .] a system of any internal structure will do, provided that a sufficient number of units can be made up from it to express the units of content. (Uldall 1944: 15)

This seems to imply that at least as many distinct units of expression are needed as there are units of content in the language. Which in turn means that any vocal or graphic systems which allow cases of homophony or homography automatically misrepresent the content system of the lan-guage. But that in turn leads to the paradoxical conclusion that neither English speech nor English writing properly express English. It is paradoxical because without English speech or English writing it is difficult to see what kind of existence the English language would have. Furthermore, if it is possible in principle that speech and writing may misrepresent the structure of a language, there seems to be no *a priori* reason to assume that we can with any assurance detect which elements of phonic or graphic manifestation correctly represent the structure of the language and which, on the other hand, do not.

Glossematics shows us what happens in linguistics when the concept of *la langue* is idealized to the point where it is assumed to exist independently of any specific materialization whatsoever. Whatever charges may be levelled against Saussure, that can hardly count as one on which he would be found guilty.

*   *   *

Hjelmslev's other major modification to the conceptual apparatus of Saussurean linguistics concerns 'rapports associatifs', which Hjelmslev proposed to replace by 'paradigmatic relations'. This latter term not infrequently occurs in what purport to be accounts of Saussure's work. Chomksy, for example, criticizes Saussure on the ground that 'transformational operations relating the deep and surface structure' of the sentence *Invisible God created the visible world* cannot 'be expressed in terms of paradigmatic and syntagmatic structures' (Chomsky 1968: 17), but evidently does not realize that 'paradigmatic' is not a Saussurean concept at all. Similarly, Barthes speaks of 'changing the name' of Saussure's 'plan associatif' to 'plan paradigmatique' (Barthes 1964b: III, 1, 1), but does not seem to see that what is involved is much more than a change in technical terminology. Culler is another who refers to 'syntagmatic and paradigmatic elements, as defined by Saussure' (Culler 1986: 87), in spite of the fact that the *CLG* contains no definition of the latter at all and Saussure never uses the term *paradigmatique* in this sense.

The reason for Hjelmslev's dissatisfaction with Saussure's 'rapports associatifs' relates to Hjelmslev's own preoccupation with reducing linguistic structure to a calculus. Asssociative relations, as defined in the *CLG*, embrace a whole range of cases: they are 'groupes formés par association mentale' (*CLG*: 173). And we are told specifically that these groups 'ne se bornent pas à rapprocher les termes qui présentent quelque chose de commun' (*CLG*: 173). On the contrary: 'Un mot quelconque peut toujours évoquer tout ce qui est susceptible de lui être associé d'une manière ou d'une autre' (*CLG*: 174). This might include even a chance similarity of sound, and nothing else. (One of the examples given is the coincidence of the final syllables of the words *enseignement* and *justement*, which otherwise have nothing in common.)

For Hjelmslev, this opened the door on far too wide a range of phenomena, quite apart from the fact that 'associations' might vary considerably from one speaker (or listener) to another. He proposed to limit it by, in effect, subordinating this second order of relations to syntagmatics and stipulating that at each place in the syntagmatic sequence a relation of exclusive disjunction ('either/or') governed the possibilities of which linguistic element could occur. This would, for the analyst, be determined by what glossematicians termed the 'commutation test'.

Exactly how this test was supposed to apply, to what extent it differed from the simpler notion of 'substitution' adopted by other linguists, and what knowledge had to be presupposed in order to implement the commutation test at all, were questions that predictably gave rise to a certain amount of theoretical debate (Siertsema 1965: 164 ff.) which cannot be entered into here. For our present purposes what matters more is that Hjelmslev's replacement of associative by paradigmatic relations implies a no less radical criticism of Saussure's basic assumptions than his proposals for reinterpreting the distinction between *langue* and *parole*. The principle of arbitrariness remains intact. But by insisting on the notion that syntagmatic relations are not independent of paradigmatic relations, and construing the latter in terms of a single, well-defined logical notion, Hjelmslev introduced a much more restricted notion of 'linearity' than Saussure had ever thought necessary or appropriate. An important step was taken in the direction of making sentence production look more recognizably like an algorithmic process than Saussure's generation would have conceded.

*   *   *

Another controversial idea that Hjelmslev developed was that sentences belonging to different languages, although differently structured, might nevertheless share what he termed a common 'purport'. Thus he held that Danish *jeg véd det ikke*, English *I do not know*, French *je ne sais pas*, Finnish *en tiedä* and Eskimo *naluvara* 'despite all their differences, have a factor in common, namely the purport, the thought itself' (Hjelmslev 1961: 50). This purport, he held, 'exists provisionally as an amorphous mass, an unanalysed entity, which is defined only by its external functions, namely its function to each of the linguistic sentences we have quoted' (Hjelmslev 1961: 50–1). The phrase 'amorphous mass' here suggests that this is an attempt to explicate a passage in the *CLG*, quoted by Hjelmslev on the previous page, which claims that 'abstraction faite de son expression par les mots, notre pensée n'est qu'une masse amorphe et indistincte' (*CLG*: 155).

Hjelmslev's claim, however, goes considerably beyond this. For it is unclear why recognizing the way in which an otherwise vague thought is given precision by its linguistic articulation into separate verbal units, and the way in which these units are combined, obliges us to suppose that it is 'the same thought' that is differently articulated in other languages. Nothing in the *CLG* suggests this. Nor does anything hint at the even more extreme position Hjelmslev adopts when he speaks in this connexion of the possibility of comparing different languages and extracting 'the factor that is common to them and that remains common to all languages, however many languages are drawn into the comparison' (Hjelmslev 1961: 50). This seems to indicate that Hjelmslev believed that there were 'universals' of purport underlying all languages.

That Saussure would have endorsed any such proposition seems extremely dubious, since it opens the door to the very nomenclaturism that Saussure explicitly rejects. Even the few examples of common purport that Hjelmslev supplies are problematic. Is it clear that *I do not know* expresses the same (unstructured) thought as *je ne sais pas*? How do we determine whether, if so, this is a thought that can be expressed in *all* languages? And why does linguistic theory need such an assumption anyway?

For Hjelmslev, it appears, the 'purport' question is one that arises out of Saussure's distinction between form and substance. He is not happy with what he takes to be Saussure's assumption that substance (either in the realm of sound or in that of thought) must 'precede language in time or hierarchical order, or *vice versa*' (Hjelmslev 1961: 50). Saussure seems to stand accused of inconsistency here; for 'if we maintain Saussure's terminology – and precisely from his assumptions' what becomes clear, according to Hjelmslev, is that substance 'can in no sense be said to have an independent existence' (Hjelmslev 1961: 50).

It is rather difficult to reconcile this with Hjelmslev's own proposals about 'purport' or with the analogies that he supplies by way of elucidation:

> Each language lays down its own boundaries within the amorphous 'thought-mass' and stresses different factors in it in different arrangements, puts the centers of gravity in different places and gives them different emphases. It is like one and the same handful of sand that is formed in quite different patterns, or like the cloud in the heavens that changes shape in Hamlet's view from minute to minute. Just as the

same sand can be put into different molds, and the same cloud take on ever new shapes, so also the same purport is formed or structured differently in different languages. (Hjelmslev 1961: 52)

But, perplexingly, these illustrations that Hjelmslev himself supplies seem, much more clearly than anything in the *CLG*, to emphasize the logical and ontological precedence of substance. The sand presumably has an independent existence before there is any question of taking a handful and distributing it in various arrangements. Similarly the water vapour has to be there in the sky before Hamlet can comment to Polonius on its changing shape.

*   *   *

To what extent Hjelmslev thought he was merely making explicit and rigorous ideas that were implicit, or at least latent, in the *CLG* is a delicate question. From one reliable witness who knew Hjelmslev well, we can infer that he was sometimes inclined to 'read too much of his own ideas into Saussure' (Fischer-Jørgensen 1966: 5). There seems to be general agreement that Hjelmslev's interpretation of Saussure's *langue* was 'one-sided' and neglected entirely its social aspects (Siertsema 1965: 10–11). At the same time, there is no doubt that Hjelmslev's 'one-sided' preoccupation with what he saw as the more abstract implications of Saussure's ideas was influential. It played an important role in shaping the view of Saussure as a more revolutionary thinker about language than Saussure's contemporaries – or perhaps Saussure himself – had ever supposed. If Sechehaye and Bally had already presented to the world a Saussure who broke radically with the linguistics of the nineteenth century, Hjelmslev went further and managed to discover a Saussure whose theoretical iconoclasm went far beyond his editors' perceptions or the linguistics of his contemporaries.

CHAPTER SIX

Jakobson's Saussure

The global itinerary of Roman Jakobson's long academic career, which eventually took him from Moscow to Harvard, via Prague and Scandinavia, made him one of the most influential disseminators of ideas about Saussure for a period of some forty years. Jakobson's debt to Saussure was immense, and he did not conceal it. His writings are peppered with references to Saussure, perhaps more copiously than the writings of any other linguist who was not actually a member of the Geneva school. But Jakobson never seemed entirely comfortable with the Saussurean inheritance, or with his own role as executor.

Part of the reason may have been a difference in intellectual temperament. Unlike Saussure, Jakobson was no theorist. He seems always to have been more interested in descriptive systematization than in theory construction: and these two things are by no means the same. Saussure, on the contrary, was primarily interested in theory construction, and very little in descriptive systematization. Nevertheless, it was Saussure who had laid out the basic programme for linguists of Jakobson's generation, and there seems to be no evidence that Jakobson ever rejected this programme as such. Where he disagreed radically with Saussure – or at least claimed to – was over the principles to be adopted in pursuing this programme. The caveat 'or at least claimed to' has to be added, because in retrospect it seems fairly clear that on a number of points Jakobson misconstrued Saussure's position.

This is hardly surprising, because Jakobson's approach to Saussure, as to everything else, was nothing if not eclectic. He picked out the bits of Saussure's teaching that he liked and rejected or dismissed the rest. It is ironic that Jakobson, whose main contribution to modern linguistics is often regarded as his development of the notion of distinctive features in phonology, should have admired above all the statement 'Les phonèmes sont avant tout des entités oppositives, relatives et négatives' (*CLG*: 164): ironic because, although Jakobson initially did not know this, the term *phonème* is due to the editors of the text and probably misrepresents Saussure's thought anyway. Years later, when Jakobson realized this mistake, he reinterpreted Saussure's statement as applying to distinctive features, thus retrospectively making a good Jakobsonian out of him (Jakobson 1962: 637). But the later misreading distorts Saussure's thinking even more seriously than the earlier one.

Jakobson also liked Saussure's distinction between syntagmatic and associative relations, but may well – like Hjelmslev, or perhaps in part because of Hjelmslev – have misunderstood that too. Nevertheless, it was to become the basis of his essay 'Two aspects of language and two types of aphasic disturbances' (Jakobson 1956).

On the other hand, the catalogue of Saussure's sins, as drawn up by Jakobson, is long and varied. Although Saussure continues to be referred to with ritual respect as *le maître*, the master's thinking about language, according to Jakobson, was deeply flawed. It was in various respects still 'Neogrammarian', 'atomistic', marred by 'naive empiricism' and 'naive psychologism'. Saussure's failure to appreciate the role of distinctive features resulted in a 'vicious circle' and had held up progress in phonology for 'a long time'. The *CLG* itself contains 'errors', 'frequent contradictions' and 'dangerous simplification'. Its terminology is 'misleading', its theses stand in need of 'far-reaching revisions', and its basic principles are 'illusory'. Even its postulation of *la langue* as something shared by a linguistic community is a 'delusive fiction'. One is in the end puzzled to know exactly what is left standing in the Saussurean edifice that might conceivably be of any lasting value. (Unless it makes sense to claim as the architect of your discipline someone who deserves that title precisely for having made at the very outset just about all the mistakes it is humanly possible to make.) This is the contradiction that lies at the heart of Jakobson's ambiguous position vis-à-vis Saussure.

In addition to the countless passing remarks about Saussure scattered throughout his publications, Jakobson devoted two pieces of work explicitly to an evaluation of Saussure's thought. The earlier dates from 1942, and is a set of lectures he gave at the École Libre des Hautes Études in New York, entitled 'La théorie saussurienne en rétrospection' (Jakobson 1942b). The later dates from 1959, and is a paper he gave at a conference in East Germany (Jakobson 1959). It is much shorter, but presumably the more mature statement. One notices immediately that certain criticisms of Saussure that he had made much of in 1942 have dropped out of sight in 1959. Why this might be is a question taken up below.

Neither of these assessments, however, offers the kind of comprehensive analysis of Saussure's thought that one might have expected. The reader is left with two overall impressions, the nature of which has already been indicated above. First, Jakobson's approach to Saussure is fragmentary: he picks out particular statements in which he is interested, but makes no coherent attempt to interrelate them. Second, he shows no interest in the Saussurean enterprise of theory-construction as such. Consequently, in Jakobson's Saussure, the trees constantly obscure a clear view of the wood.

Jakobson rejected both Saussure's principle of arbitrariness and Saussure's principle of linearity. This is already quite an achievement for someone who presented himself as a Saussurean. It is interesting to note that Jakobson's objections to these two theoretical principles were quite unrelated. In other words, he never grasped the connexion between them in Saussure's thinking about language. This is already one indication that Jakobson lacked a certain sensitivity to deeper theoretical issues. His doubts about arbitrariness seem to have been prompted by reading Benveniste, and later reinforced by reading C. S. Peirce after the Second World War. His difficulties with the notion of linearity, on the other hand, appear to derive directly from Prague-school phonology. Jakobson eventually came to accept Peirce's notion of the iconic sign. He evidently did not see that Peirce's own concept of iconicity is itself a muddle. (By his own definition, Peirce was obliged to accept signs as diverse as photographs and algebraic formulae as all being iconic.) Moreover, Jakobson did not appreciate that what Peirce took to be examples of iconicity in language would not in any case invalidate Saussure's principle. (This is because Peirce's definition of a sign is quite different from Saussure's. Even an iconic expression in Peirce's sense could still be an arbitrary sign in Saussure's sense. For Peirce, 'iconic' was not opposed to 'arbitrary'.) Jakobson's failure here is a failure to see what the theoretical issue actually is.

As regards Saussure's principle of linearity, Jakobson thought that it was disproved by the discovery – or rather rediscovery – of distinctive features in phonology. He seems to have held that this contradicted Saussure's dictum that it is impossible to pronounce two elements at once. But this interpretation pays scant respect to what the text of the *CLG* actually says. The statement (*CLG*: 170) which Jakobson quotes more than once (Jakobson 1942a: 380; Jakobson 1956: 60–1) to 'prove' Saussure's oversight, clearly applies to *words* and comes from an introductory passage on syntagmatic relations. Saussure never claimed that a speaker has to articulate a voiced stop by producing the voicing and the stop *in sequence*. Nor did Saussure deny that particular speech sounds may be analysed into components: on the contrary, the *CLG* refers explicitly to 'les éléments différentiels des phonèmes' and their 'valeur différencia-trice' (*CLG*: 68–9). Jakobson should have known all that – indeed, must have known it. The question is why he ignored it. Other linguists – Martinet, for example – realized what Jakobson seemingly failed to appreciate: that, far from invalidating the principle of linearity, the identification of distinctive features in fact *depends* methodologically on the validity of that principle.

There is an even more remarkable misreading of the principle of linearity, which occurs in another series of lectures that Jakobson gave in New York in 1942, entitled 'Six leçons sur le son et le sens' (Jakobson 1942a). Here we find a discussion of Saussure's distinction between the axes of simultaneity and succession. It may be an accident that the published version of these lectures in Jakobson's *Selected Writings* gets Saussure's diagram the wrong way round (Jakobson 1942a: 381). But in any case the text makes amply clear that Jakobson thought that any linear arrangement had to be situated on the axis of succession. Why? Apparently because in a sequence one thing 'follows' another. Jakobson seems to be alone among Saussurean commentators in proposing this peculiar misinterpretation. It is worth disinterring because it throws some light both on Jakobson's problems with the term *syntagmatique* (it suggests 'eine Zeitfolge': Jakobson 1959: 293) and on his difficulties over the distinction between synchronic and diachronic. Again, however, it is interesting that Jakobson did not himself see the connexions at the theoretical level. Had he done so, he might have realized where the source of the confusion lay. As it was, he was still claiming in 1959 that the principle of linearity involved a 'dangerous simplification' ('gefährliche Vereinfachung'). Simplification, certainly, but it was Jakobson's, not Saussure's.

Jakobson's attitude to the distinction between synchrony and dia-chrony is more ambivalent, because he wants to have both at the same time. This is certainly a feat of conceptual acrobatics if nothing else. As early as 1928 Jakobson, in company with Tynjanov (Tynjanov and Jakobson 1928: 26), was claiming: 'Pure synchronism now proves to be an illusion' (as if Saussure, like Lenin, had promised a glorious new order and failed to deliver it). Who had been taken in by the 'illusion', and exactly how? Tynjanov and Jakobson never tell us in their vaguely worded proclamation. In the late '20s, one might have thought that a case of ordering the coffin before the demise of the patient. But forty years on Jakobson was saying that Saussure's 'fallacious identification of two oppositions – synchrony *versus* diachrony, and statics *versus* dynamics

– was refuted by post-Saussurian linguistics' (Jakobson 1971: 721). Who had 'refuted' it? No answer there, either. In fact, this must count as one of the most bizarre assessments of post-Saussurean linguistics on record. For of all the articles of Saussurean doctrine, none has proved more robust than the separation of synchronic from diachronic studies, and it continues to be so in departments of linguistics all over the world. Synchrony, claimed Jakobson, 'gar nicht statisch ist' (Jakobson 1959: 275); for changes are always emerging. Quite so. But (1) Saussure does not use the word *statique* to mean 'stationary', and (2) exactly how the emerging changes could ever be identified *as such* except in a diachronic perspective Jakobson does not stop to explain. He rests content with the barren oxymoron 'dynamic synchrony' – sufficient to disown Saussure, but inadequate to suggest any genuine alternative. What is even more incongruous is that some of Jakobson's own analytic tools – for instance, the concepts of complementary distribution, free variation and neutralization – are incoherent outside a purely synchronic framework. (It would be absurd to say of a consonant of modern French that it stands in complementary distribution with any consonant of Latin.) Having your panchronic cake and eating it has always seemed an attractive prospect to some, but it does not translate into very convincing linguistic analysis.

Jakobson's rejection of the principle of arbitrariness in 1959 is direct and unequivocal, and the attack on Saussure is dramatic. It begins by objecting that Saussure's principle of arbitrariness is itself arbitrary ('ein willkürliches Prinzip': Jakobson 1959: 272). If ever Jakobson disqualified himself as a theorist, it is in this misplaced *coup de théâtre*, for it is based on verbal equivocation. The mistake is not primarily about Saussure, but about the role of theory and the status of technical terms in a theory. Reading Jakobson is rather like reading some Greek geometer who objects to Euclid's axioms on the ground that other axioms might have been chosen. Even if we are charitable enough to make the best of Jakobson's case, the reply is simple. Of course postulates are 'arbitrary', if by that one means simply that other postulates might have been selected. But on that count *all* theorizing is 'arbitrary' and Jakobson's objection is vacuous. Conceivably, for example, Saussure might have chosen as his first principle that signs reflect – or should reflect – the true nature of what they signify. (If so, he would have been Plato, not Saussure.) Jakobson here shows no indication of recognizing the most elementary difference between theory and description. This is by no means a local or temporary aberration in Jakobson's thinking. Jakobson by the late 1950s apparently wanted to claim – although he never comes out and says it in so many words – that if linguistics is to be a science there is only one way to do it.

And all other methods are wrong. Anyone who believes *that* is ultimately denying the concept of linguistic theory altogether – at least, linguistic theory as Saussure and his students understood it. The paradox is that this denial of the role of theory is itself a theoretical position, and requires theoretical arguments to defend it. This Jakobson never understood.

But is there any more substantive objection to the principle of arbitrariness? Here Jakobson wheels on Benveniste as *arbiter arbitrorum*.

> Wie es übrigens schon Benveniste in *Acta Linguistica*, I, grossartig darlegte, darf man keinesfalls vom synchronischen Standpunkt der Sprachgemeinschaft, welche die gegeben Sprachzeichen gebraucht, diesen Zeichen einen willkürlichen Charakter zuschreiben. Es is durchaus nicht willkürlich, sondern schlechthin obligat, im Französichen für 'Käse' *fromage* und im Englischen *cheese* zu sagen. (Jakobson 1959: 272)

The only trouble is that what Jakobson is here proclaiming as a definitive debunking of Saussure could equally be read as a complete misinterpretation by Benveniste.

Benveniste had started this particular hare in the article Jakobson refers to, published in Hjelmslev's periodical *Acta Linguistica* in 1939. It was entitled 'Nature du signe linguistique' (Benveniste 1939). At the time, Benveniste had just taken over Meillet's chair at the Collège de France. The fact is worth mentioning, not only because this was one of the most prestigious posts in the entire French academic Establishment but also because Meillet is sometimes described as 'the most distinguished of Saussure's pupils' (Iordan and Orr 1970: 296). In the circumstances, the publication of a paper that rejected Saussure's 'first principle' of linguistics was of some significance. Benveniste himself thought sufficiently well of this critique to republish the paper in a collection of his own essays in 1966. The introduction to this latter volume gives no indication of any second thoughts that the author might have had about the contents of 'Nature du signe linguistique' during the quarter of a century that had elapsed since its original publication.

What Benveniste argues in 'Nature du signe linguistique' appears in retrospect almost unbelievably simplistic. He says that Saussure's reasoning is 'faussé par le recours inconscient et subreptice à un troisième terme, qui n'était pas compris dans la définition initiale [sc. of the linguistic sign]. Ce troisième terme est la chose même, la réalité' (Benveniste 1939: 50). Thus although purporting to define the sign in terms of a relation between two psychological items, *signifié* (= 'concept') and *signifiant* (= 'image acoustique'), Saussure had all the timc had in view the relationship between these and an extra-linguistic item: 'la chose même, la réalité'.

Saussure a beau dire que l'idée de «sœur» n'est pas liée au signifiant *s-ö-r*; il n'en pense pas moins à la réalité de la notion. (Benveniste 1939: 50)

What exactly Benveniste takes to be the reality ('la chose même') of the notion 'sister' we are never told. It hardly becomes any clearer when Benveniste analyses the notorious example of *bœuf/Ochs* (CLG: 100), which has occasioned many misgivings (De Mauro: 442ff.). According to Benveniste:

c'est seulement si l'on pense à l'animal «bœuf» dans sa particularité concrète et «substantielle» que l'on est fondé à juger «arbitraire» la relation entre *böf* d'une part, *oks* de l'autre, à une même réalité. (Benveniste 1939: 50)

This is philosophically ingenuous, to say the least. What Benveniste calls 'l'animal «bœuf»' is already an abstraction, i.e. a classification, as nominalists had been insisting since the Middle Ages. Saussure's (post-nominalist) point, which Benveniste seems to miss entirely, is that it is a *linguistic* classification (i.e. dependent on the particular *langue* in question). There is no question of somehow entertaining the concept «bœuf» without entertaining the concept of an animal with certain physical properties; and Saussure had never suggested otherwise. But the nature of those properties – whether they are 'real' or imaginary – is irrelevant to the constitution of the *signifiant* (be it *bœuf*, *Ochs*, or any other) which any given language correlates with this concept. Benveniste concludes:

Il y a donc contradiction entre la manière dont Saussure définit le signe linguistique et la nature fondamentale qu'il lui attribue. (Benveniste 1939: 50)

To this the appropriate reply is: no, the only contradiction is between the Saussurean notion of *la langue* as a system of values and the (one) jarring sentence in the text (*CLG*: 100) which speaks of 'the same' *signifié* in two different languages. But if the same *animal* has different designations on either side of a linguistic frontier, that is simply a reflection of the classification imposed by the vocabularies of the two languages in question.

According to Benveniste:

Entre le signifiant et le signifié, le lien n'est pas arbitraire; au contraire, il est *nécessaire*. (Benveniste 1939: 51)

But in the *CLG* the warning against possible misinterpretation of the term *arbitraire* is quite specific (*CLG*: 101). It is there made abundantly clear that we must not interpret the term *arbitraire* to imply that individuals – or even communities – exercise a free choice over the linguistic sign. When we see how lucidly and unambiguously the question is dealt with in the *CLG*, it is difficult to believe, as later commentators were not slow to remark, that there is any basis here for an opposition between *arbitraire* and *nécessaire* in Benveniste's sense. Saussure already says quite plainly that users have no choice in the matter. Benveniste's error was immediately pointed out by one of Saussure's editors, in a paper published the following year (Bally 1940), but neither Benveniste nor Jakobson seems to have taken any notice of it.

An even clearer indication that Jakobson never really understood Saussure's thinking comes not from what he says about the arbitrariness of the linguistic sign but from what he fails to say. Neither in 1942 nor in 1959 does Jakobson mention Saussure's crucial distinction between *arbitraire absolu* and *arbitraire relatif.* Consequently he never gets to grips with Saussure's theory of grammatical structure. Given these omissions, Saussure is easily pilloried as a linguist who held the ridiculous view that a language is a fortuitous set of associations between sounds and concepts, which somehow manages to stand still in spite of changing all the time. What emerges is a caricature of Saussure, not a portrait.

*   *   *

It would be a mistake to discuss these points of confrontation as if they were floating free in a sempiternal academic vacuum. They were not. They had a very concrete political and social context, which it would be foolish or irresponsible for any historian to ignore. This context includes Jakobson's personal career before, during and after the Second World War.

When we look at what was going on, it begins to explain why, for instance, Jakobson decides to retreat behind the skirts of Benveniste, rather than confront Saussure directly on the issue of arbitrariness. Benveniste was not only a European linguist, but a French linguist, teaching in Paris. All Jakobson's published attacks on Saussure are directed from the safe distance of the east coast of America. While he was based in Europe, Jakobson's attitude to Saussure had been, albeit critical, quite positive. For instance, his paper 'Signe zéro' (Jakobson 1939) spells out the importance of Saussure's recognition that a *signifiant* does not have to be realized concretely as a sound. Before the Second

War, Jakobson's attitude could hardly have been otherwise: for Jakobson's great mentor and collaborator, Trubetzkoy, had based his *magnum opus* on Saussurean principles. Anyone who wishes can undertake the intellectual exercise of going through the *Grundzüge der Phonologie* (Trubetzkoy 1939) deleting one after another all the steps in the argument that rest on the tacit acceptance of Saussure's twin principles. At the end, nothing is left. Once Saussure is discarded, it would not even be possible to define a phoneme – at least, not in the way Trubetzkoy does. Thirty years later, Jakobson would claim credit for having introduced Trubetzkoy to the work of Saussure (De Mauro: 433). But wherever he got them from, Trubetzkoy certainly recognized the value of Saussure's famous theoretical principles and made good use of them.

With Trubetzkoy dead and Europe three thousand miles distant, Jakobson's linguistic perspective – understandably – begins to shift. American linguists were attending his lectures in New York. (They included Hockett, Hoenigswald and Garvin.) Jakobson was having to come face to face with an approach to linguistics that had made no impact at all in pre-war Europe. But his own academic position in the USA was still very insecure. It was not until 1946 that he was given a chair at Columbia. It would be surprising if these circumstances had nothing to do with a move away from what Americans regarded as a typically European brand of linguistics. This may not have been opportunism, but it was certainly opportune.

In Jakobson's New York lectures, we find not only complimentary remarks about Whitney, Sapir and Bloomfield, but the first signs of a flirtation with behaviourism. Pavlov is credited with having demonstrated that even dogs can distinguish between sounds, provided they are habituated to treating the distinctions as having a meaning. One of the charges Jakobson levels against Saussure is his failure to realize that language exists in the individual as a set of personal 'habits': it is these habits, says Jakobson, and not the collective system of *langue*, which directly underlie *parole*. The word *habit*, it goes without saying, is a constant leitmotiv in the later Bloomfield's behaviourist account of language. In short, having belatedly detected this major lacuna in Saussurean theory, Jakobson neatly allows the current trend in American linguistics to fill it. Again not opportunism, but strikingly opportune.

On reading 'La théorie saussurienne en rétrospection', one has the impression of a linguist trying hard to exorcize the ghost of Saussure. Trying hard, but not succeeding very well. The lack of success perhaps has something to do with the method deployed. The method consists in trying to convict Saussure of self-contradiction. Whenever the *CLG* – as often – presents a rather complex idea for examination, Jakobson will first cite a partial version of it, producing a quotation – out of context – which captures just one facet of the point. This isolated quotation is then discussed as if that represented Saussure's final pronouncement on the matter. Jakobson will then produce another quotation from the *CLG* which presents the rest of what is said on the subject, and invite us to see the first and second quotations as incompatible. Thus 'Saussure' is constantly shown as apparently condemning himself out of his own mouth.

This game can, of course, be played to discredit any thinker whose thinking is at all subtle and nuanced. By 1959 Jakobson had realized – or perhaps been told – that games of this kind do not in the end convince anyone, and the arguments that featured prominently in 1942 are no longer in evidence. Or perhaps he had seen that the technique is dangerous, because it cuts both ways and the critic can easily trip himself up. An example of this occurs when Jakobson takes issue with Saussure over whether linguistic change originates in *langue* or in *parole*. Jakobson first of all cites without qualification the Saussurean dictum '*c'est la parole qui fait évoluer la langue*'. He then proceeds to focus on the *CLG* account of analogical change, as if analogical innovations were the only changes Saussure had in mind. This explanation of analogy, he points out, presupposes an already existing matrix of forms. But, asks Jakobson, where does this matrix come from? It is already supplied by *la langue*. Ergo, Saussure has contradicted himself. It is not *la parole* which is responsible for the evolution of *la langue*, but *la langue* which is responsible for its own evolution.

Jakobson was evidently so pleased with this demonstration that he failed to notice that he had argued himself into a self-contradiction of his own. If any system contains within itself its own potential developments, and brings them to fruition in its own good time, in response to some inner necessity, then nothing alters the system as such: *plus ça change, plus c'est la même chose*. A language, thus construed, is no longer an instrument of communication responding to the external needs of its users, but an organism obeying internal laws of its own. We are back again to the Neogrammarian position which Jakobson condemns, but which is uncomfortably close to his own.

This is not the only argument that backfires in 'La théorie saussurienne'. Jakobson decides to take issue with Saussure's way of defining 'l'objet de la linguistique'. The *CLG* starts by drawing attention to the variety of perspectives from which it is possible to consider an utterance of the French word *nu* and the variety of questions it is possible to ask about it (*CLG*: 23). Thus it is illusory to suppose that when someone pronounces the word *nu* we have an independently given linguistic object. Actually, we can distinguish and inquire about three or four quite different things: a sound, the expression of an idea, a derivative of Latin *nudum*, and so on. None of these, it is pointed out, intrinsically takes precedence or priority. But this is quite wrong according to Jakobson, and shows that Saussure approached language in exactly the same way as the Neogrammarians, with their '*esprit atomisant*'. (The pejorative implication of the phrase '*esprit atomisant*' is particularly interesting, coming as it does from a linguist who was to make such a song and dance about distinctive features in phonology.)

When it comes to explaining exactly *why* Saussure is wrong on this initial point, Jakobson resorts to a contorted argument by analogy. He compares the utterance of a word to a bus. It would be ludicrous, he claims, to point out that a modern bus can be examined as a metal construction, a means of transport, a successor to the old horse-drawn tram, etc. For we all know perfectly well what the function of a bus is, and that is all that really matters. Linguistics, proclaims Jakobson, swept along on the wings of his own analogy, 'envisage tous les éléments constitutifs d'un autobus pas rapport aux besoins du transport' (Jakobson 1942b: 400).

As often, Jakobson does not seem to realize that all he has succeeded in doing is tripping himself up. What are 'the needs of transport'? How are these needs defined, and by whom? No one would get very far in analysing the structure of a bus on this basis: unless the 'needs of transport' were taken to subsume in advance all questions of cost, production, mechanics, competition, road safety, availability of materials, labour, etc. But then we are back with Saussure's problem: where do we start, and which of these questions has priority? Jakobson's comparison between the word and the bus is already grotesque; but if we take that comparison at all seriously, it actually proves Saussure's point, not Jakobson's. For in order even to recognize Jakobson's bus, i.e. to distinguish it as a certain type of vehicle, we have to belong to a culture familiar with the forms of locomotion peculiar to an advanced industrial society. In short, Saussure's conclusion here is perfectly valid: 'Bien loin que l'objet précède le point de vue, on dirait que c'est le point de vue qui crée l'objet' (*CLG*: 23). In order to recognize the word *nu*, we have to be familiar with French. And being familiar with French is not something that is conferred automatically on hearing or uttering the sounds [ny], any more than it is assured by being able to grasp the concept of nakedness. Words do not – any more than buses – constitute an 'objectively given' order of reality, with 'objectively given' identities. Jakobson never seems to have grasped this basic point and its theoretical implications. He never sees that Saussurean theory is an attempt to spell out just how our recognition of the word is possible, i.e. how the *point de vue* creates the *objet*. Instead of giving Saussure any credit for pinpointing the problem, Jakobson blandly refuses to concede that there is any problem in the first place.

'Naive' is one of the derogatory terms Jakobson applies to Saussure: but we have to ask ourselves whether this is not a case of pot calling the kettle black. Is it not Jakobson who is being far more naive than Saussure on this particular issue? But that particular brand of naivety would doubtless have gone down well with some of the Americans in Jakobson's audience in 1942. The positivism which provided the philosophical basis for Bloomfieldian linguistics has exactly this order of naivety. For Bloomfield the behaviourist, equally, there is no problem about *identifying* the object of study; for language is simply *given* as an observable form of behaviour. (In fact, among the Bloomfieldians and post-Bloomfieldians only Zellig Harris ever recognized that there might be a theoretical problem here, and he opted to treat it as one that could be resolved methodologically.) The American linguistics to which Jakobson transferred his allegiance during the war wanted, in effect, to reduce linguistic theory to descriptive methodology. Jakobson in 1942 is perfectly happy to go along with that reduction (thus distancing himself from Hjelmslev and other European linguists who were trying to develop a neo-Saussurean approach). And what better way to mark the change of allegiance than by showing *in extenso* that the *CLG* was full of contradictions from beginning to end?

*   *   *

By 1959, however, the academic climate in the USA had changed. Jakobson's Saussure had changed too. The emphasis has now switched from trying to show that Saussure was inconsistent to trying to show that Saussure was not very original. Kruszewski is posthumously rehabilitated in order to take the credit for having already formulated the important distinction between 'similarity and contiguity' – thus in effect retracting the debt to Saussure that Jakobson had acknowledged in his paper on two types of aphasia (Jakobson 1956: 61). What is interesting is that Kruszewski is not mentioned at all in Jakobson's earlier attack on Saussure in 1942.

In 1959 a respectful forelock is duly tugged in the direction of recent developments in the USA. 'The theory of syntactical transformations' is described as 'one of the most topical problems of linguistic analysis'. Which was doubtless how it looked in Boston in 1959. But what Jakobson omits to mention, having just dismissed Saussure's principle of linearity as worthless, is that the American transformational grammar of the late '50s was essentially committed to that principle. More than that: the operations invoked by the transformational grammarians of that period *do not make sense* except in a theoretical framework which presupposes the linearity of the linguistic sign (i.e. as 'surface structure'). Did Jakobson fail to realize that? If he did, this merely confirms his lack of theoretical acumen. If he did not, it indicts his criticism of Saussure's principle as disingenuous. The entire apparatus of transformational analysis of the period Jakobson is referring to was based on simple left-to-right rewrite rules. The *modus operandi* of such rules is inescapably linear.

What leaps to the eye on comparing the comments on Saussure in 1959 to those made in 1942 is that in the later paper there is, quite astonishingly, no discussion of the Saussurean distinction between *langue* and *parole*. This had featured prominently in 1942, where Jakobson tries hard to prove from the text of the *CLG* that Saussure thought that only the speaker was engaged in the *acte de parole* and the hearer was excluded. There Jakobson had also claimed that Saussure advocated a study of *langue* without reference to *parole*. And, for good measure, that Saussure claimed that *parole* lacked homogeneity. When we turn to the text (*CLG*: 25), we find that Jakobson has engineered this interpretation by substituting the word *parole* for the word *langage* in the passage cited.

Perhaps between 1942 and 1959 Jakobson had come to realize that all these criticisms were unfounded. But there were also more positive reasons for the loud silence about *langue* and *parole*. One of Jakobson's favourite themes during the early part of his American career was the distinction between speaker-oriented and hearer-oriented analysis. This was never, in fact, translated into any specific methodological proposals for language description. But the internal logic of that perspective actually required the distinction between *langue* and *parole* for its validation. (It would not do to suppose that the speaker had one *langue* but the hearer another. For on that assumption there would be no common 'code' as the basis of dialogue.) Jakobson may have realized, in short, that in attacking Saussure's distinction between *langue* and *parole* he was cutting off his nose to spite his face. It may also have become clear to him by 1959 that he would in any case get no support for any opposition between speaker-oriented and hearer-oriented descriptions from within the swelling cohorts of American transformationalists. On the contrary, the leader of those cohorts was committed to a theoretical scenario in which speaker and hearer must be assumed to have access to the *same* set of linguistic rules.

* * *

In conclusion, it is worth quoting the *profession de foi* that Jakobson highlights in his 1959 paper on Saussure.

> Überhaupt glaube ich, *dass es heutzutage unsere Grundaufgabe ist, ja unser Schlag-wort sein sollte, realistisch zu werden, eine durchaus realistische Sprachwissenschaft aufzubauen und jeden Fiktionalismus in der Linguistik zu bekämpfen.* (Jakobson 1959: 276)

But this was no rallying call to 'realism' in any philosophical sense. Rather it was a submission to the current *Realpolitik* of American academia. As one of Jakobson's admirers says, Jakobson put himself firmly 'on the side of God's truth' (Mel'chuk 1985: 180). And for a God's-truth linguist, Saussure in retrospect could hardly seem other than the great apostle of hocus-pocus. Later Jakobson airily dismissed the 'God's truth' contro-versy as misconceived, insisting that any linguistic opposition is 'code-given' (Jakobson 1962: 650). But this itself is, patently, a God's-truth position.

What Jakobson may not have realized in 1959 was that behaviourism was already out, mentalism was back in, and generative linguistics was in this respect set to become *plus catholique que le pape* – more Saussurean than Saussure. To the end Jakobson never understood what Saussure had tried to do for linguistics. This incomprehension is summed up in his contemptuous remark about 'the master': 'he succumbed to the tradi-tional belief in the linear character of language' (Jakobson 1956: 60–1). The comment epitomizes Jakobson's failure to see the difference between taking a truism for granted and selecting it as a theoretical postulate. One might as well say of Euclid: 'he succumbed to the traditional belief that space is continuous'.

Caught early on in the web of Saussurean theory, Jakobson never in the end managed to extricate himself. On the one hand, he did not see its potential and develop it further as, for example, albeit in quite different ways, both Guillaume and Hjelmslev did. On the other hand, although ostensibly rejecting the principles of Saussurean linguistics, Jakobson never managed to put any alternative principles of his own in their place.

This is doubtless one reason why the Jakobsonian inheritance – in spite of Jakobson's wide-ranging interests and numerous graduate students – never included anything that could be called a 'Jakobsonian school' of linguistics.

CHAPTER SEVEN

Lévi-Strauss's Saussure

It was to Jakobson that Claude Lévi-Strauss owed his introduction to the work of Saussure. According to Lévi-Strauss's own account, before attending Jakobson's lectures, 'je ne savais à peu près rien en linguistique' (Lévi-Strauss 1976: 191). The lectures in question were 'Six leçons sur le son et le sens' (Jakobson 1942a) and the unlikely venue for this introduction was New York, where both Jakobson and Lévi-Strauss found themselves wartime exiles. From the start, therefore, Lévi-Strauss's reading of Saussure had a Jakobsonian slant to it. Jakobson's lectures were for Lévi-Strauss 'la révélation de la linguistique structurale'. Thus by 1942 Saussure was firmly identified as the pioneer of 'structuralism' and 'structural linguistics' as an established intellectual enterprise that could be 'revealed' to neophytes (as distinct from being a chain of rather tentative speculations about what might follow from taking some of Saussure's suggestions seriously).

The relevance of these details in the present context is that they bear on the fact that Lévi-Strauss is commonly cited as one of the most prominent examples of the influence of Saussure's teachings outside the domain of linguistics proper.

> The implications of Saussure's work on language are seen at their clearest in the work of Lévi-Strauss, who has declared Saussure to be one of the two truly formative influences in his intellectual life (the other being a sixteenth-century French Protestant missionary to Brazil, who produced the first recognizably modern ethnographic account of an indigenous population). (Sturrock 1979: 11)

As the foremost exponent of modern 'structural anthropology', Lévi-Strauss seems to have chosen two heroes who between them epitomize a certain approved model of scientific endeavour in the twentieth century: on the one hand, the humble field worker who spends all his time in observation and the accumulation of factual information; on the other, the lofty theorist whose intellectual task is to 'make sense of' the 'data' that the field worker has patiently collected. Lévi-Strauss, it seems not extravagant to suggest, sees himself as fulfilling both roles: on the one hand, a meticulous accumulator of 'data' and, at the same time, a Saussure of anthropological theory.

More specifically, Lévi-Strauss is credited with promoting the notion that the 'social practices and institutions studied by anthropologists' are 'amenable to the same kind of analysis Saussure had pioneered in linguistics' (Johnson 1997: 5–6). Whether this is a plausible account of the relationship between Lévi-Strauss's ideas and Saussure's is the basic question addressed in the present chapter.

The term 'structural anthropology', deliberately calqued on 'structural linguistics', certainly leaves little room for doubt about which study is envisaged as model. Any doubt there might be is dispelled by the forthright and frequently quoted opening statement of the article Lévi-Strauss published in 1945 in the newly founded linguistic journal *Word* (in the creation of which Jakobson had played a leading role):

Dans l'ensemble des sciences sociales auquel elle appartient indiscutablement, la linguistique occupe cependant une place exceptionnelle: elle n'est pas une science sociale comme les autres, mais celle qui, de loin, a accompli les plus grands progrès; la seule, sans doute, qui puisse revendiquer le nom de science et qui soit parvenue, à la fois, à formuler une méthode positive et à connaître la nature des faits soumis à son analyse. (Lévi-Strauss 1945: 37)

It is a rarity in the annals of academia for a leading figure in one discipline to acknowledge publicly the superiority of a neighbouring discipline, as Lévi-Strauss did on this occasion. It is even rarer for such a figure to admit, albeit indirectly, that his own discipline is not yet a science, even though it claims to be. Lévi-Strauss then went on to quote Marcel Mauss's observation (in 1924) to the effect that sociology would have made much further progress if sociologists had followed the lead given by linguists. What is slightly surprising about that reference is that the lead to which Mauss was alluding was one that had been abandoned in the structural linguistics that Lévi-Strauss so much admired. Indeed, later in the same article Lévi-Strauss states:

L'erreur de la sociologie traditionnelle, comme de la linguistique traditionnelle, est d'avoir considéré les termes, et non les relations entre les termes. (Lévi-Strauss 1945: 57)

This pronouncement sounds at first to have a very Saussurean ring to it. But, given Saussure's status as one of Lévi-Strauss's intellectual heroes, perhaps something more overtly Saussurean might have been expected. When one looks into the matter more carefully, some odd features of Lévi-Strauss's supposed regard for Saussure begin to emerge. For example, in Lévi-Strauss's 1945 paper Saussure is not mentioned except in a brief footnote. It is not Saussure but Trubetzkoy whom Lévi-Strauss identifies as 'the illustrious founder of structural linguistics'.

By implication, it would seem, Saussure's linguistics is pre-structuralist as far as Lévi-Strauss is concerned. This appears to be borne out by the footnote mentioned above, which claims laconically that the founders of modern linguistics, Ferdinand de Saussure and Antoine Meillet, had between 1900 and 1920 been content to place their discipline 'sous le patronage des sociologues', and that it was not until the 1920s that Mauss in anthropology began to 'reverse this tendency', i.e. to look to linguistics for a lead.

As an account of the relevant history of ideas, this is both remarkable and puzzling. Saussure, one feels, would have been surprised and distressed to learn that he was held responsible for setting up a modern linguistics that was tributary to the anthropology of his day (i.e. the anthropology of Tylor, of Rivers, of the Bureau of American Ethnology, of Mauss himself). For while it might be argued that in the USA linguistics at the beginning of the century owed a serious academic debt to anthropology, that could hardly be said of the European tradition to which Saussure belonged. European linguistics came out of the long-established study of ancient texts in universities, not out of the practical problems of dealing with dispossessed indigenous communities and their half-destroyed cultures, artificially preserved in North American 'reservations'.

Furthermore, in the *CLG* anthropology is explicitly referred to as one of the disciplines *not* to be confused with linguistics:

> la linguistique doit être soigneusement distinguée de l'ethnographie et de la préhistoire, où la langue n'intervient qu'à titre de document; distinguée aussi de l'anthropologie, qui n'étudie l'homme qu'au point de vue de l'espèce, tandis que le langage est un fait social. (*CLG*: 21)

Linguistics, the reader of the *CLG* is told, must define its 'objet' in such a way that it does not include a heterogeneous miscellany of unrelated things; for this would open the door to other sciences, such as psychology, anthropology, normative grammar and philology (*CLG*: 24). Finally, whereas Lévi-Strauss in his 1945 paper stresses the ways in which linguistics has been of assistance to anthropology 'ever since the work of Schrader' (i.e. c. 1890), the *CLG* strikes a much more sceptical note:

> la langue apporte-t-elle des lumières à l'anthropologie, à l'ethnographie, à la préhistoire? On le croit très généralement; nous pensons qu'il y a là une grande part d'illusion. (*CLG*: 304)

None of this sounds very much like Lévi-Strauss's Saussure of 1945, who was supposedly content for linguistics to be placed under the patronage of sociology.

As for Meillet, he might well have been astonished to find himself regarded in 1945 as one of the twin founders of modern linguistics at all. For although an erstwhile student and confidant of Saussure's, his reaction to the publication of the *CLG* had been far from enthusiastic (Meillet 1916). Given that, alongside Saussure, Lévi-Strauss's other intellectual hero was the patient fact-gathering missionary in Brazil, it is worth considering a little further Lévi-Strauss's identification of Meillet as the co-founder of modern linguistics. For it is on the question of 'facts' that Meillet is most sharply critical of Saussure. Lévi-Strauss's coupling of Meillet with Saussure might accordingly be seen as reflecting Lévi-Strauss's own view of the need to balance the demands of theoretical generalization with respect for the detailed examination of specific evidence.

*   *   *

By the time he published 'Histoire et ethnologie' in the *Revue de Métaphysique et de Morale* in 1949, Lévi-Strauss seems to have revised his view of Saussure's historical role. In this article the publication of the *CLG* is hailed as marking the advent of structural linguistics, and Trubetzkoy, thus demoted without either apology or explanation, is praised only (in a footnote) for the minor achievement of having shown for the Indo-European languages what Franz Boas had long since demonstrated for the American Indian languages – that common features did not necessarily have to be explained by common origin. Boas, not mentioned at all in the earlier article in *Word*, now emerges into the limelight and upstages all other linguists in 'Histoire et ethnologie'. The reason is interesting. It is not because Boas was also an anthropologist (on the anthropological front Lévi-Strauss criticizes him for his 'timidity') but because Boas, here credited with laying down the foundations of American linguistics, is said by Lévi-Strauss to have shown that linguistic structure exists at a level below the consciousness of the speaker (Lévi-Strauss 1949: 26).

It would have been less questionable if Lévi-Strauss had contented himself with saying that that was what Boas asserted, rather than what Boas had been able to show. But, as elsewhere, Lévi-Strauss is keen to point to linguistics as having achieved advances that anthropology must try to emulate. So for this purpose Boas, although not formally or theoretically committed to structuralism, is presented as a kind of structuralist *avant la lettre*. According to Lévi-Strauss, he anticipated 'le développement ultérieur de la pensée linguistique'.

Lévi-Strauss points out that eight years before the publication of the *CLG* Boas had already stated that

«La différence essentielle, entre les phénomènes linguistiques et les autres phénomènes culturels, est que les premiers n'émergent jamais à la conscience claire, tandis que les seconds, bien qu'ayant la même origine inconsciente, s'élèvent souvent jusqu'au niveau de la pensée consciente, donnant ainsi naissance à des raisonnements secondaires et à des ré-interprétations.» (Lévi-Strauss 1949: 26)

Boas had furthermore recognized that

«Le grand avantage de la linguistique à cet égard est que, dans l'ensemble, les catégories du langage restent inconscientes; pour cette raison, on peut suivre le processus de leur formation sans qu'interviennent, de façon trompeuse et gênante, les interprétations secondaires, si fréquentes en ethnologie qu'elles peuvent obscurcir irrémédiablement l'histoire du développement des idées.» (Lévi-Strauss 1949: 26–7)

Although this important difference might at first sight seem to put an obstacle in the way of simply transferring linguistic methods of analysis to other 'phénomènes culturels', Lévi-Strauss sweeps the objection aside with the bland assurance that the difference is only one of degree and does not lessen 'la valeur exemplaire de la méthode linguistique pour les recherches ethnologiques'. But why Lévi-Strauss is so pleased with Boas for insisting on the unconscious character of linguistic structure does not emerge until the end of 'Histoire et ethnologie'. According to Lévi-Strauss 'l'activité inconsciente de l'esprit consiste à imposer des formes à un contenu'. Moreover these forms are 'fondamentalement les mêmes pour tous les esprits, anciens et modernes, primitifs et civilisés'. In order to reveal this activity it is both necessary and sufficient to grasp 'la structure inconsciente, sous-jacente à chaque institution ou à chaque coutume.' This is not to be confused with what members of a society happen to believe – or have been taught – about their own institutions and customs.

> Or on sait que, chez la plupart des peuples primitifs, il est très difficile d'obtenir une justification morale, ou une explication rationnelle, d'une coutume ou d'une institution: l'indigène interrogé se contente de répondre que les choses ont toujours été ainsi, que tel fut l'ordre des dieux, ou l'enseignement des ancêtres. Même quand on rencontre des interprétations, celles-ci ont toujours le caractère de rationalisa-tions ou d'élaborations secondaires: il n'y a guère de doute que les raisons inconscientes pour lesquelles on pratique une coutume, on partage une croyance, sont fort éloignées de celles qu'on invoque pour la justifier. (Lévi-Strauss 1949: 25)

The goal of the anthropologist, Lévi-Strauss tells his readers, is 'd'atteindre, par-delà l'image consciente et toujours différente que les hommes forment de leur devenir, un inventaire de possibilités incon-scientes'. Thus conceived, anthropology becomes a kind of psycho-analysis of the collective mind, rather than mere documentation of strange customs, beliefs, artifacts, etc. The importance of modern linguistics for the anthropologist is that the linguist has shown that such an enterprise is feasible, i.e. it is possible to analyse 'scientifically' and exhaustively the unconscious collective structures underlying certain ubiquitous forms of social behaviour.

*   *   *

By his insistence on the unconscious nature of linguistic structure, Lévi-Strauss could be seen – depending on one's point of view – either as opening up new academic vistas for interdisciplinary studies or as biting off more than anthropology could chew. It was certainly an insistence that opened the flood gates of structuralism to sundry experts on 'the unconcious'. Ever since Boas raised the question of what speakers of a language are – or are not – conscious of, it had been a controversial issue in linguistics, having obvious implications for the development of lin-guistic methodology, the reliability of introspective evidence, etc. Bloom-field held that it was no use asking speakers for the meaning of a linguistic form (Bloomfield 1933: 160); but this is a relatively weak version of the claim. That is to say, although speakers might think they knew the answer and be willing to give it, their answer might be wrong. (Bloomfield's example is a hypothetical informant's supposition that *cran-* in *cranberry* means 'red'. Bloomfield is evidently not willing to accept either (1) that if a speaker thinks that *cran-* means 'red' then *ipso facto* it *does* mean 'red' for that speaker, or (2) that *cran-* might have different meanings for different speakers.) A stronger and more recent version emerges in Chomsky's thesis that some grammatical rules are not only followed by speakers unconsciously, but are rules that could not even be brought to the level of consciousness (Chomsky 1965: 8). Which presumably means that even if speakers had examples pointed out to them they would fail to grasp them. (How, in that case, the linguist would be aware of the rule in the first place is one of many unanswered questions in Chomskyan linguistics.)

The problem with bringing the unconscious into the linguistic picture has always been that nobody knows very much about what goes on in that realm anyway. So this is an instance of explaining *obscurum per obscurius*. In Lévi-Strauss's case one might have supposed that light might be cast on the claim by reference to related and roughly contemporary 'structural' claims in the realm of psychology, in particular by Jacques Lacan. Lacan says, for example, of kinship terms:

> À l'alliance préside un ordre préférentiel dont la loi impliquant les noms de parenté est pour le groupe, comme le langage, impérative en ses formes, mais inconsciente en sa structure. (Lacan 1953: 156)

This is a formulation that Lévi-Strauss, one supposes, would have been more than happy to endorse; and it is relevant to note that, although Lévi-Strauss is not specifically mentioned on this occasion, the writings of Lacan are sprinkled with approbatory references to the work of 'mon ami Lévi-Strauss'. The question is: what is being claimed by insisting that a 'law' is 'imperative in its forms' but 'unconscious in its structure'? And what exactly hinges on the acceptance or rejection of that claim?

Several interpretations might be proposed, and their plausibility varies according to whether the consciousness involved is seen as that of the individual or the collectivity. Saussure distinguished between the two in his lectures (*CLG3*: 120), although his dictum 'chacun de nous a en soi la langue' is open to more than one reading. Lévi-Strauss holds out 'the hope of overcoming the opposition between the collective nature of culture and its manifestations in the individual'. But his solution would hardly have appealed to Saussure, since it involves supposing that

> the so-called 'collective consciousness' would, in the final analysis, be no more than the expression, on the level of individual thought and behavior, of certain time and space modalities of the universal laws which make up the unconscious activity of the mind. (Lévi-Strauss 1951: 65)

This would be rather like maintaining that the features of the way an individual walks reduce to the manner in which the individual skeleton and musculature respond to the universal laws of physiology and gravity. Oddly, what would be missing from any such account is recognition of a *cultural* dimension to the activity in question.

There are obvious problems in making sense of the notion of a collective consciousness, but in this instance they can be left on one side, since Saussure in any case seems to accept the concept. Thus any major difference between Saussure's position and that adopted by Lévi-Strauss and/or Lacan does not seem to lie here. It is perfectly possible – at least in theory – for an individual always to behave in a certain way without realizing that the form of behaviour in question is in fact socially mandatory. But there is both a logical and a psychological difficulty in the notion that the community does not realize it either. In both the individual and the collective case, it is hard to see how the 'forms' of the 'law' could be 'imperative' unless that imperative character were recognized. The notion of an 'unrecognized' imperative seems to imply that the 'law' in question actually has a physical or biomechanical basis which is not understood. (Thus, hypothetically, it might be believed that death by drowning was due to the malevolence of Neptune rather than to the failure of the human lungs to function when filled with water.) But that hardly applies to 'laws' of the kind that are involved where questions of kinship and marriage are concerned. A prohibition on, say, sexual intercourse with one's sister is bound to be a social imperative, not a physiological imperative: if it were not at least physiologically possible there would be no point in prohibiting it. Quite apart from the fact that in some societies marrying one's sibling is both common and approved.

Defenders of Lévi-Strauss might wish to argue that, likewise, if it were not linguistically possible to split infinitives, there would be no point in grammarians condemning the practice. But the question of the reasons for the prohibition raises further issues. Presumably it is possible, both with incest and with split infinitives, for individuals to be ignorant or mistaken as to *why* such a prohibition is in force. Again it makes little sense to suppose that the whole community remains in ignorance or error, unless perhaps what is meant by that is that the prohibition in question springs from underlying fears or motives that are not consciously recognized.

Since Lacan is a Freudian, that might be his basic assumption regarding kinship. But whether it would be plausible to maintain that for social imperatives in general is another question. It is in any case difficult to see what Lévi-Strauss or anthropology as a whole would stand to gain by commitment to such an assumption, not to mention general linguistics.

Lacan's pronouncements about linguistics are neither clear nor consistent. Like Lévi-Strauss, he sometimes writes as if he considered linguistics to be the pilot discipline in modern attempts to understand human behaviour:

> La linguistique peut ici nous servir de guide, puisque c'est là le rôle qu'elle tient en flèche de l'anthropologie contemporaine, et nous ne saurions y rester indifférent. [. . .]
>
> N'est-il pas sensible qu'un Lévi-Strauss en suggérant l'implication des structures du langage et de cette part des lois sociales qui règle l'alliance et la parenté conquiert déjà le terrain même où Freud assoit l'inconscient?
>
> Dès lors, il est impossible de ne pas axer sur une théorie générale du symbole une nouvelle classification de sciences où les sciences de l'homme reprennent leur place centrale en tant que sciences de la subjectivité. (Lacan 1953: 165)

Linguistics Lacan defines as 'l'étude des langues existantes dans leur structure et dans les lois qui s'y révèlent', but specifically excludes information theory and what he calls 'toute sémiologie plus ou moins hypothétiquement généralisée'. This might seem to indicate a reluctance to accept Saussure's view of linguistics as a branch of a more general science of signs. Historically, however, Lacan identifies the emergence of modern linguistics with the appearance of what he calls its foundational 'algorithm', and this is Saussure's definition of the linguistic sign as a pairing of *signifiant* with *signifié* (Lacan 1957: 253).

At other times Lacan seems to be more sceptical about the role of linguistics, referring to it as *linguisterie* ('linguistery') and insisting on writing 'la langue' as one word (*lalangue*) in order – he says – to identify it as the 'object' studied in linguistics (Lacan 1974: 16). Which seems to suggest that what linguists study under this rubric may be a suspect abstraction of some kind. It is noticeable that the terms Lacan uses when referring to language are *parole* and *langage*, rather than *langue*. The unconscious, he tells us, depends on *langage*, about which only little is known ('dont on ne sait que peu') (Lacan 1974: 16). The unconscious is something that only creatures with *langage* have (Lacan 1974: 15). Culture, which is the distinguishing characteristic of human societies, may well be reducible to *langage* (Lacan 1957: 252). And then there is perhaps the most famous dictum of all; Lacan's claim that the unconscious is structured like a *langage*.

Both Lacan and Lévi-Strauss seem to regard the crucial breakthrough made by modern linguistics as being the 'discovery' of the phoneme (Lévi-Strauss 1945: 39 ff.; Lacan 1953: 165). But this is hardly a discovery for which Saussure can be given credit. And even if it were, what light does this discovery throw on the claim that the speaker is handling a system which is 'imperative in its forms, but unconscious in its structure'?

It could be argued that phonemic rules are imperatives in the sense that disregarding them renders speech unintelligible. So far so good. But in what corresponding sense is the speaker unconscious of phonemic structure? It seems unlikely – nor do either Lévi-Strauss or Lacan suggest – that there are deep-seated psychological factors (fears, desires, etc.) underlying particular phonemic contrasts, and that what the speaker is unaware of are these hidden psychological foundations. If that were so, then presumably profound psychological differences would have to be posited for speakers of different languages, since one of the conclusions most linguists seem to be agreed about is that no two languages share the same inventory of phonemic oppositions or phonemic rules. It would then, one supposes, be a central task for psychoanalysis to try to uncover the latent psycho-phonemics of our language. But this does not seem to feature in Lacan's programme for exploring the unconscious.

The question remains as to whether, if the unconscious is 'structured like a *langage*', it has basic units *like* phonemes. If not, then the structural parallel itself becomes not only weak but obscure. But if so, what form do these psycho-phonemic units take? How do they combine into psycho-morphemes? The answers to such questions, and even the outlines of answers, are missing from Lacan's writings. According to one Lacanian apologist:

> Thanks to the efforts of the Lacanian school of psychoanalysis, we can now understand how the unconscious is formed at the beginning of life, what it is composed of, and what its precise modes of arrangement and functioning are [. . .] (Lemaire 1977: 247–8)

If that were true, it ought at least to be clear whether the structure of the unconscious includes something corresponding to a limited set of (inherently meaningless) phonemes. But it isn't. To that extent, Lacan is not much help to Lévi-Strauss.

Is there, then, a less problematic interpretation of the claim that speakers are unconscious of phonemic structure, even though they obey its imperatives quite consistently? Yes, there is; but it is an interpretation which hardly seems strong enough for Lacan's theoretical purposes, or for Lévi-Strauss's either. It reduces, in fact, to the rather trite claim that speakers who have not had the benefit of a course in modern linguistics will not be able to state the phonemic rules of their own language. This does seem to be at least part of what Lévi-Strauss has in mind, at least to judge by his congratulating Boas in 'Histoire et ethnologie' for demonstrating that 'la structure de la langue reste inconnue de celui qui parle jusqu'à l'avènement d'une grammaire scientifique' (Lévi-Strauss 1949: 26).

Lévi-Strauss wishes to go further, however. According to him, even the introduction of a scientific grammar makes no difference, because even the scientific grammarian is powerless to apply that conscious knowledge:

> even the scholar's linguistic knowledge always remains dissociated from his experience as a speaking agent, for his mode of speech is not affected by his ability to interpret his language on a higher level. (Lévi-Strauss 1951: 57)

Thus what Lévi-Strauss calls 'absence of consciousness' still holds even for those who, through education, are aware of 'the grammar or the phonemics' of their language. So 'linguistic knowledge', on this view, ends up as being roughly on a par with having some medical knowledge of how one's own digestive system works: it makes no difference, because one cannot control one's digestive processes anyway.

Lévi-Strauss does not seem to see that this is a dangerous argument to advance, if only because it can so easily be rejected outright. That is to say, it leaves itself open to the riposte that being able to distinguish the spoken forms *pin* from *bin*, *bin* from *tin*, *tin* from *din* . . . and so on for all the other 'minimal pairs' in the language *does* show the speaker's consciousness of its phonological structure *and in the only way that matters for practical communicational purposes.*

Furthermore, if the contention about 'unconscious structure' amounts to no more than distinguishing between knowing and not knowing what the scientific grammarian knows, it hardly amounts to anything worth getting excited about. For at least two reasons. One is that 'scientific grammar' itself gives conflicting accounts of phonemes and phonemic rules. The number of phonemes in English is not a question of the same order as the number of atoms in a molecule of carbon (i.e. a question to which, the assumption is, there is just one correct answer, but an answer that the first researchers may have got wrong). For the 'psychological reality' of the phoneme is itself a debated issue, not a truth established in linguistics that other disciplines are now entitled to take as incontrovertible. The second reason is that if being conscious of linguistic structure is equated with being aware of what the 'scientific grammarian' knows, what the unsophisticated speaker lacks is merely an acquaintance with the latest analyses current in academic circles. It begs all kinds of questions to equate this ignorance with being 'unconscious' of phonological or grammatical structure. (That would be rather like claiming that villagers are unconscious of the topography of the locality where they live until a municipal surveyor has been sent along to map it.)

*   *   *

It now begins to become clear why, in Lévi-Strauss's assessment, Saussure does not score as many points as Boas. There is nothing in the *CLG* which declares unambiguously that linguistic structure is below the level of consciousness. On the contrary, as Lévi-Strauss reads it, the *CLG* equates synchronicity with consciousness. Although that remains unstated in 'Histoire et ethnologie', it is made explicit in Lévi-Strauss's inaugural lecture at the Collège de France (1960), where we are told that the *CLG* set up

> une opposition absolue entre deux catégories de faits: d'une part, celle de la grammaire, du synchronique, du conscient; de l'autre, celle de la phonétique, du diachronique, de l'inconscient. Seul le système conscient est cohérent; (Lévi-Strauss 1960: 26)

But this will not suit Lévi-Strauss's book at all. As the first 'structural anthropologist' he wants the synchronic to be unconscious and coherent too – in fact, much more coherent, more deeply logical than the chaotic diversity that appears on the surface of cultural consciousness. It is interesting to note that some commentators on Saussure have reached a conclusion which is almost the opposite of Lévi-Strauss's: they see Saussure as *denying* that *la langue* is 'a product of the conscious mind' and maintaining on the contrary that 'it works by unconscious laws' (Pettit 1975: 10). This ought to have been a conclusion much more to Lévi-Strauss's liking; but somehow he reaches a quite different one. Rather than condemn Saussure outright on this score, however, Lévi-Strauss suggests that the two categories of fact that appear in the *CLG* are the work of the editors, who may have 'forced and schematized' Saussure's thought. Thus Saussure is posthumously granted an anthropological pardon from the first holder of France's new Chair in the subject; clearly a symbolic act in the tradition of ritual generosity that newly enthroned monarchs were at one time expected to show towards convicted offenders.

However, an apologist for Saussure's editors might well object that what is 'forced and schematized' is Lévi-Strauss's version of what appears in the *CLG*. Two questions therefore arise here. Did the editors misrepresent Saussure's position on this issue? Does Lévi-Strauss misrepresent the editors' account?

In support of his criticism of Saussure's editors, Lévi-Strauss refers to Godel's analysis of the manuscript sources, published in 1957, but gives no precise reference. Turning to Godel, one looks in vain for anything that bears on points relevant to the controversial question of consciousness. Turning to the *CLG* text itself, one finds a far more complicated picture than Lévi-Strauss's simplistic summary suggests. The following points are worthy of note.

1. As regards the distinction between synchronic and diachronic, the claim in the *CLG* is indeed that this is 'absolute and admits no compromise' (*CLG*: 119). But what this means is that the linguist must at all costs not confuse them:

> Vouloir réunir dans la même discipline des faits aussi disparates serait donc une entreprise chimérique. Dans la perspective diachronique on a affaire à des phénomènes qui n'ont aucun rapport avec les systèmes, bien qu'ils les conditionnent. (*CLG*: 122)

This is what demands the absolute separation of diachronic from synchronic facts. The 'conscience collective' that Saussure invokes merely supplies the (theoretical) guarantee of homogeneity of the synchronic system. (How, in practice, the linguist is to obtain an assurance of that homogeneity in any given case is a problem Saussure never tackled.)

2. There is no correspondence of the kind Lévi-Strauss implies between 'diachronic' and 'phonetic'. What the *CLG* says is (a) that 'tout ce qui est diachronique dans la langue ne l'est que par la parole' (*CLG*: 138), and (b) that 'la phonétique, et la phonétique tout entière, est le premier objet de la linguistique diachronique' (*CLG*: 194). But it does not follow from either or both of these statements that diachronic phenomena are exclusively phonetic. (Lévi-Strauss perhaps did not realize that in the terminology of the *CLG phonétique* is not phonetics in the modern sense.)

3. The *CLG* does insist that in synchronic linguistics the linguist must endeavour to determine (and be solely concerned with) those linguistic units and relations which have psychological reality for the linguistic community. But this reality includes both conscious and unconscious levels of activity:

> On peut dire que la somme des classements conscients et méthodiques faits par le grammairien qui étudie un état de langue sans faire intervenir l'histoire doit coïncider avec la somme des associations, conscientes ou non, mises en jeu dans la parole. (*CLG*: 189)

A similar conclusion can be drawn from the account given in the *CLG* of the process of speech production:

> Quand quelqu'un dit *marchons!*, il pense inconsciemment à divers groupes d'associations à l'intersection desquels se trouve le syntagme *marchons!* Celui-ci figure d'une part dans la série *marche! marchez!*, et c'est l'opposition de *marchons!* avec ces formes qui détermine le choix; d'autre part, *marchons!* évoque la série *montons! mangeons!* etc., au sein de laquelle il est choisi par le même procédé; dans chaque série on sait ce qu'il faut faire varier pour obtenir la différenciation propre à l'unité cherchée. Qu'on change l'idée à exprimer, et d'autres oppositions seront nécessaires pour faire apparaître une autre valeur; on dira par exemple *marchez!*, ou bien *montons! (CLG:* 179)

Here we are told that the speaker 'unconsciously' thinks of various associative series in which *marchons!* features. The adverb does not appear in the corresponding passages in the students' notes. Is this a case where the editors have 'forced' Saussure's thought? If so, it should be noted, they are forcing it in the opposite direction to that which Lévi-Strauss claims (i.e. this does *not* bear out the equation of 'synchronic' with 'conscious'). The adverb was doubtless inserted in the *CLG* text to *avoid* attributing to Saussure the implausible picture of the speaker actually rehearsing mentally all the possible choices before eventually deciding on one (a process which, if it had to take place consciously for every single choice involved in every syntagma, would presumably result in our speaking much more cautiously than we do – perhaps agonizingly slowly).

Anyone wishing to justify the editors' attempt to make this clear can do so by pointing out that in presenting the famous example of the word *enseignement* and its related associative series, Saussure seems explicitly to have invoked the notion of 'unconscious' associative relations, as the students' notes (Engler: 2026) bear witness:

> – Ce mot [sc. *enseignement*] appellera d'une façon inconsciente pour l'esprit idée d'une foule d'autres mots [. . .]
> – *enseignement* appelle inconsciemment pour l'esprit une foule d'autres mots [. . .]
> – un mot comme *enseignement* appellera d'une façon inconsciente pour l'esprit en particulier l'idée d'une foule d'autres mots [. . .]

But – to come back to the *acte de parole* – whether the speaker is aware or unaware of running through a list of possibilities makes little difference to Saussure's case: for the fact is that *in some way or other* – perhaps partly consciously, partly unconsciously – the speaker manages to make a selection and reject or block all the other possibilities which were potential candidates for any particular syntagmatic slot.

There are certainly, on the other hand, cases in which the speaker is presented as being aware of synchronic relationships. For example:

> les sujets ont conscience que la relation qui unit *enseigner* à *enseignement* ou *juger* à *jugement* n'est pas la même que celle qu'ils constatent entre *enseignement* et *jugement* [. . .] (*CLG*: 189)

But would Lévi-Strauss himself wish to deny this? To attribute this kind of awareness to the speaker is by no means to suppose that the speaker consciously categorizes linguistic forms as 'noun', 'verb', etc. This is quite clear from the relevant passage in Caille's notes, cited by Engler:

> Non pas qu'un sujet conscient manie les idées de *verbe*, de *substantif*, etc. Mais il n'en résulte pas que ces classements ne puissent pas rentrer à des distinctions formant la grammaire. Mais il se trouvera qu'*il y aura un accord* entre cette opération, *(l'activité) inconsciente* et continue *des matériaux accumulés et les opérations conscientes du linguiste sauf sur un point:* < *le grammairien fait intervenir le passé que le sujet parlant ignore* > . (Engler: 2173)

This throws a great deal of light on the whole question of what is to be understood by *un sujet conscient* and *conscience* in Saussure's discussions of language. It also provides *prima facie* evidence that there is no basis for accusing the editors of distorting Saussure's views on the subject.

A similar conclusion emerges from examination of other passages. For instance, on the subject of analogical innovation the *CLG* text says:

> elle suppose la conscience et la compréhension d'un rapport unissant les formes entre elles. (*CLG*: 226)

But this has to be interpreted in the light of the more explicit statement later in the same section:

> Toute création doit être précédée d'une comparaison inconsciente des matériaux déposés dans le trésor de la langue où les formes génératrices sont rangées selon leurs rapports syntagmatiques et associatifs. (*CLG*: 227)

Here the relevant passage in Riedlinger's notes has:

> Il faut un acte < inconscient > de comparaison non seulement pour créer mais pour comprendre les rapports. (Engler: 2522)

Once again the editors emerge as having shown scrupulous respect for the evidence available to them and Lévi-Strauss's complaint about their 'forcing' Saussure's thought appears to be groundless.

Thus when one examines what the *CLG* actually says and the evidence of the students' notes, several points relevant to Lévi-Strauss's account of Saussure's 'two categories of facts' are thrown into relief. The most important is that as far as Saussure was concerned the extent to which individual speakers are conscious of the synchronic structure of *la langue* and of their own use of it in the processes of *parole* was not a big issue; in fact, one might almost say that it was not an issue at all. For what matters – as far as the (Saussurean) linguist is concerned – is to establish the distinctions actually operative in the way a community puts its *langue* to use for communicational purposes. (But that – *pace* Meillet – is not the same as examining ever more closely the minutiae of *parole*.)

In other words, once the linguist has established that speakers regularly distinguish between one sign (S_1) and another sign (S_2) it makes no difference exactly how they implement that distinction phonetically. Furthermore, whether they have reflected intelligently on this distinction and are so aware of it that they can *describe* how they make it (by, for example, saying that, whereas S_1 begins with a voiceless bilabial plosive, S_2 by contrast begins with the corresponding voiced plosive) is completely irrelevant. It is perfectly possible that different individuals in the community will make the distinction between S_1 and S_2 somewhat differently from one another: and it is perfectly possible that some individuals will be more aware of the distinction than others are. That is linguistically of no importance, provided they all make the distinction somehow and provided the variations between individuals in that respect do not result in their ending up with non-matching inventories of signs. This is the thrust of the most famous epigram in the *CLG*: *dans la langue il n'y a que des différences*. What the linguistic community shares is a common respect for the differences, not some uniform mode of implementing those differences in *parole*. (In practice, as the *CLG* points out, a single speaker may pronounce the same word differently on different occasions. Again, whether this is done consciously or unconsciously does not matter. What matters is that the hearers do not mistake it for some other word.) Saussurean doctrine as formulated in the *CLG* is perfectly consistent on this point, and if Lévi-Strauss had appreciated the rationale underlying that consistency he too might have come to see why making consciousness and unconsciousness an issue for synchronic analysis is a *faux pas* for any 'structuralist'.

Where, on the other hand, Saussure *does* make an issue of (one aspect of) consciousness is when it impinges on the question of linguistic change. A move in a game of chess is made deliberately to achieve a certain result, i.e. in order to change the state of the board in a way advantageous to the player. But this is not, in Saussure's view, how linguistic change operates. There is no foresight involved, either by the individual or by the collectivity.

> Il n'y a qu'un point où la comparaison soit en défaut; le joueur d'échecs *a l'intention* d'opérer le déplacement et d'exercer une action sur le système; tandis que la langue ne prémédite rien; c'est spontanément et fortuitement que ses pièces à elle se déplacent – ou plutôt se modifient. (*CLG*: 127)

Lévi-Strauss perhaps interpreted this as implying that synchronic phenomena, since they are radically different from diachronic phenomena, must in Saussure's view always involve consciousness. But if so, this is his own *non sequitur*. What the *CLG* maintains is simply that there is no teleological dimension to linguistic change. Although it may – retrospectively – look as though certain changes were directed towards a certain goal (e.g. the abolition of a grammatical distinction, or the regularization of a conjugation, or a more symmetrical phonological system) this illusion is a product of hindsight. What actually happened was that change sparked a reorganization. But this is classic (Darwinian) evolutionary theory: a kick from behind rather than a tug from in front.

Putting all this together, one sees that Saussure was never in a position to supply exactly what Lévi-Strauss wanted: namely, a mandate for his own ambitious programme for anthropology. This would, in effect, by a kind of argument from extrapolation, establish the anthropologist as being in charge of the 'scientific' investigation of human social behaviour in general (just as the linguist was in charge of that subsection dealing with linguistic behaviour). So although linguistics provided the exemplar, the result envisaged would be ultimately to install the anthropologist in the superordinate role (i.e. when, in the fullness of time, anthropologists had applied 'structuralist' methodology across the entire range of phenomena open to anthropological investigation). In the end, linguistics-cum-anthropology would cover all things designated 'cultural'.

Lévi-Strauss cannot resist the opportunity of chiding Saussure for failing to recognize this. The way he put it in his inaugural lecture at the Collège de France is a masterly example of ironical innuendo.

> Qu'est-ce donc que l'anthropologie sociale?
> Nul, me semble-t-il, n'a été plus près de la définir – bien que ce soit par prétérition – que Ferdinand de Saussure, quand, présentant la linguistique comme

une partie d'une science encore à naître, il réserve à celle-ci le nom de *séméiologie*, et lui attribue pour objet d'étude la vie des signes au sein de la vie sociale. [. . .]

Nous concevons donc l'anthropologie comme l'occupant de bonne foi de ce domaine de la séméiologie que la linguistique n'a pas déjà revendiqué pour sien. (Lévi-Strauss 1960: 18)

Saussure, in other words, brilliant though he was, did not realize that the rest of what he called 'semiology' was actually social anthropology. The anthropologist's programme is thus a semiological programme in the Saussurean sense (in spite of Saussure's lamentable failure to recognize this).

*   *   *

For such a programme to carry conviction, it is necessary somehow to establish the semiological character of the anthropologist's 'data'. And it is here that Lévi-Strauss reveals his Achilles' heel. Instead of producing evidence and mounting arguments, he proceeds by way of rhetoric and metaphor. All patterns of social behaviour become 'languages'. A kinship system is a 'langage' (Lévi-Strauss 1945: 58). A society's cuisine is 'comme la langue' (Lévi-Strauss 1956: 99) And this, understandably, has evoked the derision of linguists. 'Que peut signifer', asks Mounin, 'un énoncé comme celui-ci: «La cuisine française est diachronique»?' (Mounin 1968: 79). The answer is that French cuisine is seen as contrasting 'structurally' with Chinese cuisine, which is – Lévi-Strauss declares – 'synchronic' (Lévi-Strauss 1956: 100). But what in turn does that mean? Insofar as one can make any sense of the contrast, it seems to mean that French meals are served in a succession of courses, whereas in Chinese meals all the dishes are served at once. Which suggests that Lévi-Strauss's expertise in the matter was limited to eating in some very mediocre 'Chinese' restaurants.

If the contrast between 'synchronic' and 'diachronic' cuisine were intended as some kind of academic ethnic joke, it might possibly raise a smile. Unfortunately, it is clear that Lévi-Strauss advances this in all seriousness. He proposes to set up units called 'gustemes' (presumably the gastronomic equivalent of phonemes) for the analysis of food across cultures. But this is by no means the only example in his work – although perhaps it is the most ludicrous – of the anthropological misappropriation of the vocabulary of structuralism. Although he constantly appeals to the Saussurean opposition between synchronic and diachronic, he is manifestly reluctant to accept Saussure's version of that crucial distinction. He even cites Trubetzkoy and Jakobson as his authorities for rejecting it (Lévi-Strauss 1960: 26). But it is one thing to reject the Saussurean distinction (even if for dubious reasons): quite another is carrying on using the Saussurean terms all the same. If this is structuralism, it is bad structuralism by any standards.

In a similar vein, Lévi-Strauss's critics have pointed out his manifest failure to respect the structuralist implications of other terms.

Faithful to the terminology of Saussure, he tends to refer to symbolic phenomena as 'signifiers', and one might assume that the investigation is into an underlying code which pairs these signifiers with their 'signifieds'. Yet, if the reader begins looking for the signifieds, he soon realizes that the underlying code relates signifiers to other signifiers: there *are* no signifieds. Everything is meaningful, nothing is meant. (Sperber 1979: 28)

But in that case, the last thing Lévi-Strauss is being is 'faithful to the terminology of Saussure'. It has also been pointed out that insofar as Lévi-Strauss tries to apply the model of structural linguistics to the analysis of kinship systems, the attempt is manifestly abortive.

It is not a semiological analysis because there is nothing in kinship to correspond properly to the sentence in language. What holds in common between language and kinship systems is something very abstract – suggestive perhaps but not semiological. [. . .] The 'language' of kinship in the sense required by the analogy is the set of possible kinship arrangements, the 'sentence', if it can be called that, the arrangement of a particular community. This arrangement is not a proper analogue to the sentence because it is not something the construction of which requires knowledge of the language. [. . .] The only one aware of the 'language' of kinship and able to see the arrangement of a community in significant contrast with other arrangements is the man who is informed about various communities and knows about the operation of different arrangements: typically the professional anthropologist. (Pettit 1975: 70–1)

In other words, Lévi-Strauss's 'linguistic' analysis – seen from a Saussurean perspective – commits the basic mistake of confusing the investigator's perspective with that of the community; or, more exactly, projecting the former upon the latter.

Perhaps most serious of all is Lévi-Strauss's equivocation over the concept of 'system'. It goes without saying that this is intimately connected with his treating almost any pattern of social behaviour as a 'language'. In respect of such patterns of social behaviour as are manifest in gesture, dress, games, etc. the move is fairly innocuous, and perfectly compatible with Saussure's examples of semiological systems. The trouble is that in these uncontroversial examples one is dealing with conventions of which the practitioners are conscious – *and have to be*. It is hard to see how drivers could consistently obey traffic signals without understanding – and knowing *that* they understand – the system. But this does not, on the face of it, square with Lévi-Strauss's insistence on the unconscious nature of semiological structure.

To wriggle out of this difficulty, Lévi-Strauss is obliged to claim that there is more to the system than meets the eye, i.e. more than its users are aware of. For instance, he reads a great deal into traffic lights by drawing attention to the cultural associations of the colours red and green. Red evokes danger, violence and blood, whereas green evokes hope, serenity and 'le déroulement placide d'un processus naturel comme celui de la végétation' (Lévi-Strauss 1956: 108). To be sure, the driver may not be thinking of these associations when approaching the traffic lights, but – the implication seems to be – they are nevertheless part of the meaning of the signal at some unconscious level.

This, however, brings Lévi-Strauss into conflict with another Saussurean doctrine: the arbitrariness of the sign. Confronted with this problem, he makes a half-hearted attempt to have it both ways at once. Yes, the traffic signal is arbitrary (red *could* have been assigned the meaning 'go'); but it nevertheless retains an 'inherent value'. So it is both arbitrary and not arbitrary. Or, more exactly, 'je dirai que le signe linguistique est arbitraire *a priori*, mais qu'il cesse de l'être *a posteriori*' (Lévi-Strauss 1956: 105).

Lévi-Strauss's problem here is that, up to a point, he wants to invoke the doctrine of arbitrariness just as Saussure does, i.e. as part of the denial that one needs to look for a 'natural' basis in order to explain the meanings of signs or the structure of sign systems. He wants to claim, for example, that kinship systems are not 'natural' systems, and writes:

> Un système de parenté ne consiste pas dans les liens objectifs de filiation ou de consanguinité donnés entre les individus; il n'existe que dans la conscience des hommes, il est un système arbitraire de représentations, non le développement spontané d'une situation de fait. (Lévi-Strauss 1945: 61)

Here, surprisingly, we see individuals credited with conscious awareness of the system. We likewise see 'arbitrary' opposed to 'objective' and identified with 'cultural': it is the old *topos* of Nature versus Nurture, which runs throughout the whole history of anthropological thought. Saussure is an ally here, because he is a linguist who rejects the need to look for any foundation *outside* language in order to explain linguistic phenomena. But Lévi-Strauss also wants to say that the structure of kinship systems conforms to certain universal patterns; hence the attempt to leave himself room to say that they are not, at some deeper level, arbitrary after all.

In order to support his see-saw position on arbitrariness, Lévi-Strauss summons both Jakobson and Benveniste to his assistance. But none of this does his case much good, since he is conflating different applications of the term 'arbitrary'. Some of these are clearly irrelevant to the sense in which, for Saussure, the linguistic sign is arbitrary. For instance, Lévi-Strauss wants to allow for the possibility that sounds 'imperceptibly' (i.e. unconsciously) affect meanings. Here he invokes the phenomena of synesthesia and again cites in support a number of authorities, ranging from Mallarmé to Karl Marx, including Jakobson once more. According to Jakobson, vowels have 'colours' (white, yellow, blue, etc.) which correspond to articulatory positions in the mouth (Lévi-Strauss 1956: 105–6). Lévi-Strauss's implication seems to be that all this would be inexplicable if the linguistic sign were 'really' arbitrary. Furthermore, even if we consider words arbitrary at one level, says Lévi-Strauss (his example is *pomme de terre* 'potato'), we often find that further investigation reveals a rationale behind the choice. Thus, according to Lévi-Strauss, the coining of the term *pomme de terre* 'traduit les conditions techniques et économiques très particulières, qui ont marqué l'acceptation définitive de ce produit alimentaire dans notre pays' and also 'les formes verbales en usage dans les pays d'où la plante a été surtout importée', plus the use of the word *pomme* in French terms for various fruits (*pomme de pin* 'pine cone', *pomme de chêne* 'acorn', *pomme de coing* 'quince', etc.). 'Un choix où s'expriment des phénomènes historiques, géographiques, sociologiques en même temps que des tendances proprement linguistiques, peut-il être vraiment considéré comme arbitraire?' he demands rhetorically (Lévi-Strauss 1956: 104).

Saussure thus emerges, in Lévi-Strauss's interpretation, as a linguist who, although a pioneer of structuralism, failed to realize the extent to which – and the subtle mechanisms by which – the unconscious mind seeks to impose motivation on signs. Defenders of Saussure will doubtless counter that this merely shows how superficial Lévi-Strauss's reading of Saussure is: in particular, it ignores Saussure's distinction between the 'arbitraire absolu' and the 'arbitraire relatif', the chapter in the *CLG* on popular etymology, and most of what the *CLG* says about associative relations and analogy. Furthermore, although apparently rejecting Saussure's principle of arbitrariness, Lévi-Strauss not only fails in turn to clarify the distinction between arbitrary and non-arbitrary signs, but unwittingly multiplies problems for his own brand of 'structuralism'. For if everything from synesthesia to current trade conditions may *perhaps* be semiologically relevant – albeit at an unconscious level – to the choice of a sign and its 'value', it becomes quite unclear how the semiologist is ever to set about determining what the structure of any given system actually is, or indeed what determines semiological relevance at all. Thus what begins to disintegrate in Lévi-Strauss's anthropology is the crucial theoretical notion of 'structure' itself.

At times Lévi-Strauss seems uneasily aware of this. The problem already surfaces in his 1945 paper:

> Le système de parenté est un langage; ce n'est pas un langage universel, et d'autres moyens d'expression et d'action peuvent lui être préférés. Du point de vue du sociologue, cela revient à dire qu'en présence d'une culture déterminée, une question préliminaire se pose toujours: est-ce que le système est systématique? Une telle question, au premier abord absurde, ne le serait en vérité que par rapport à la langue; car la langue est le système de signification par excellence; elle ne peut pas ne pas signifier, et le tout de son existence est dans la signification. Au contraire, la question doit être examinée avec une rigueur croissante, au fur et à mesure qu'on s'éloigne de la langue pour envisager d'autres systèmes, qui prétendent aussi à la signification, mais dont la valeur de signification reste partielle, fragmentaire, ou subjective: organisation sociale, art, etc. (Lévi-Strauss 1945: 58)

Contrary to what Lévi-Strauss suggests here, it is not *only* with respect to language that the question 'Is the system systematic?' is absurd. The notion of system on which Saussurean semiology is based is a holistic notion: Saussurean theory admits no partial or incomplete systems. The system *is* the whole in terms of which constituent units and relations are defined: they have no other status. Once that theoretical keystone of wholeness is removed, the coherence of structuralism collapses. The self-stultifying question 'Is the system systematic?' is symptomatic of that collapse: it is no coincidence that it remains unanswered throughout Lévi-Strauss's *œuvre*.

Part of the problem with Lévi-Strauss's appropriation of Saussurean structuralism – but, ironically, a part which Lévi-Strauss seemingly fails to appreciate – hinges on the fact that they are speaking different 'languages'. There are two different 'idiosynchronic systems', as Saussure might have put it. Although both theorists use terms such as *langage*, *société* and *communication*, their basic assumptions with respect to language, society and communication differ widely. For Saussure, it seems fair to say, Lévi-Strauss would be a theorist who not only shirks the definition of crucial terms but constantly speaks and argues in metaphors in order to evade it. Consider, for example, the following passage from Lévi-Strauss's essay on 'Social Structure':

> A society consists of individuals and groups which communicate with one another. [. . .] In any society, communication operates on three different levels: communication of women, communication of goods and service, communication of messages. Therefore, kinship studies, economics, and linguistics approach the same kinds of problems on different strategic levels and really pertain to the same field. Theoretically at least, it might be said that kinship and marriage rules regulate a fourth type of communication, that of genes between phenotypes. Therefore, it should be kept in mind that culture does not consist exclusively of forms of communication of its own, like language, but also (and perhaps mostly) of *rules* stating how the 'games of communication' should be played both on the natural and on the cultural levels. (Lévi-Strauss 1953: 296)

The assimilation of the 'communication of women' to the 'communication of goods and services', and that in turn to the 'communication of messages', already flags a problem about distinguishing communication from mere exchange. The subsequent intrusion of genetics, together with the oblique reference to Wittgenstein in the final sentence, risks reducing the whole passage to a jumble of mixed metaphors. In order to validate these metaphors and, at the same time, justify the *therefores* in the argument, it would be necessary to imagine that Lévi-Strauss is already writing a new kind of language – using an idiosynchronic system (still called 'French', however) in which certain lexical relations between key terms have already been restructured. In that way – perhaps – one can make his argument 'make sense'. But a less charitable view would be that this is the kind of writing that would not pass muster in an undergraduate essay, for the very good reason that it betokens woolly thinking. Why it should do so any the less when written by an eminent anthropologist it is difficult to see. (There are those who praise Lévi-Strauss's metaphorical excursions for their 'poetic' qualities. One must presume they cannot tell the difference between good poetry and bad.)

Is it, then, a bold example of 'bricolage'? *Bricolage* is Lévi-Strauss's favourite figurative term for the process by which cultural odds and ends are re-used and fashioned into something different. But even this figurative use of the word is question-begging. In the non-figurative world of the home handyman, *bricolage* would presumably be recognized as a counterproductive activity and soon abandoned if it always required dismantling one serviceable apparatus in order to put together another that worked less well or not at all. But that, it seems, is exactly the outcome of Lévi-Strauss's *bricolage* of Saussure. In Lévi-Strauss's work

Saussure's ideas are never followed through, but the Saussurean term is often retained even when the original idea has been dropped. What results is neither an application nor an extension of Saussurean theory, but its reduction to a heap of terminological spare parts for the anthropological *bricoleur*.

Lévi-Strauss's position in the history of anthropology is doubtless by now as secure as Saussure's in the history of linguistics. But that is no reason for perpetuating the academic fiction that Lévi-Strauss's anthropology is 'Saussurean'. On the contrary, in spite of his constant borrowing of Saussurean terminology, Lévi-Strauss's universalist panchronic approach is in many respects at odds with the basic tenets of Saussurean doctrine.

CHAPTER EIGHT

Barthes's Saussure

Half a century after Saussure's death, Roland Barthes proposed a new academic discipline, of neo-Saussurean inspiration, which he originally called *trans-linguistique*. Whether or not this was ever more than an academic gimmick, it purported to be based on a radical rethinking of Saussure's position, and as such became extremely influential for a whole generation of French (and subsequently British and American) students. By appealing to Saussurean theory and appropriating Saussurean terminology Barthes introduced a form of cultural analysis which, as in the case of Lévi-Strauss, was in many respects quite unSaussurean although ostensibly flaunting Saussurean credentials.

Translinguistics was to be based on a reversal of the relationship which Saussure had posited between linguistics and semiology. The rationale for this reversal was explained in the preface Barthes wrote for a number of the periodical *Communications* (Barthes 1964a). Here he speaks of 'absorbing' semiology into translinguistics. The proposal was subsequently incorporated into his *Éléments de sémiologie* when the latter text was published in book form (Barthes 1964b). The term *trans-linguistique* was evidently intended to capture what Barthes originally seems to have had in mind; namely, that the areas appropriate for semiological research in the first instance were not non-linguistic areas but, on the contrary, those in which language itself was used as an instrument with which to articulate further systems of signs. The materials for such a semiology were, he suggested

> tantôt le mythe, le récit, l'article de presse, bref tous les ensembles signifiants dont la substance première est le langage articulé, tantôt les objets de notre civilisation, pour autant qu'ils sont parlés (à travers la presse, le prospectus, l'interview, la conversation et peut-être même le langage intérieur, d'ordre fantasmatique). (Barthes 1964a: 2)

The passage continues:

> Il faut en somme admettre dès maintenant la possibilité de renverser un jour la proposition de Saussure: la linguistique n'est pas une partie, même privilégiée, de la science générale des signes, c'est la sémiologie qui est une partie de la linguistique: très précisément cette partie qui prendrait en charge les *grandes unités signifiantes* du discours; de la sorte apparaîtrait l'unité des recherches qui se mènent actuellement en anthropologie, en sociologie, en psychanalyse et en stylistique autour du concept de signification. (Barthes 1964a: 2)

These latter remarks are significant on at least two counts. One is the way in which (Saussurean) linguistics is seen as being at the centre of a whole range of interdisciplinary enterprises in virtue of providing a basic theory of the sign and signification. The other is that, in spite of this emphasis on interdisciplinarity, what Barthes proposes may be read as sniping at both Lévi-Strauss ('anthropologie') and Lacan ('psychanalyse') over the contributions of their respective disciplines to the modern reorientation of the human sciences. For their claims were based on accepting the Saussurean map of inquiry, in which linguistics appeared as a province of semiology. Whereas Lévi-Strauss claimed the whole of non-linguistic semiology for anthropology, and Lacan saw linguistics as dealing with only the superficially visible part of a semiological whole which had its basis in the domain of the unconscious, Barthes takes a different view. In effect, he sees not only anthropology and psycho-analysis but sociology and stylistics too as subfields where, in practice if not in theory, the techniques and concepts of linguistics are currently being extended beyond the Saussurean domain of *langue* proper. It is in this sense that he proposes a reversal of Saussure's scheme and proclaims semiology to be a part of linguistics rather than linguistics a part of semiology.

Although Barthes is commonly given credit for this reversal as an original contribution to the development of semiology, the idea was in fact borrowed from Hjelmslev. In *Omkring sprogteoriens grundlæggelse* (1943) – probably read by Barthes in the American translation (*Prolegomena to a Theory of Language*) which appeared in 1953, or in the revised edition of 1961 – Hjelmslev had distinguished between a 'broader' and a 'narrower' conception of linguistics. The latter was, roughly, the traditional conception of the discipline as established in the universities. In the broader conception, however, linguistics was to deal not just with those natural languages historically attested but with all semiotic systems having a comparable structure. This broader linguistics is identified with 'semi-ology' (Hjelmslev 1961: 108). Hjelmslev actually went much further than

Barthes in envisaging this broader linguistics as pivotal to all human investigations, not only of human society but of the human environment in general: 'we are thus led to regard all science as centered around linguistics' (Hjelmslev 1961: 78).

Barthes eventually redefined his conception of *trans-linguistique*. In an interview (May 1966) defending the views expressed in *Éléments*, he redefined it as the study of 'impure' semiological systems, utilizing more than one 'substance', i.e. language + plus + something + else: 'On pourrait donner à l'étude des substances mêlées de langage le nom de translinguistique' (Barthes 1994: 117). This, he admitted, involved 'une certaine déviation du project sémiologique saussurien'. It also involved a certain departure from Barthes's original programme, inasmuch as translinguistics now seems to be not the superordinate discipline but a sister discipline standing in contrast to the study of 'pure' semiological systems. Later still, translinguistics undergoes a further redefinition. In 1970, Barthes identifies it as 'linguistique du discours' and claims that all translinguistic systems are based on 'la linéarité du message' (Barthes 1994: 968). Furthermore, it now seems to be the task of translinguistics to deal with the context or situation of messages, and in general with their 'extra-linguistic' referential features (Barthes 1994: 972). By this stage, it hardly needs pointing out, translinguistics has ceased to be a recognizably Saussurean enterprise at all.

Barthes's venture into translinguistics had doubtless been prepared, and perhaps even prompted, by the readiness of both Lévi-Strauss and Lacan to call the semiological systems in which they were interested 'languages'. Barthes can be seen in one sense as merely insisting that if the term *langages* is indeed to be taken seriously, then what we are dealing with in these forms of investigation is an extension of linguistics – a conclusion that Lévi-Strauss and Lacan had left themselves little room to avoid. For neither had taken it upon himself to explain what *additional* theoretical apparatus (i.e. other than that supplied by linguistics) is necessary for analysing the 'languages' in question.

Barthes speaks (in 1967) of the need to give 'un contenu technique, et non plus métaphorique' to this notion of 'languages', as in the so-called 'languages' of the cinema, of photography, of painting, etc. (Barthes 1994: 453). But he himself is one of the worst culprits when it comes to applying the term *langage* to anything and everything. Linguists were not slow to single out for ridicule statements like: 'Le colt est langage' (Mounin 1968: 81).

Barthes evidently sees the 'translinguistic' extension of linguistics into the neighbouring territories of anthropology, psychoanalysis, etc. as natural and perhaps inevitable, inasmuch as the semiological systems in which these disciplines show an interest are heavily dependent for their existence and functioning on the availability of words. In the original proposal of 1964, Barthes claims that 'tout système sémiologique se mêle de langage' and that it is difficult to conceive of 'un système d'images ou d'objets dont les signifiés puissent exister en dehors du langage' (Barthes 1964a: 2). Subsequently this claim took even more extreme forms. The study of non-linguistic signs was condemned outright: 'l'étude des signes non linguistiques est une abstraction, une utopie' (Barthes 1994: 452). Presumably a utopia for bourgeois academics. Taken this far, Barthes's conception of semiology can hardly be said to have any Saussurean backing at all.

Dismissing as marginal or trivial such obviously non-linguistic sign systems as traffic lights (a dig at latter-day Saussureans like Buyssens), Barthes apparently sees all 'serious' semiological systems as having in common an involvement with words and a capacity for generating their own forms of discourse (*discours*). Discourse, he tells us in 1974, was from his very first book (*Le degré zéro de l'écriture*, 1953) onwards 'l'objet constant de mon travail' (Barthes 1995: 37): but it was not until 1956 that he first read Saussure. So although Barthes was born in 1915, he apparently did not make his acquaintance with the *CLG* until after becoming familiar with the work of later linguists and also that of scholars in other fields who were already invoking Saussure. This is not without interest in assessing Barthes's interpretation of Saussure. It was an interpretation already shaped from the beginning by the glosses provided by such linguists as Jakobson, Benveniste and Martinet and, outside linguistics, by Lévi-Strauss and Lacan.

The first mention of Saussure in Barthes's writings is in the final essay of *Mythologies* (1957). He later described this essay as 'peut-être vieilli scientifiquement', but one which expressed his 'éblouissement' at that time. No less significant is his own account of the reasons why he found Saussure so exciting. He saw in Saussure's teaching a way of developing scientifically ('scientifiquement') the denunciation of petit-bourgeois myths ('la dénonciation des mythes petits-bourgeois'). This newly revealed approach was semiology, seen by Barthes as the 'analyse fine des processus de sens grâce auxquels la bourgeoisie convertit sa culture historique de classe en nature universelle' (Barthes 1995: 37).

In other words, Barthes saw semiology as a Marxist weapon in the ideological war against the oppressors:

la sémiologie m'est apparue alors, dans son avenir, son programme et ses tâches, comme la méthode fondamentale de la critique idéologique. (Barthes 1995: 37)

It was from his reading of Saussure, Barthes wrote in 1970, that he became convinced that

en traitant les 'représentations collectives' comme des systèmes de signes on pouvait espérer sortir de la dénonciation pieuse et rendre compte *en détail* de la mystification qui transforme la culture petite-bourgeoise en nature universelle. (Barthes 1993: 563)

Saussure, whose own social credentials were distinctly haut-bourgeois, would have been amazed and alarmed. But realizing this doubtless contributed not a little to Barthes's excitement. (Turning the intellectual products of the enemy against them is a particularly intoxicating strategy of combat.)

The final essay of *Mythologies* does indeed reflect, as Barthes puts it, 'éblouissement' (rather than clarity) concerning the scope and programme of semiology. Its relevance to mythology takes off from Barthes's introductory definition of what a myth is.

Qu'est-ce qu'un mythe, aujourd'hui? Je donnerai tout de suite une première réponse très simple, qui s'accorde parfaitement avec l'étymologie: *le mythe est une parole*. (Barthes 1993: 683)

The author feels obliged to add immediately an apologetic footnote, conceding that there are 'mille autres sens du mot *mythe*', and adding cryptically: 'Mais j'ai cherché à définir des choses, non des mots'. This is already taking a leaf from Saussure's book. The *CLG* offers exactly the same excuse in defence of Saussure's use of the terms *langue* and *parole*:

Il est à remarquer que nous avons défini des choses et non des mots [. . .]. Aucun mot ne correspond exactement à l'une des notions précisées plus haut; c'est pourquoi toute définition faite à propos d'un mot est vaine; c'est une mauvaise méthode que de partir des mots pour définir les choses. (*CLG*: 31)

Commentators have been rather slow to point out that this apparent commitment to the traditional doctrine of 'real definition' (as it is sometimes known) stands out as an anomaly in Saussure's thinking. From a theorist who takes Saussure's resolutely anti-nomenclaturist stance on lexical meaning, and proclaims unreservedly the holistic nature of linguistic systems, the last thing one would expect is this pusillanimous capitulation to surrogational semantics. Presenting (even parenthetically) such an apologia for Saussure's own metalanguage makes nonsense of the theory of *valeurs* spelt out so lucidly elsewhere in the *CLG*. Barthes's realization of this paradox seems to have played some role in his eventual disengagement from Saussurean semiology. In the early days of *Mythologies*, the paradox passed unnoticed in the general 'éblouissement'. But by 1974 Barthes is saying that

> il appartient à la sémiologie, et peut-être, de toutes les sciences humaines, aujourd'hui, à la Sémiologie seule, de mettre en cause son propre discours: science du langage, des langages, elle ne peut accepter son propre langage comme un donné, une transparence, un outil, bref un métalangage.' (Barthes 1995: 39)

Is this the *mea culpa* of one who now realized how he had misled so many shoals of students?

Barthes's definition of myth as 'une parole' is in fact taken (without acknowledgment) from Lévi-Strauss. Although the final essay in *Mythologies* makes no reference to Lévi-Strauss, it is heavily indebted to him, and in particular to Lévi-Strauss's paper on 'The structural study of myth'. Lévi-Strauss had written: 'myth *is* language: to be known, myth has to be told; it is a part of human speech' (Lévi-Strauss 1955: 209).

The cryptic statement 'to be known, myth has to be told' contains in germ the whole translinguistic agenda, which proceeds to apply that principle not just to myth but to all semiological systems. The passage in Lévi-Strauss continues: 'In order to preserve its specificity, we must be able to show that it is both the same thing as language, and also something different from it' (Lévi-Strauss 1955: 209).

This is, in effect, exactly what Barthes set out to show in the final essay of *Mythologies*. At the same time, however, he extends the domain of mythology beyond that recognized by Lévi-Strauss (who is concerned with what were traditionally recognized as myths – the Oedipus myth, the myths of the American Indians, etc.) to include the contemporary 'myths' of Western culture. He also enlarges the scope of *parole* to include both verbal and non-verbal forms of expression. In this connexion it is worth pointing out that in Saussurean terminology we find *la parole, acte de parole, circuit de la parole*, but never *une parole*. What Barthes's use of the indefinite article invites us to do is envisage Saussure's *parole* as one among many. Saussure never, in fact, proposed a technical term that would stand to any other semiological system as *parole* does to *langue*. So *une parole* is one – quite subtle – way of extending the Saussurean concept.

Barthes's programmatic declaration in *Mythologies* states:

Comme étude d'une parole, la mythologie n'est en effet qu'un fragment de cette vaste science de signes que Saussure a postulée il y a une quarantaine d'années sous le nom de *sémiologie*. La sémiologie n'est pas encore constituée. Pourtant, depuis Saussure même et parfois indépendamment de lui, toute une partie de la recherche contemporaine revient sans cesse au problème de la signification: la psychanalyse, le structuralisme, la psychologie eidétique, certaines tentatives nouvelles de critique littéraire dont Bachelard a donné l'exemple, ne veulent plus étudier le fait qu'en tant qu'il signifie. Or postuler une signification, c'est recourir à la sémiologie. (Barthes 1993: 684–5)

However, Barthes's enthusiasm for the project soon gains the upper hand over clarity. Not content with defining myth in terms of 'parole', he proclaims 'le mythe est un système de communication, c'est un message'. Can it, one wonders, be both at once? Not unless we read this as McLuhan *à la française*, which would be a far cry from reading it as an exegesis of Saussure. Pelion is then piled upon Ossa when the text continues with: 'On voit par là que le mythe ne saurait être un objet, un concept, ou une idée; c'est un mode de signification, c'est une forme' (Barthes 1993: 683).

So in no time at all Barthes's myth is 'parole', system of communication, message, mode of signification and form all rolled into one. Spiraling vertiginously out of control, Barthes's exposition soon begins to run into conceptual difficulties. Their immediate source seems to be the pronouncement in the *CLG* that 'la langue est une forme et non une substance' (*CLG*: 169). Somehow Barthes manages to transfer this to signs in general and here proclaims semiology to be a science of 'forms': 'La sémiologie est une science des formes, puisqu'elle étudie des significations indépendamment de leur contenu' (Barthes 1993: 685).

The first part of this claim is already problematic enough (since a science of 'forms' is not quite the same thing as a science of 'form'), but the reason immediately supplied in the second part verges on gobbledegook. For it is quite unclear in what sense one could make a serious study of *significations* independently of studying what is signified (however broadly or narrowly that study might be circumscribed). As if realizing that the investigation of contentless forms is a somewhat bleak and unattractive prospect (even if it were possible in theory), Barthes immediately tries to rescue himself from this difficulty of his own making by partially extricating mythology from the domain of semiology. He does so by recognizing a historical dimension in myth-making.

This idea too seems to be derived from Lévi-Strauss, who cites the example of the French Revolution. According to Lévi-Strauss a myth always refers to events alleged to have taken place long ago. But what gives the myth an operational value is that the specific pattern described is timeless; it explains the present and the past as well as the future. This can be made clear through a comparison between myth and what appears to have largely replaced it in modern societies, namely, politics. When the historian refers to the French Revolution, it is always as a sequence of past happenings, a non-reversible series of events the remote consequences of which may still be felt at present. But to the French politician, as well as to his followers, the French Revolution is both a sequence belonging to the past – as to the historian – and a timeless pattern which can be detected in the contemporary French social structure and which provides a clue for its interpretation, a lead from which to infer future developments. [. . .] It is that double structure, altogether historical and ahistorical, which explains how myth, while pertaining to the realm of *parole* and calling for an explanation as such, as well as to that of *langue* in which it is expressed, can also be an absolute entity on a third level which, though it remains linguistic by nature, is nevertheless distinct from the other two. (Lévi-Strauss 1955: 209–10)

The above passage gives a clearer exposition of the 'semiological' approach to myth than Barthes ever succeeded in giving. It explains the sense in which a myth can have a specific historical content, but at the same time – and in virtue of having that content – function as a permanent explanatory model. In Barthes's far less lucid account, we are invited to contemplate a mythology straddling, as it were, the two very different domains of semiology and ideology:

elle fait partie à la fois de la sémiologie comme science formelle et de l'idéologie comme science historique: elle étudie des idées-en-forme. (Barthes 1993: 685)

But we are left none the wiser about what kind of entity an 'idée-en-forme' is supposed to be (psychological? social? or neither? or both?), or how such an entity comes into existence, or how anyone would recognize one. To make matters worse, all this falls under the heading: 'Le mythe comme système sémiologique'. So in the course of just three jumbled pages of exposition, 'le mythe' has been identified not only as 'une parole' as well as a 'système sémiologique', but, even more astonishingly, as a 'système sémiologique' of which the content is to be studied not in semiology but in the neighbouring 'historical' discipline of ideology.

With hardly a pause for breath, Barthes proceeds to give examples intended to show, presumably, how a semiologist can apply the distinctions between *signifiant*, *signifié* and *signe* across a variety of different *paroles*. For this purpose, Saussure, Freud and Sartre are his selected theorists. Saussure's *signifié* is the concept, his *signifiant* the 'image acoustique', while his *signe* is the 'rapport du concept et de l'image'

(Barthes 1993: 686). The first two of these identifications are – as far as they go – unexceptionable, while the third is a disaster. Barthes seems not to have grasped at this point the difference between a relation and a unit in the system, and hence fails to see that for Saussure the *signe* is indeed not only a linguistic unit but *the* linguistic unit, and *not* a mere 'rapport' between its constituent parts. *A fortiori*, the fundamental Saussurean tenet that in *la langue* semiological relations take priority over – and determine – units sinks without trace in Barthes's exposition. Thus in the excitement generated by his belated discovery of semiology, and perhaps in the simultaneous attempt to reconcile Saussure with Lévi-Strauss, Barthes had not only missed the most original theoretical feature of Saussure's account of linguistic structure, but reinstated precisely the concept that Saussure was at pains to reject, i.e. the sign as a mere correlation between antecedently given items (formal and semantic).

This semiological misconception is promptly projected on to Freud. For Freud, Barthes tells us, the *signifiant* is the apparent content of the dream, the *signifié* is its hidden sense, while the *signe* is the correlation between these two, i.e. 'le rêve lui-même, dans sa totalité'. Sartre is subjected without further ado to the same brisk treatment. According to Barthes, in Sartre's theory of literature the *signifié* is some traumatic event (*crise*) in the author's experience, the *signifiant* is the literary form (*discours*) in which this is expressed, while the relation between these two defines the literary work (*œuvre*). The latter, i.e. the whole work, is presumably the *signe*.

Having enlisted Saussure, Freud and Sartre as fellow semiologists in the space of a single paragraph, Barthes returns to the subject of mythology. It still remains to explain what is special about the myth as 'parole': 'ce n'est pas n'importe quelle parole: il faut au langage des conditions particulières pour devenir mythes, on va les voir à l'instant (Barthes 1993: 683). These 'conditions particulières' turn out once again to be borrowed from Lévi-Strauss, who, in his paper on 'The structural study of myth', identifies the 'structural' mythologist's basic assumptions as follows:

> (1) If there is a meaning to be found in mythology, it cannot reside in the isolated elements which enter into the composition of a myth, but only in the way those elements are combined. (2) Although myth belongs to the same category as language, being, as a matter of fact, only part of it, language in myth exhibits specific properties. (3) These properties are only to be found *above* the ordinary linguistic level, that is, they exhibit more complex features than those which are to be found in any other kind of linguistic expression. (Lévi-Strauss 1955: 210)

Mytheme was the term Lévi-Strauss proposed for these higher-order units which he identified as the 'gross constituent units' of myth. Barthes did not adopt this term but retained the notion of 'gross constituent units' (cf. the 'grandes unités signifiantes du discours' postulated in Barthes 1964a: 2). The distinguishing feature of mythical *parole*, according to Barthes, is that it typically employs second-order signs: '*c'est un système sémiologique second*' (Barthes 1993: 687).

How does this work? The second-order system is based on treating a first-order sign (i.e. the unit comprising *signifiant*-plus-*signifié*) as being in turn merely the *signifiant* of another sign. It is the association of this latter *signifiant* with a second-order *signifié* which constitutes the sign of myth. This second-order system Barthes proposes to call (confusingly) *méta-langage*. (What part ignorance played in this proposal is far from clear: by 1957 the term *metalanguage* was already established in linguistic theory, but in a quite different sense. Barthes, who had not discovered Saussure until 1956, may not have been well enough read in linguistics to realize this. By 1959 he was certainly aware of it, since he gives the more usual account of the distinction between object language and metalanguage in a brief article entitled 'Littérature et métalangage': Barthes 1993: 1245.)

Thus 'parole mythique', according to Barthes, is always, or typically, articulated 'metalinguistically'. To compound terminological confusion yet further, Barthes proposes to call the sign of the first-order system *sens* when considered as a first-order item, but *forme* when considered as the *signifiant* of the second-order item; to use the term *concept* to designate the *signifié* of *both* the first-order *and* the second-order items; and to adopt *signification* as the term for the second-order sign as a whole. It is hardly surprising that even his most enthusiastic admirers subsequently seemed unwilling to follow Barthes the mythologist into this terminological jungle.

The first example Barthes gives of a second-order sign is sufficiently striking to impress any reader making a first acquaintance with this new brand of post-Saussurean semiology. Whereas Lévi-Strauss's second-order 'mytheme' is, quite straightforwardly, a sentence expressing some basic fact or event in the myth (e.g. that Oedipus kills his father), nothing so uncomplicated features in Barthes's account, although the example he gives is also a sentence: the Latin sentence *quia ego nominor leo*. Barthes invites us to imagine him as a fifth-form schoolboy finding this sentence in his Latin grammar. Although he understands at one level what this sentence means (i.e. 'because I am called lion'), he also realizes that this is of incidental importance compared with the fact that the sentence is there to illustrate the grammatical rule of attributive agreement in Latin. *That* is its meaning: conveying any information about being called 'lion' is quite inessential. (Many other sentences would have served the purpose.)

> la phrase ne me *signifie* nullement son sens, elle cherche fort peu à me parler du lion et de la façon dont il se nomme; sa signification véritable et dernière, c'est de s'imposer à moi comme présence d'un certain accord de l'attribut. Je conclus que je suis devant un système sémiologique particulier, aggrandi, puisqu'il est extensif à la langue. (Barthes 1993: 688)

With this unfortunate example Barthes immediately confuses several issues at one stroke. In the first place, the status of second-order signs has nothing to do – *pace* Barthes – with their syntagmatic complexity as such. A single word or suffix could equally well be cited in a grammar book as an example of a certain grammatical type. Second, it is unclear from Barthes's exposition whether we are supposed to know the second-order meaning only from what the grammar book says. In itself, the clause *quia ego nominor leo* exemplifies other features of Latin besides attributive agreement.

More generally, the problem with this example as an illustration of second-order signs is that it is quite overtly metalinguistic *not* in Barthes's peculiar sense of 'méta-langage' but in the more usual one. In other words, this is an example from a foreign language (Latin) cited in a textbook which is itself written in French. The special (second-order) status of the sentence *quia ego nominor leo* is already linguistically marked from the outset. What Barthes fails to see is that all he has succeeded in doing is giving an example of a special kind of speech act (namely, quotation). This (or any similar example) can hardly stand as a paradigm case of the second-order sign without forcing *both* semiology *and* mythology into a linguistic straitjacket far more restrictive than would presumably be welcome even to Barthes. For it reduces myth to a form of what traditional grammarians called *oratio obliqua*.

Alongside this, Barthes offers an example of a second-order non-verbal mythical sign. This is a picture on the cover of *Paris-Match* showing a black soldier, in French military uniform, saluting the national flag. This sign means, according to Barthes, that France is an imperial power, whose soldiers serve her loyally, irrespective of race, their zeal in so doing providing a refutation of detractors who decry French colonialism and its alleged repression of native peoples. Here what is open to question, clearly, is how we know whether this *is* the meaning of the image, or only Barthes's personal interpretation of it.

The disparity between this overtly political example and that of the Latin clause is striking. But perhaps intentional. Or so it might be claimed. But in that case it exposes Barthes to the charge of substituting metaphor for serious argument. For we do not read *Paris-Match* as we read a Latin grammar, and no amount of 'semiology' can elide the difference. Furthermore, any assimilation of the two does less than justice to either type of publication. It was doubtless the realization that such comparisons could easily be dismissed by critics as superficial and worthless that was to lead Barthes to attempt the more serious 'scientific' endeavour of *Éléments de sémiologie*.

Whether Barthes's Marxism ever went any deeper than the thickness of a typewriter ribbon is open to doubt. Be that as it may, it is not difficult to see how, from the overtly radical position Barthes initially adopted, both Lévi-Strauss and Lacan might be judged to have made poor use of the resources of structural semiology in exposing the hypocrisies of bourgeois discourse.

What does Barthes mean by 'discourse'? At first it seems that this is simply a non-technical synonym for Saussure's *parole*. In *Éléments*, Barthes paraphrases and quotes with approval a passage from the *CLG* as follows:

> la *Parole* est essentiellement un acte individuel de sélection et d'actualisation; elle est constituée d'abord par les 'combinaisons grâce auxquelles le sujet parlant peut utiliser le code de la langue en vue d'exprimer sa pensée personnelle' (on pourrait appeler *discours* cette parole étendue), et ensuite par les 'mécanismes psycho-physiques qui lui permettent d'extérioriser ces combinaisons' [. . .]. (Barthes 1993: 1472)

If this were all, one might suppose that for Barthes the analysis of discourse would be – or would be part of (as indeed the final essay of *Mythologies* seemed to imply) – a *linguistique de la parole*. However, in *Éléments* Barthes goes out of his way to make the point that there is no such enterprise as a *linguistique de la parole*, and even – more surprisingly still – attributes this denial to Saussure.

> On notera (fait important lorsque l'on passera aux perspectives sémiologiques) qu'il ne saurait y avoir (du moins pour Saussure) une linguistique de la Parole, puisque toute parole, dès lors qu'elle est saisie comme procès de communication, est *déjà* de la langue: il n'y a de science que de la Langue. (Barthes 1993: 1473)

This is puzzling, since one of the chapters in the *CLG* actually has as its title 'Linguistique de la langue et linguistique de la parole'. Furthermore, as Barthes must have been aware, Bally and Sechehaye in their Preface to the first edition lament the lack of material on a *linguistique de la parole*. Lectures on this topic had been promised to the students attending the Third Course, but never delivered. Furthermore, what Saussure told his listeners was not that a *linguistique de la parole* was out of the question, but (1) that it was not to be confused with *linguistique de la langue*, and (2) that it could be useful to anyone engaged in *linguistique de la langue* (*CLG3*: 92). None of this squares with Barthes's account. Nor does the reason Barthes gives ('puis que toute parole [. . .] est *déjà* de la langue') correspond to a rationale attributable to Saussure.

It is at this point – if not before – that anyone familiar with the text of the *CLG* will begin to have doubts about Barthes as an interpreter of Saussure. What Barthes here presents as Saussure's view is in fact lifted straight from Martinet's *Éléments de linguistique générale*, which had been published in Paris four years earlier.

> Cette distinction, fort utile, entre langue et parole peut entraîner à croire que la parole possède une organisation indépendante de celle de la langue, de telle sorte qu'on pourrait, par exemple, envisager l'existence d'une linguistique de la parole en face de la linguistique de la langue. Or il faut bien se convaincre que la parole ne fait que concrétiser l'organisation de la langue. (Martinet 1960: 30–1)

But Martinet had made no attempt to pass this off as Saussure's position. The interesting question is why Barthes found it convenient to do so.

Some light is thrown both on this and on Barthes's reversal of the relationship between linguistics and semiology when we turn to Barthes's first full-length semiological study, *Système de la mode* (1967). This analyses 'fashion', its discourse and its associated values, as a cultural product of bourgeois commerce. The choice of topic is itself an eloquent comment on what was lacking in the semiology of Lévi-Strauss and Lacan. Here straight away semiology is made to seem more directly relevant to familiar features of contemporary society, saturated with 'advertising'. Semiology becomes an analytic tool for exposing the verbal manipulation to which the public is subjected by means of organized professional 'publicity'. In short, *Système de la mode* is both a manifesto and an object lesson in the art of hoisting bourgeois culture with its own petard: an achievement of which any Marxist-inspired radical could be proud.

In order to underwrite this achievement, however, it seemed necessary to Barthes to establish its 'scientific' credentials. In retrospect, *Éléments* appears as providing such a basis for *Système de la mode*. What better strategy than to purloin the 'scientific' equipment of academic bourgeois culture? Since structural linguistics was widely hailed as one of the great 'modern' advances in establishing a science of human activities, what could be smarter than showing that, when rightly applied, structuralism revealed all too plainly the deceptions and equivocations of bourgeois society? For this *coup de théâtre* to work, it was necessary to show that one's analysis was founded on the very premisses that bourgeois academia respected. Barthes's astuteness lay in spotting Saussure as the respected theorist on whom this trick could be played.

Unfortunately, the text of the *CLG* did not provide *exactly* chapter and verse for Barthes's programme. So he had to produce an updated and 'improved' version of Saussurean doctrine. His two initial 'improvements' are logically related, if we consider them as steps in Barthes's radical agenda. First, the 'inversion' by which semiology becomes 'translinguistics' is designed to protect *Système de la mode* (and any future essays in the same genre) against attacks by linguists. In other words, it blocked the objection that *Système* did *not* provide anything recognizable as orthodox linguistic analysis. (Barthes was never a linguist, but he needed linguistic theory as a platform.) It wrong-footed those for whom Saussurean linguistics had become academic orthodoxy. At the same time, it presented Barthes's interpretation as being *in advance of* contemporary linguistics. (One could upstage any professor at the Sorbonne by implying, in effect, that the professor did not really understand Saussure's message.) This was a technique Barthes borrowed from Lacan (where the guru in question was not Saussure but Freud).

Denying the possibility of a *linguistique de la parole* is related to this, because it is one way of reducing all linguistics to *linguistique de la langue*. That suited Barthes because it pre-empted the criticism that *Système de la mode* was no more than a biased critique of a certain carefully selected range of texts. Lacan had already demonstrated how much academic capital could be accrued in post-war Paris by setting up as the only true interpreter of Freud. Barthes saw a similar opportunity awaiting whoever could pass muster as the one true interpreter of Saussure. This was unlikely to convince linguistic theorists, but it attracted Parisian students of the 1960s, for whom the abstruse technicalities of the discipline of linguistics were already proving rebarbative. Barthes belonged to the first generation of Parisian gurus who realized that the fast lane to media eminence sidetracked the academic establishment and appealed to its captive student audience (grossly swelled by post-war governments in the endeavour to expand university education). As a semiological insight, this is on a par with Maynard Keynes's capacity for making money out of his own market analyses. Whereas Keynes, however, was an original and powerful economic thinker, nothing comparable can be said of Barthes as a linguist.

What Barthes does in *Éléments* is offer a simplified version of Saussurean structuralism, stripped down to four basic dichotomies. These are: (1) *langue* versus *parole*, (2) *signifiant* versus *signifié*, (3) *système* versus *syntagme*, and (4) *dénotation* versus *connotation*. Of these, the fourth is not Saussure's at all but Hjelmslev's. It is clear in retrospect that this brief fourth section is included solely to accommodate the second-order signs of translinguistics. For the one second-order system that Saussure does in fact discuss at some length – namely writing – is passed over in silence (a quite remarkable omission for the author of *Le degré zéro de l'écriture*). The lacuna was soon to be spotted by Derrida, who made high drama out of it.

Leaving that on one side, however, what is immediately obvious from this project – even in embryo – is its inability/refusal to respect the most fundamental feature of Saussurean doctrine, i.e. the way in which the various distinctions logically hang together. Barthes speaks of 'extracting' these concepts from linguistics in order to apply them in the domain of semiology:

> Les *Éléments* qui sont présentés ici n'ont d'autre but que de dégager de la linguistique des concepts analytiques dont on pense *a priori* qu'ils sont suffisamment généraux pour permettre d'amorcer la recherche sémiologique. (Barthes 1993: 1469)

But this 'extraction' is precisely what risks misrepresenting the concepts themselves, just as the accompanying '*a priori*' assumption effaces the underlying logic which led to their being set up in the first place. Barthes's approach, despite his disclaimers, involves the *de-structuring* of Saussurean structuralism.

One no longer sees, for example, how the distinction between *signifiant* and *signifié* is derived from Saussure's principle of 'arbitrariness'. On the contrary, it almost seems that arbitrariness is a contingent consequence of the way the basic relationship between *signifiant* and *signifié* has been defined. Barthes, it is clear, has not much room for the principle of arbitrariness anyway, since the second-order signs of his translinguistics are far from arbitrary: they reflect and promote the repulsive ideology of the bourgeoisie. So in order to downplay the essential Saussurean connexion between the notions of arbitrariness and systematicity Benveniste and Lévi-Strauss are wheeled on (Barthes 1993: 1493) to cast doubt on whether Saussure was right about arbitrariness; while Hjelmslev is recruited to show that, even if Saussure was right, that principle cannot be applied to second-order signs in any case. Here we see the handiwork of a 'theorist' wielding intellectual scissors, who supposes that ideas about language can be cut up and pasted together again in any collage that he or his public find attractive. Distinctions like '*signifiant* versus *signifié*' are thus cut out from their original Saussurean text and reappear as exhibits in the semiologist's museum of 'basic concepts'.

This is the misconceived strategy that vitiates the whole approach to 'structuralism' in *Éléments*. By trying to patch up Saussure's distinctions with Hjelmslev's, and reconcile both with those of Jakobson and Martinet (not to mention occasional appeals *en passant* to C. S. Peirce and the Stoic philosophers of antiquity), Barthes demonstrates his own failure to realize that the 'basic concepts' he ends up expounding are, at best, lowest common denominators drawn from quite diverse linguistic enterprises, and at worst incoherent muddles.

Along with this decontextualization, inevitably, go quite different implications about systematicity and *valeur*. Having (rightly) pointed out that Saussure distinguishes between *valeur* and *signification*, Barthes claims that *signification* (which he construes as the relation holding between *signifiant* and *signifié*) is a question of 'substance', whereas *valeur* is a question of 'form'. Taking up Saussure's example of the lexical contrast in English between *mutton* and *sheep* (to which French has no parallel) Barthes draws from this the extraordinary conclusion that *mutton* and *sheep* are paradigmatically related as *signifiants*, but not as *signifiés* (Barthes 1993: 1496). In Barthes's *Système de la mode*, the embarrassing Saussurean concept of *valeurs* emanating from the structure of the system is disposed of even more peremptorily in a single paragraph. This is achieved by the *ex cathedra* declaration that in the bourgeois world of fashion journalism there are no such things:

le signe de Mode apparaît défini en dehors de toute 'valeur': car si le signifié est explicite (mondain), il ne comporte jamais une variation de valeur analogue à celle qui oppose '*mutton*' et '*sheep*' [. . .]. La 'valeur' est un facteur de complexité; la Mode ne la possède pas [. . .] (Barthes 1994: 308)

So here Barthes manages to produce for his audience the ultimate Saussurean nonsense: a semiological system without *valeurs*.

Système de la Mode is an odd example of a supposedly ground-breaking work that had already passed its sell-by date before it was offered to the general public. Barthes evinces an uneasy awareness of this in the *Avant-*

propos (Barthes 1994: 131). This might in part be attributed to the fact that previously, when *Éléments* had been launched as a book, the author had already been faced with probing questions that clearly caught him unprepared. An interviewer asked him, for example, why a sociologist like Friedan found it unnecessary to appeal to 'semiology' in order to explain how advertisers presented the products of the fashion industry to its consumers. Barthes, who seemed never to have heard of Friedan, responded with a lame reply to the effect that sociologists were concerned with the 'parole' of fashion, whereas he was concerned with its 'langue'. Another shrewd question asked whether Saussurean models of the sign had not already been invalidated by Chomsky's criticisms. Barthes's evasive answer (May 1966) shows that he had not yet caught up with current developments in semantics at MIT:

> Pour Chomsky lui-même le signifié est actuellement encore un 'résidu' et ce n'est pas mince; mais lorsque la sémantique sera structurale, ce résidu disparaîtra. (Barthes 1994: 120)

Eventually Barthes's interpretation of Chomsky's position turned out to be no less odd than his interpretation of Saussure's. Although he soon picked up the MIT jargon and started invoking 'generation', 'transformation rules' and Bostonian *topoi* such as the infinite number of sentences in a natural language, Barthes evidently thought that the purpose of the generative apparatus was to render an account of 'performance' (i.e. *parole*). In 'Introduction à l'analyse structurale des récits' (November 1966) he speaks of the art of the narrator as one of 'generating' *récits* from the linguistic structures available:

> le pouvoir d'engendrer des récits (des messages) à partir de la structure (du code); cet art correspond à la notion de *performance* chez Chomsky [. . .] (Barthes 1994: 75)

The 'new' (i.e. Chomskyan, post-Saussurean) linguistics was then offered to Barthes's acolytes in an article in *Les lettres françaises* in 1967 as a 'linguistique moins taxonomique', because it is focussed not on the classification of signs but on the 'règles de production de la parole' (Barthes 1994: 454). If Chomsky ever read this, it must have given him considerable amusement. One might, doubtless, say that Barthes's initial misreading of Saussure made his subsequent misreading of Chomsky almost inevitable. But what underlies both is the conflation between 'linear' concatenation and individual expression (i.e. the assimilation of syntagmatics to execution). This is rather like confusing the case of the mathematician who spells out *sotto voce* (in the course of making a calculation) that 'three-times-two-equals-six' with the mathematical *proposition* which identifies the product of three and two as six. (The latter has nothing intrinsically 'linear' in it at all.) Barthes evidently thinks that both Saussure and Chomsky made the mistake of confining linguistics to the sentence as its upper bound. (In this he anticipates what was subsequently called 'text linguistics'.) His error is to suppose that going beyond the sentence involves going beyond the code to the message. Hence his definition of *discours* as the 'objet' of translinguistics in 'La linguistique du discours' (1970):

> toute étendue finie de parole, unifiée du point de vue du contenu, émise et structurée à des fins de communication secondaires, culturisées par des facteurs autres que ceux de la langue. (Barthes 1994: 969)

At the same time, when taxed with objections, Barthes's first line of defence is to fall back on the claim that what interests him as a semiologist is the *langue* underlying the *parole*. But where this line is to be drawn never emerges very clearly. He even speaks in 'Entretien sur le structuralisme' (1966) of 'intermediary' areas between the two:

> Il s'agira de décrire et d'analyser ces mondes intermédiaires de la connotation, ces syntagmes figés comme les appelait Saussure, ces sous-codes, ces idiolectes qui finissent par former eux-mêmes une langue. (Barthes 1994: 118)

As if not content with defending semiology by appeal to the quite unSaussurean notions of 'connotation' and 'idiolect' (neither of which has anything to do with the 'fixed' syntagmas that Saussure does recognize), Barthes goes on to admit, as if making a great concession to the claims of sociology:

> Il est exact qu'à mesure que l'on s'approche de la parole, le monde avec ses lois économiques et autres, pénètre dans le langage. (Barthes 1994: 118)

And then, as if history had long ago settled the matter in his favour:

> Le problème qui se présente à nous était déjà celui d'Aristote dans la *Rhétorique*: comment coder les grandes unités de parole? (Barthes 1994: 118)

So now you see it: now you don't. Here we have *parole*: there we have *langue*. If you press me on one, I will hide behind the other. Or, if forced to become a semiological refugee, I will retreat to the no-man's-land in between; or even, as a last resort, to the *ars rhetorica* tradition. This makes a dog's dinner of semiology: what thinkers with the acumen of Aristotle or Saussure would have thought of their names being taken in vain to recommend such a programme hardly bears contemplation.

It must have been a disappointment for Barthes eventually to realize that, far from sharing his enthusiasm for semiology, critics to his left in the political spectrum regarded both his 'translinguistics' and semiological analysis in general as bourgeois obfuscation. Barthes's response to these critics is feeble: all he can say by 1974 (in 'L'aventure sémiologique') is that any objective analysis of the ideological content of semiology must itself employ semiological methods (Barthes 1995: 37). The question is whether his own highly eclectic semiological methods were ever well-founded in the first place.

CHAPTER NINE

Chomsky's Saussure

There seems to be no indication that Noam Chomsky, founder of modern generative linguistics, had ever read or paid any attention to the work of Saussure until the appearance, in 1959, of the first English translation of the *CLG* (Baskin 1959). Since Bloomfield's review of 1923, the only serious discussion of Saussure's work to be published in America had been an isolated article by Rulon Wells in the journal *Word* (Wells 1947). Although Jakobson had lectured on Saussure in New York during the war, his lectures did not appear in print until much later. Even in the late 1950s, the authors of American linguistics textbooks maintained a discreet silence concerning Saussure's contribution to their discipline. In Gleason's *An Introduction to Descriptive Linguistics* (Gleason 1955) the only European theorists mentioned are Hjelmslev, Firth, Trubetzkoy and Daniel Jones. In Hockett's *A Course in Modern Linguistics* (1958) the *CLG* does not even appear in the Bibliography (although publications by European linguists such as Jakobson, Jespersen, Martinet and Meillet do). In Hill's *Introduction to Linguistic Structures* (Hill 1958) Saussure is not mentioned once (whereas references to the work of Bloomfield, Sapir, Jespersen, Bloch, Joos and others abound).

In Chomsky's first major publication, *Syntactic Structures* (Chomsky 1957), apart from immigrants such as Jakobson and Halle, who were already installed in academic posts in the United States, the only European linguists mentioned are Jespersen and Hjelmslev. According to Joseph's detailed analysis of Chomsky's references to Saussure (Joseph 1990: 63–75), Saussure is mentioned for the first time in Chomsky's paper on 'Formal properties of grammars' (Chomsky 1963). This had earlier been noted by De Mauro, who spoke of 'une véritable profession de foi saussurienne' (De Mauro: 400). Here we see the beginnings of the modern academic fable of 'Chomsky the Saussurean', to which Joseph adds his own more subtly critical contribution.

If 'profession de foi saussurienne' is something of an overstatement, nevertheless Chomsky's early allusions to Saussure give at least the impression of a cautious welcome in from the cold. The reason for the welcome is hardly in doubt. Having recently published a swingeing attack on behaviourism in linguistics (Chomsky 1959), Chomsky was looking retrospectively for pre-Bloomfieldian champions of 'mentalism' who could be posthumously resurrected as avatars heralding his own approach to linguistic theory. The welcome was only a cautious one, however, because the *CLG* did not *prima facie* look at all like a generativist treatise in embryo.

As Joseph observes, Chomsky straight away expressed certain reservations. The most important concerned Saussure's failure to present *langue* as a system of generative rules. Chomsky, however, failed to mention Saussure's conception of *langue* as a *social* phenomenon (Joseph 1990: 66). But neither De Mauro nor Joseph comments on the interesting fact that right from the start, even when describing *langue* in the individual, Chomsky either misunderstood or misrepresented the Saussurean distinction between *langue* and *parole*. The former, according to Chomsky, was 'the grammatical and semantic system represented in the brain of the speaker', whereas the latter was 'the actual acoustic output from his vocal organs and input to his ears' (Chomsky 1963: 327). The terminology of this description suggests that for Saussure 'grammar' and 'semantics' were somehow independent, or at least separable, components of the synchronic 'system' (as indeed they were for Chomsky, who had argued strongly in his early work for the autonomy of grammar), whereas on the contrary the *CLG* presents a quite different notion of grammar (*CLG*: 185 ff.) in which it is far from autonomous and there is no opposition between the 'grammatical' and the 'semantic'. Furthermore, there is no mention in Chomsky's account of the 'image acoustique' or where it stands in relation to the dichotomy between *langue* and *parole*. Finally, if we interpret Chomsky's account by reference to the analysis of the *circuit de la parole* (*CLG*: 27–8), it would seem that Chomsky thought *parole* was limited to the 'external' or physical sections of the circuit.

These gaps and discrepancies do not seem unconnected: they reveal that, far from seeing himself as a Saussurean, from the outset Chomsky was more concerned to see Saussure as a possible Chomskyan.

The other pre-Bloomfieldian linguist mentioned with approval at about the same time is Humboldt, on whom Chomsky dwells at some length. Chomksy even goes so far as to say that his own approach is 'basically Humboldtian' (Chomsky 1964: 61). Later commentators, with the wisdom of hindsight, sometimes maintained that affinities with the work of Saussure and Humboldt were already apparent in *Syntactic*

Structures. One of them even claimed that he had recognized this before Chomsky himself:

> by virtue of my own background, I immediately related Chomsky's notion of generative grammar to the ideas of Saussure and Von Humboldt, whereas it was only much later that Chomsky himself became aware of the connection. (Lyons 1977: 171)

Here is the fable of 'Chomsky the Saussurean' already in full flow and dispensing even with the concurrence of the principal actor himself: Chomsky was from the start a Saussurean, whether he realized it or not. The Saussurean element in Chomsky's thinking was allegedly to be found in Chomsky's insistence that 'the theory of grammar should reflect the ability that all fluent speakers of a language possess to produce and understand sentences which they have never heard before' (Lyons 1977: 36–7). Saussure, apparently, 'had also insisted upon the importance of this property of creativity' (Lyons 1977: 37).

What this facile assimilation overlooks is that in Saussure's case it was in *parole*, i.e. in the activity of the individual, that linguistic creativity was manifest, not in 'grammar' (i.e. *langue*). In the *CLG* there is no question of 'formalizing' creativity as a communal system of rules. (From a Saussurean perspective, that might even be seen as a kind of contradiction.) For anyone interested in the history of ideas, it is fascinating to see here how a radical difference can in retrospect be presented as a continuity. It is all the more fascinating in view of the evidence that Chomsky himself realized that, whatever else Saussure might have been, he was not *stricto sensu* a generativist. Chomsky makes it quite clear (in Chomsky 1964) that he (Chomsky) does not approve what he interprets as Saussure's conception of *la langue* as 'a store of signs' (Chomsky 1964: 59). At the same time Chomsky explains *why* he cannot accept this: because that conception 'makes it impossible to come to grips with the recursive processes underlying sentence formation' (Chomsky 1964: 59). For Chomsky, these 'recursive processes' – never mentioned once in the *CLG* – are the soul or mainspring of grammar.

It seems a mistake for Saussure's defenders to argue, as some of them seem inclined to (De Mauro: 401), that 'rule-governed creativity' in the Chomskyan sense is already recognized, at least implicity, in the *CLG*. That only compounds the confusion: the confusion being caused by Chomsky's question-begging application of the notion 'creativity' to the operation of an algorithm. Anyone who supposes that Saussure would have endorsed that cannot have realized the full implications of Saussure's favourite comparison between language and chess. It is not in following the rules of chess that the players display any creativity: it is in using the rules to contrive situations on the board that open up opportunities for them and cause problems for their opponents – a quite different matter, and one of chess *parole*, not of chess *langue*.

So why, given Saussure's apparent insensitivity to the importance of generative rules, did Chomsky want Saussure on board his generativist ship at all? The answer is that one of the theoretical mainstays of the whole generativist programme for the next twenty years was to be the distinction (not yet mentioned in Chomsky 1957) between linguistic 'competence' and linguistic 'performance'. Linguistic theory, allegedly, was primarily concerned with the former, not the latter; and 'competence' could be conveniently identified with Saussure's *langue*, just as 'performance' could loosely be identified with Saussure's *parole*.

To sum up thus far, there were originally not just one but two reasons why Chomsky wanted Saussure on his side. 1. Saussure was a prominent 'mentalist', who had never fallen into the trap of behaviourism, as Bloomfield and his generation had done. 2. Saussure had insisted on a distinction (*langue* versus *parole*) that could be used to lend theoretical credibility to a generativist programme that proposed to concentrate on abstract systems of 'rules' and pay little heed to their implementation in actual speech situations. What commentators have failed to point out is that these two reasons, far from complementing each other, created a certain tension which is reflected in Chomsky's ambivalence towards Saussure. Saussure's apparent indifference to recursivity showed that being a 'mentalist' did not automatically make one a generativist, while at the same time Saussure's view of *parole* raised the whole question of how much could safely be assigned to the rule-system alone and how much to the individual. Thus Saussure's patronage brought along with it certain problems for Chomsky.

The attempt to solve them gives rise to Chomsky's outlandish doctrine of linguistic 'creativity'. Unwilling to espouse the allegedly Saussurean concept of *langue* as an inert inventory of items, and equally unwilling to relegate generative processes to *parole*, Chomsky resorted to distinguishing between two types of creativity, one being 'rule-governed' and the other 'rule-changing'. The former kind of creativity supposedly 'leaves the language entirely unchanged', while the latter 'actually changes the set of grammatical rules (e.g., analogic change)' (Chomsky 1964: 59). But if we look carefully at how Chomsky describes the former type of creativity, we see that he commits what Saussure would have regarded as a cardinal mistake: the conflation of *faits de langue* with *faits de parole*. Chomsky tells us that rule-governed creativity is the kind of creativity involved 'in the production – and understanding – of new sentences, an activity in which the adult is constantly engaged' (Chomsky 1964: 59). Presumably by 'new' Chomsky means sentences not previously encountered by the individual in question.

There are several difficulties with this account. In the first place, it would seem that the production and understanding of 'old' sentences do not qualify for Chomsky as manifestations of creativity: so normal speech would seem to comprise both 'creative' and 'uncreative' procedures, the latter including by definition repeating oneself and repeating what others have said, not to mention using such familiar forms of expression as *What time is it?*, *Please shut the door*, *Sit down*, *Who is that?*, *Today is Monday*, *What did she say?* and countless more. Thus it seems that according to Chomsky one can accomplish a great deal in linguistic communication without being creative at all. The more one says and hears, the more sentences presumably have to be struck off the 'new' list and relegated to the uncreative roster. How unconvincing this concept of creativity is becomes evident if one imagines applying it to other human activities where rules are followed. The chess of a grand master evidently becomes less and less creative as his career advances, because most of the moves he will make are ones he has already made or seen at some time in the past. Only if moving a queen (legitimately) from one particular square to another happens to be a move never encountered in his entire chess experience will that move be creative (in the 'rule-governed' sense). From this it is obvious that Chomsky is here conflating the notions 'creative' and 'previously unattempted'.

In the second place, a further difficulty follows from this. There is no possibility of distinguishing the 'rule-governed' from the 'rule-changing' on this basis. For whatever is 'new' in the individual's linguistic experience at any given time will include both. That is to say, in terms of innovation *there is no difference* between an original coinage and a first-time application of the 'rules'. This is very evident in children's speech. Has the child who says *sheeps* (where an adult might be expected to say *sheep*) gone creatively beyond any previous learning, or merely applied mechanically a previous pattern of familiar forms? Such questions have no answers. To realize this is not just to pinpoint a marginal problem for psychologists studying the early phases of language acquisition. It throws open the whole question of what one means by 'creativity' in respect of language *and of sign systems in general*.

Third, even if we set the above doubts on one side, it is difficult to see that this 'creative' linguistic activity which, Chomsky tells us, adults 'constantly' engage in can be anything other than *parole*. This brings us to the paradox at the centre of Chomsky's theoretical recruitment of Saussure. In spite of his disclaimers, Chomsky is actually endorsing Saussure's view of the creativity of *parole*; but apparently failing to realize what he is doing. The term *rule-governed creativity* is nothing but the lexical expression of a theoretical muddle.

Is there any way to extricate Chomsky from his own dilemma? Let us grant that it was always a nonsense to speak of rule-following *per se* as 'creative': nevertheless, selecting *which* rule to follow might arguably be held to involve an element of judgment that deserved to be called 'creative'. Would this be enough to rescue Chomsky's 'fundamental distinction' (Chomsky 1964: 59)? Only at the cost of demanding of Chomskyan grammar a whole new component, i.e. one which did not merely set out the 'rules' in general but specified how the appropriate 'rule' is selected in any given case. And that would require something that Chomsky is just as anxious to avoid as Saussure was: namely, relating linguistic proficiency to actual contexts of communication. To revert to the chess analogy, it would certainly be possible to devise a set of useful 'rules' for players to follow when confronted with certain situations on the chessboard. But these would be rules of strategy, not rules of chess (in the sense in which moving the king one square at a time is a rule of chess). Chomsky shows no interest in strategic rules of this kind where language is concerned; and even if he did it would be open to a Saussurean to claim that such rules belonged to a *linguistique de la parole*, not to a *linguistique de la langue*.

* * *

Competence and *performance* were certainly not Bloomfieldian terms. Nor do they appear anywhere in Hamp's *Glossary of American Technical Linguistic Usage 1925–1950* (Hamp 1957). Ambrose-Grillet's *Glossary of Transformational Grammar* (Ambrose-Grillet 1978) quotes from Chomsky 1965 for the definition of both terms. But in Chomsky 1964 we find a reasonably explicit statement:

> On the basis of a limited experience with the data of speech, each normal human being has developed for himself a thorough competence in his native language. This competence can be represented, to an as yet undetermined extent, as a system of rules that we can call the *grammar* of his language. (Chomsky 1964: 51)

Again, to anyone familiar with the *CLG* it is immediately obvious that 'competence' is not *langue* in the Saussurean sense but, rather, the individual's personal mastery of a language (which, for Saussure, is always incomplete). It is interesting to note that the expression *mastery of a language* is used previously by Chomsky in this very same passage. There he claims:

> Normal mastery of a language involves not only the ability to understand immediately an indefinite number of entirely new sentences, but also the ability to identify deviant sentences and, on occasion, to impose an interpretation on them. (Chomsky 1964: 50)

Nowhere in the *CLG* will the reader find any such characterization of what the 'sujet parlant' needs in order to engage in the *circuit de la parole*. But a more important point to note about the Chomskyan account of 'normal mastery' is this: there is nothing 'creative' about it other than the ability to 'impose an interpretation' on deviant sentences. In other words, it seems that this 'imposition' is not merely a matter of *recognizing* the meaning (perhaps because deviant sentences do not, strictly speaking, have a meaning?) but of making the best of a bad job – a task at which some individuals, having wider experience or greater powers of imagination, might 'on occasion' be better than others. So, given a 'deviant' sentence, you and I (otherwise regarded by our contemporaries as equally well-qualified native speakers of English) might nevertheless fail to come up with the same list of possible interpretations. Furthermore, it is difficult to see that this varied ability to 'impose an interpretation' on any random deviant sentence is likely to be unconnected to our corresponding abilities to think up and produce 'deviant' sentences, as and when we consider appropriate. To spell the point out once again, Chomsky's (1964) account of 'normal mastery' of a language, far from coinciding with Saussure's definition of *langue*, actually combines or conflates *langue* with *parole*.

This seems to be confirmed by Chomsky's discussion of 'degrees of grammaticalness', published three years earlier (Chomsky 1961), where he insists on the psychological difference between what goes on when we interpret a 'grammatical' utterance and what goes on when we are confronted with one which is not.

> Given a grammatically deviant utterance, we attempt to impose an interpretation on it, exploiting whatever features of grammatical structure it preserves and whatever analogies we can construct with perfectly well-formed utterances. We do not, in this way, impose an interpretation on a perfectly grammatical utterance

(it is precisely for this reason that a well-chosen deviant utterance may be richer and more effective). (Chomsky 1961: 384–5)

One of Chomsky's examples of effective deviance is Dylan Thomas's 'a grief ago'. The paper goes on to argue that such phenomena call for linguists to take seriously the following question: 'by what mechanism can a grammar assign to an arbitrary phone sequence a structural description that indicates its degree of grammaticalness, the degree of its deviation from grammatical regularities, and the manner of its deviation' (Chomsky 1961: 386). So what is being proposed programmatically is that a grammar has to deal not only with the 'correct' sentences of a language but also with (at least some of) the 'mistakes' (either random or deliberate) that speakers might conceivably perpetrate.

Now mistakes of either kind, not to mention attempts to make sense of them by constructing analogical interpretations, are patently *faits de parole* in Saussurean terms. Nor did traditional grammar books treat it as part of their brief to explain just how bad or how trivial certain grammatical errors would be; or, on the other hand, how richly suggestive a poet's creative tampering with conventional forms of expression might on occasion be, and why.

To go very far down this slippery path seems inevitably destined to blur any distinction between a speaker's 'mastery' of the language and what can or could be done on the basis of that 'mastery'. One might sooner or later end up suggesting that it is the function of a grammar to explain puns, verbal jokes and wordplay of all kinds. Chomsky seems dimly to have glimpsed the danger of the bottomless pit. His technical 'solution' to the 'problem' of degrees of grammaticalness was to incorporate into the grammar a 'hierarchy of categories'. (How this was supposed to work is irrelevant for purposes of the present discussion.) But in a shy footnote he raises the question : 'What is the natural point where continued refinement of the category hierarchy should come to an end?' His unenlightening answer is: 'This is not obvious' (Chomsky 1961: 387). No, indeed; for there is no such 'natural point'. A grammar can do as much or as little as the grammarian decides it shall do. Grammars of *parole* are perfectly feasible.

Here we see Chomsky grappling uneasily with a problem that the generativist notion of 'grammar' made it difficult for him to come to terms with, or even see clearly at all. Did Dylan Thomas have a different grammar, which allowed him to generate the expression *a grief ago*? It is no insuperable task to write a retrospective 'grammar' (in the Chomskyan sense) of the poetic usage of Dylan Thomas, Shakespeare or any other writer. For a grammar thus conceived is a set of algorithms. But that leads directly to the conundrum that every speaker, it appears, has or may have his or her own grammar. In other words, the narrowly algorithmic conception of grammar is difficult to reconcile with the notion that a language is *not* a possession of individuals but of a community (as Saussure had pointed out). Putting a variety of different algorithmic systems together does not magically create a single algorithmic system for the collectivity.

Thus there seems to be fairly incontrovertible evidence that up to 1964, at least, Chomsky was still groping (unsuccessfully) for a way of disengaging the specialized domain of grammatical analysis from the vast and heteroclite study of language and languages in general. In this sense he was, indeed, re-enacting in part a scenario that had been both scripted and played out by Saussure two generations previously. But, as De Mauro points out, he seems to have failed to realize that Saussure's theoretical enterprise was aimed at getting back to basics; whereas Chomsky tamely accepted most of the intellectual baggage of the Western grammatical tradition (concepts such as 'noun', 'verb', 'subject', 'predicate', etc.) and dressed it up in his own terminology. Had Chomsky studied Saussure's work more carefully, or perhaps earlier in his career, he might have avoided the inevitable recycling of ancient material. Unfortunately, by the time Saussure appeared on Chomsky's intellectual horizon Chomsky was already committed to certain epistemological allegiances and to certain quasi-mathematical modes of formalism. So the best he could eventually make of the Saussurean dichotomy between *langue* and *parole* was to recast it as the distinction between a system of rules, on the one hand, and, on the other, actions in (occasionally imperfect) conformity with those rules.

That must have seemed, at first sight, to map neatly on to a general distinction American psychologists were drawing at the time between one's 'competence' *at* doing something and one's actual 'performance' *in* doing it. G. A. Miller, for example, one of Chomsky's early collaborators, discusses a universal human ability he calls 'planning'. Some people, he assumes, will be more 'competent' at this than others. Success will depend in part on the amount of detail in the plan. However, there is no direct correlation because:

> There is little need to plan in detail an activity you know you are competent to perform, that you have successfully performed many times before [. . .]. One goes just far enough in elaborating a plan to reassure oneself that one is competent to perform each subpart. (Miller 1962: 301)

Miller refers here to a recently published paper by the clinical psychologist R. W. White, entitled 'Motivation reconsidered: the concept of competence' (White 1959).

On reading Chomsky's famous review of Skinner (Chomsky 1959) one is struck by the fact that if Chomsky had been acquainted at that time with the work of Saussure he could have summed up the whole thrust of his critique (as doubtless any European linguist at the time would have done) by saying that Skinner's basic mistake was to suppose that language could be treated as *parole* without any reference to *langue*.

In this paper Chomsky does occasionally use the terms *perform* and *performance* (both of humans and of animals: 'chimpanzees were taught to perform complex tasks . . .', 'monkeys can learn object discriminations and maintain their performance at a high level of efficiency . . .', 'no known neural structure capable of performing this task . . .', 'the performance of the speaker, hearer, and learner . . .') but no systematic distinction is drawn between *performance* and *competence*. The latter term does not in fact occur.

When Chomsky belatedly realized that generative linguistics needed some basic theoretical distinction of the same kind that Saussure had drawn, he lost no time in equating competence with *langue* and performance with *parole*:

> The generative grammar internalized by someone who has acquired a language defines what in Saussurian terms we may call *langue* (with a qualification to be specified below [. . .]). In performing as a speaker or hearer, he puts this device to use. Thus as a hearer, his problem is to determine the structural description assigned by his grammar to a presented utterance (or, where the sentence is syntactically ambiguous, to determine the correct structural description for this particular token) and using the information in the structural description, to understand the utterance. (Chomsky 1964: 52)

The qualification referred to here relates, as mentioned above, to conceptualizing a language as a system of generative rules. Chomsky goes on to congratulate Saussure not only on distinguishing *langue* from *parole* so clearly but on having got his priorities right into the bargain.

> Clearly the description of intrinsic competence provided by the grammar is not to be confused with an account of actual performance, as de Saussure emphasized with such lucidity [. . .]. Nor is it to be confused with an account of potential performance. The actual use of language obviously involves a complex interplay of many factors of the most disparate sort, of which the grammatical processes constitute only one. It seems natural to suppose that the study of actual linguistic

performance can be seriously pursued only to the extent that we have a good understanding of the generative grammars that are acquired by the learner and put to use by the speaker or hearer. The classical Saussurian assumption of the logical priority of the study of *langue* (and the generative grammars that describe it) seems quite inescapable. (Chomsky 1964: 52)

This whole paragraph must rank as one of the most confused pieces of linguistic theorizing to appear in print since Horne Tooke. It conflates (1) knowledge of a language, with (2) practical command of a language and (3) description of a language. The term *mastery*, and indeed *competence* itself, would suggest that Chomsky was at first aiming to discuss (2), but came to confuse (2) with certain forms of propositional knowledge, i.e. (1). But this is not 'competence' in the sense in which psychologists like Miller were originally using the term: there 'competence' is an evaluative word. People who are competent at planning are good at it, regardless of how inept their performance (i.e. execution) may be. Furthermore, there is no general norm or level of excellence for planners: competence varies from individual to individual. Incompetence is relative. It is difficult to resist the conclusion that Chomsky's appeal at this point to Saussure's *langue* was an attempt to lend theoretical credibility to a notion that he was having difficulty in defining satisfactorily.

This attempt was in any case wrecked by Chomsky's insistence on bringing in (3). Whatever a fluent speaker of English may have 'internalized' (to use Chomsky's own expression) it is certainly not the contents of a treatise by Lowth, Cobbett, Nesfield, C. C. Fries or any other English grammarian (unless indeed the speaker in question had been foolish enough to memorize some such description, or parts of it, by rote). And even if some grammatical description (however obtained) had been 'internalized', that would not *eo ipso* guarantee any practical command of the language. (A computer disc could hold such a description and nevertheless be unable to engage in discourse, whether in English or any other language.) According to Chomsky, as cited above, a hearer has to 'determine the correct structural description' for any utterance heard. But what is the connexion between the description and understanding what was said? 'Understanding' seems to be for Chomsky the result of some further operation; but here again we are left lost in a maze of inadequately defined notions.

That is only the beginning of the labyrinth into which we are ushered by Chomsky's 'Current issues in linguistic theory'. What use it would be for a hearer to have determined the 'correct structural description' – for, say, the English speaker's utterance 'Good morning!' or 'Warm again, isn't it?' – is not vouchsafed. Nor in what language this 'correct structural description' is couched. For the language-learner, with whose problems Chomsky seems to be particularly concerned, this latter question would presumably be of particular importance. Or is there assumed to be a universal 'language of thought' that does not need to be learnt, and in which a 'correct structural description' of English can be formulated? If so, Chomskyan linguistic theory seems wedded from the outset to a metaphysics that Saussure would have regarded not merely as dubious but as incoherent. Whichever side one takes in such arcane debates, the relevant point here is how incongruous it would be – and always was – to think of enrolling Saussure as an ally in propounding the generativist case.

The incongruity has several historical – and rhetorical – layers. Although Chomsky begins by equating Saussure's *langue* with 'the generative grammar internalized by someone who has acquired a language', only a couple of pages later he is complaining that Saussure failed entirely to conceptualize *langue* as a generative system (Chomsky 1964: 59–60). So now you see it, now you don't. It is rather like hailing Jesus Christ as a Marxist, and then adding in a whisper that, of course, unfortunately Jesus Christ understood nothing about economics. But we are left to infer that if he *had* done, then he would have endorsed Marx. (Who else?) Likewise, Chomsky in 1964 is keen to hail Saussure as a precursor, while at the same time conceding that Saussure knew nothing about the mathematics of recursion. Four years later, Chomsky can afford to dismiss Saussure as having an 'impoverished and thoroughly inadequate conception of language' (Chomsky 1968: 18), i.e. impoverished and inadequate as compared to Chomsky's own.

The Saussurean sign in any case pairs an acoustic image with a concept, *not* a description of an acoustic image with a description of a concept. Chomsky's picture of the hearer seeking to 'determine the correct structural description' for a sequence of sounds bears no relation to the *CLG* account of the Saussurean *circuit de la parole*. There the acoustic image in the hearer's brain simply triggers the corresponding concept (*CLG*: 28): there is no search for a 'correct structural description'. It may be that Chomsky thought that this part of the circuit had been omitted from the *CLG* account in the interests of simplicity, but that its presence was implied by other comments in the *CLG*. If so, it is difficult to see which those comments might have been, and Chomsky himself never identifies them. Furthermore, although the speech circuit account is conceded in the *CLG* to be only an incomplete analysis, it is also said to include all the essential elements. In other words, it is adequate for purposes of distinguishing *langue* from *parole*: for this ('trouver dans l'ensemble du langage la sphère qui correspond à la langue') is presented as its main purpose (*CLG*: 27). If we take this seriously, we have little option but to conclude that the portions of the circuit enclosed in circles in the diagram presented (*CLG*: 28) – and only those – represent operations involving *la langue*. The rest falls into the domain of *parole*.

What Chomsky says about the hearer, however, implies something not identified in the Saussurean speech circuit; namely, a search process. The question that inevitably arises is: does this search belong to competence or performance? The answer might seem to be that it must belong to performance, since Chomsky speaks not only of a 'problem' for the hearer to tackle but of then 'using the information' obtained by its solution in order to 'understand the utterance'. Nowhere does the Chomskyan account suggest that this is all taken care of automatically without any effort on the hearer's part. Understanding the utterance would seem to involve deciding, on the basis of the evidence available, such questions as which of two available structural descriptions of an ambiguous sentence was correct 'for this particular token'. Now a 'particular token', like a 'presented utterance', can hardly be other than a performance item; and presumably resolving the ambiguity might well require other performance-related information, such as the identity of the speaker, the circumstances obtaining at the time, etc.

As against this, we also have Chomsky's explicit statement that the 'internalized' grammar assigns assessments of deviation to at least some ill-formed sentences. So at least part of the hearer's task seems to be already taken care of and requires no individual initiative. To that extent, we are dealing with competence, not performance. None of this maps on to the *CLG* diagram of the speech circuit at all. In short, the attempt to equate Chomskyan *competence* with Saussurean *langue* was misguided from the start. Chomsky's Saussure never offered what Chomsky was looking for.

* * *

Chomsky's proclaimed appreciation of the 'lucidity' of Saussure's distinction also calls for comment. For, as Saussure's critics had always pointed out, the distinction as formulated in the *CLG* is far from lucid. According to some, it was downright puzzling, since it appealed to conflicting criteria. The puzzle is perhaps best summarized by Culler, who presents it in the following terms:

Saussure himself invokes various criteria in making the distinction: in separating *langue* from *parole* one separates the essential from the contingent, the social from the purely individual, and the psychological from the material. But these criteria do not divide language in the same way and they thus leave much room for dispute. By the first *la langue* is a wholly abstract and formal system; everything relating to sound is relegated to *parole* since English would still be essentially the same language if its units were expressed in some other way. But clearly, by the second criterion we should have to revise this view: the fact that /b/ is a voiced bilabial stop and /p/ a voiceless bilabial stop is a fact about the linguistic system in that the individual cannot choose to realize the phonemes differently if he is to continue speaking English. And by the third criterion one would have to admit other acoustic features to *la langue*, since differences between accents and pronunciations have a psychological reality for speakers of a language. (Culler 1986: 81)

Chomsky appears to have grasped very little – if anything – of all this when he decided to explain his own inchoate distinction by reference to Saussure's. But the theoretical picture is even worse than Culler paints it: all the doubts about where to draw the line on the phonetic side are matched by corresponding doubts on the semantic side. For example, is it part of one's linguistic competence to recognize the name *George Washington* as that of a former president of the United States? Or is that recognition merely relevant to *parole*? Or perhaps not to *any* enterprise which it falls to the linguist to explain or investigate? Or, then again, is it 'linguistic' knowledge which would enable one to identify not the bearer of the name *George Washington* but just, say, the likelihood that the bearer will be a male person (or a ship, or a dog, or a racehorse) but not perhaps a patent medicine or a brand of petrol?

The best-case scenario that could be made out for Chomsky here would be that he realized he had no answers to such questions and recognized that Saussure had no answers either, and *therefore* invoked Saussure's *langue* as a convenient and respectable façade behind which to conceal the linguistic problems in question. However, it is open to question whether Chomsky had even understood this much about Saussure's distinction.

Part of the reason for doubting it is that Chomsky had evidently not read the *CLG* (or Baskin's translation) carefully enough to see that Saussurean linguistics leaves ample room for allocating to *la langue* the whole range of syntagmatic 'types' that generative rules à la Chomsky would be invoked to explain. The *CLG* is quite explicit on this point:

il faut attribuer à la langue, non à la parole, tous les types de syntagmes construits sur des formes régulières. (*CLG*: 173)

It is open to argument, doubtless, whether a given combination is to be regarded as constructed 'sur des formes régulières'. But that does not affect the general point. It is clear – contrary to Chomsky's claim – that, given some interpretation of 'forme régulière', this general point will cover all kinds of 'recursive' combinations:

> il s'agit toujours d'unités plus vastes, composées elles-mêmes d'unités plus restreintes, les unes et les autres étant dans un rapport de solidarité réciproque. (*CLG*: 177)

There is no envisageable limit to this process of composition. So Chomsky's much-lauded 'insight' concerning the non-finite nature of syntax turns out to coincide – unsurprisingly – with his poor eyesight in reading Saussure.

Various commentators have noted the connexions between Chomsky's view of language and his political commitments (see, for example, Sampson 1979). In 1973, in an article entitled 'Saussure, le signe et la démocratie', Barthes pointed out the contrast between Saussure's reliance on analogy as a force shaping *la langue* and Chomsky's insistence on the 'creativity' of the speaker's internalized grammar. Barthes saw an ideological dimension in this difference, relating Chomsky's position to his rejection of state authority and Saussure's to the latter's acceptance of Tarde's sociology and his (traditional Swiss) belief in democracy (Barthes 1994: 1584–7). Whatever one makes of this, it might go some way towards explaining in Chomsky's case what otherwise seems, for a linguist, a perverse rejection of the notion that languages are forms of communicational activity identified with particular communities. Such a notion, declares Chomsky dismissively, is a 'mere artifact' and has no place in 'the theory of language' (Chomsky 1986: 26). All one can say is that Saussure would have regarded any such dismissal as a crippling impoverishment to any 'theory of language'.

*   *   *

This is not the place to trace the subsequent tribulations that beset Chomsky's attempts (beginning with Chomsky 1965) to clarify his own distinction between *competence* and *performance*. That would involve a tedious thirty-year detour into the related distinction between 'deep structure' and 'surface structure', which generativists eventually abandoned anyway. According to Pinker, nowadays 'many linguists – including in his most recent writings, Chomsky himself – think one can do without deep structure per se' (Pinker 1994: 120–1). That must be, for all concerned, at least a relief, if not a consummation devoutly to be wished. (What one thinks of the many years of misguided effort that went into exploring and even extending Chomsky's blind alley is another question.) As soon as the hallowed distinction between 'deep structure' and 'surface structure' goes, there is no longer any need to castigate Saussure for his allegedly 'impoverished and inadequate' conception.

This chimes with Joseph's conclusion that, by examining the discrepancies between Chomsky's various comments on Saussure over the years, one can trace a correlation with changes in Chomsky's own theoretical position. As Chomsky began to focus on 'I[nternalized]-language' (as opposed to 'E[xternalized]-language') as the proper object of linguistic inquiry Saussure's *langue* as a social construct came to seem increasingly irrelevant. And as the distinction between deep structure and surface structure withered away in Chomsky's own thinking, Saussure's indifference to recursive processes in syntax ceased to matter. Chomsky always 'read' Saussure according to his own current agenda (Joseph 1990: 74). That does not quite answer the question of whether Chomsky ever understood what the Saussurean agenda was.

In any case, there is more to it than plotting the development of Chomsky's Saussure against changes in the generativist programme. For Saussure was only one figure in a history of linguistics that Chomsky invented to serve his own purposes (as Saussure had done before him). Of the most important *dramatis personae* in Chomsky's historiography, one – Humboldt – has already been mentioned. The other was Descartes, who receives star billing in *Cartesian Linguistics* (Chomsky 1966). This brings us to the other key facet of Chomsky's self-presentation. He wished to be seen not only as an anti-behaviourist in psychology but also as a 'rationalist' in philosophy. Since Descartes was the rationalist philosopher *par excellence*, clearly Descartes had to be brought into the generativist camp somehow.

The problem was that Descartes had bequeathed little or nothing in the way of work on language; so Chomsky proclaimed the Port-Royal grammar of Lancelot and Arnauld to be a posthumous Cartesian testament, and proceeded to discover therein the antecedents of Chomskyan 'deep' and 'surface' structure. Descartes had already been identified as precursor of generativism in 'Current issues in linguistic theory', albeit in a very roundabout way. There we are told that the realization that the 'creative' aspect of language 'is its essential characteristic' can be traced back at least to the seventeenth century, where we find the Cartesian view that man alone is more than mere automatism, and that it is the possession of true language that is the primary indicator of this (see Descartes, *Discourse on Method*, part V) [. . .] (Chomsky 1964: 51)

Anyone who turns to the passage in Descartes that Chomsky cites, looking for the expected confirmation, will be in for a surprise. The way Descartes brings language into his argument falls a long way short of substantiating Chomsky's claim: it might even be regarded as contradicting it. For what Descartes argues is that we would always be able to tell a human being from a machine that merely looked and behaved like a human being by noting the way it modified its verbal responses *rationally* in accordance with the demands of the situation. This has nothing to do with the 'creativity' of a language system as such. The same argument would apply to the use of any signs, verbal or non-verbal, and presumably also to the use of other devices, such as tools, which might give an indication of the rationality of the user when confronted with the unexpected. At the linguistic level, all this is once again a matter of *parole*, not of *langue*.

Descartes's argument, as Turing and others later realized, can in any case be stood on its head. Should not a machine that can handle words as well as a human being be reckoned as having the ability to think? (It is interesting to note that in the annual competition for the Loebner Prize in computer intelligence, which is based on the Turing test, no machine has so far been mistaken for a human being, but several human beings have been mistaken for machines. Presumably those humans thus misclassified were not being sufficiently 'creative', in spite of being equipped with flawless internalized Chomskyan grammars.)

Whether to regard *Cartesian Linguistics* as an ingenious piece of special pleading or evidence of the author's historical ignorance will not be debated here. Some critics have inclined to the latter view (Aarsleff 1970). According to Koerner, Chomsky in 1978 privately cited the hostile reception of *Cartesian Linguistics* by certain scholars as his reason for giving up further work in the history of linguistics (Koerner 1999). This in turn suggests that Chomsky's primary interest in the history of linguistics was in any case limited to a trawl for selected items of evidence in support of his own agenda. If this evidence could immediately be shown to be unreliable by experts, the agenda itself might be discredited: so here discretion was clearly the better part of academic valour. Be that as it may, it is worth noting that the same three figures on whom Chomsky's historiography relies so heavily – Descartes, Humboldt and Saussure – can be seen as related in a quite different way. An interesting comparison is between Chomsky's history of linguistics and Voloshinov's.

In *Marxism and the Philosophy of Language* (Voloshinov 1929), Saussure is presented as an 'abstract objectivist'. Abstract objectivism for Voloshinov is characterized by four main theses. 1. 'Language is a stable, immutable system of normatively identical linguistic forms'. 2. 'The laws of language are the specifically linguistic laws of connection between linguistic signs within a given, closed linguistic system'. 3. 'Specifically linguistic connections have nothing in common with ideological values (artistic, cognitive, or other)'. 4. 'Individual acts of speaking are [. . .] merely fortuitous refractions and variations or plain and simple distortions of normatively identical forms' (Voloshinov 1929: 57).

Abstract objectivism stands opposed to 'individualistic subjectivism', for which the corresponding four theses are the following. 1. 'Language is activity, an unceasing process of creation (*energeia*) realized in individual speech acts'. 2. 'The laws of language creativity are the laws of individual psychology'. 3. 'Creativity of language is meaningful creativity, analogous to creative art'. 4. 'Language as a ready-made product (*ergon*), as a stable system [. . .] is [. . .] the hardened lava of linguistic creativity, of which linguistics makes an abstract construct in the interests of the practical teaching of language as a ready-made instrument' (Voloshinov 1929: 48).

The most important proponent of individual subjectivism, according to Voloshinov, was Humboldt. Thus Saussure and Humboldt represent, for Voloshinov, diametrically opposed theoretical approaches to language. Furthermore, abstract objectivism is basically Cartesian; for Voloshinov, Saussurean synchrony is 'the revival of the Cartesian spirit in the area of linguistic investigation' (Matejka 1986: 167). For Chomsky, on the other hand, it is Humboldt who is the Cartesian and whose work marks 'the terminal point of the development of Cartesian linguistics' (Chomsky 1966: 86).

Both Voloshinov and Chomsky invoke rather vague and facile distinctions between 'rationalism' and whatever supposedly stands in opposition to it, e.g. 'empiricism'. Both had their own theoretical objectives, in the interests of which they found it not only expedient but extremely easy to rewrite selected chapters in the history of ideas. As one might expect, their main objections to Saussure are characteristically different. Whereas Chomsky, the anarchist, has no time for Saussure's insistence on *langue* as a social product (Chomsky 1986: 16), for the Marxist Voloshinov, Saussure's failure is a failure to appreciate the social nature of the utterance (Voloshinov 1929: 60–1). On the one hand, we have a Saussure too socially oriented; on the other, not socially oriented enough. Which of the two Saussures – Voloshinov's or Chomsky's – is thus the more distorted must be a moot point; but perhaps no more than that needs to be said.

CHAPTER TEN

Derrida's Saussure

Saussure is, for Derrida, one of the founders of modern linguistics and, as such, one of the culprits responsible for perpetuating in the name of 'science' an ancient, ethnocentric and flawed view of the relationship between speech and writing. In *De la grammatologie* (1967), observes a recent commentator, Derrida sets himself an ambitious task:

> to question and contest a tradition of Western thought in which writing has consistently been cast in a role subordinate to that of speech. Whereas speech is habitually associated with reason and rationality (the Greek notion of *logos*) and the voice is perceived as being closer to the inner 'truth' of individual consciousness, writing is considered to be a secondary extension or supplement to the voice, an auxiliary technology employed by human reason but not essential to it. Speech is the guarantor of presence and of authenticity, whereas writing represents artifice and absence, the alienation and deferment of presence. In *Of Grammatology*, Derrida's critique of this historical subordination of writing, which he calls 'logocentrism', takes the form of close, sustained readings of thinkers representing different instances or 'moments' of the logocentric tradition, the most substantial of which are the readings devoted to Saussure, Lévi-Strauss and Jean-Jacques Rousseau. (Johnson 1997: 4–5)

Exactly how 'close' and how well 'sustained' these readings are, at least in Saussure's case, is a matter of some interest in the present context. Before tracing in detail exactly how Derrida's 'reading' of Saussure is articulated, we should note that Derrida's Saussure is the Saussure of the *CLG*. All the references Derrida gives are to this one text. Derrida concedes, in a footnote (Derrida 1967: 107), that there may be some doubt as to the reliability of the *CLG* as a record of Saussure's teaching, and refers briefly to Godel's *Sources manuscrites* of ten years earlier. Nevertheless, he declines to go into this question on the ground that Saussure (presumably the Saussure of the *CLG*) 'domine encore la linguistique et la sémiologie contemporaines'. This comment hardly inspires confidence that Derrida had kept up to date with linguistics before launching his remarkable anti-Saussurean polemic.

As regards 'contemporary semiology', Derrida was evidently acquainted with at least Barthes's 'reversal' of Saussurean priorities, since he writes with something approaching enthusiasm:

> Ce renversement cohérent, soumettant la sémiologie à une «trans-linguistique», conduit à sa pleine explicitation une linguistique historiquement dominée par la métaphysique logocentrique, pour laquelle en effet il n'y a, il ne devrait y avoir «de sens que nommé». Dominée par la soi-disant «civilisation de l'écriture» que nous habitons, civilisation de l'écriture soi-disant phonétique, c'est-à-dire du logos où le sens de l'être est, en son telos, déterminé comme parousie. Pour décrire *le fait et la vocation de la signification* dans la clôture de cette époque et de cette civilisation en voie de disparaître dans sa mondialisation elle-même, le renversement barthésien est fécond et indispensable. (Derrida 1967: 75)

This unqualified approval of Barthes is somewhat unexpected, particularly since the other neo-Saussurean theorist discussed in detail in *De la grammatologie*, i.e. Lévi-Strauss, comes in for such harsh treatment. Derrida doubtless approves of Barthes because he sees Barthes's 'renversement' as fulfilling 'la plus profonde intention du *Cours*'. So although Barthes's semiology is arguably even more logocentric than Saussure's, Barthes is allowed to escape without criticism because he unwittingly demonstrates, as it were, the belated historical germination of the tares that Derrida detects in Saussure's work.

*   *   *

Before Saussure is ever mentioned by name in *De la grammatologie*, Derrida is already discussing language and writing in Saussurean terms: *signe, signifiant, signifié, langue, parole*, etc. are straight away (Derrida 1967: 16 ff.) assumed to belong to a vocabulary with which the reader is familiar and which therefore does not call for preliminary discussion or explanation. But this immediate adoption of Saussurean terminology betokens neither flattery nor respect; for Saussure's own terms will shortly be turned against him. When Saussure himself at last makes his first appearance in the course of Derrida's exposition, it immediately follows a preliminary account of Aristotle's *symbolon*, and the point in question is one about which Saussure would certainly have had doubts:

> La notion de signe implique toujours en elle-même la distinction du signifié et du signifiant, fût-ce à la limite, selon Saussure, comme les deux faces d'une seule et même feuille. (Derrida 1967: 23)

With this bland, indirect reference to *CLG*: 157, Derrida manages at one stroke to assimilate Saussure's theory of the linguistic sign to Aristotle's. The assimilation had already been prepared verbally for several pages by the use of the terms *signifiant* and *signifié*; so that when their originator is eventually introduced *in propria persona*, he is automatically presented as the person who has to take responsibility for the way that distinction has hitherto been employed in Derrida's exposition. We are not dealing here with accidental infelicities of style but with a calculated rhetorical technique of which there are many other examples in Derrida's writing. In political journalism it is known as the 'smear'. Rather than actually demonstrate a connexion between person *A* and person *B*, the journalist implies connexion by means of lexical association. The technique is all the more effective when the lexical association can be based on terms that either *A* or *B* actually uses. This dispenses with any need to argue a case; or, if any case is argued, its conclusion is already tacitly anticipated in the terms used to present it. So here, Aristotle's *symbolon* is presented *ab initio* as an instance of the *signifiant*. The concessive 'fût-ce à la limite' is calculated to forestall all reactions of protest on the part of the reader sufficiently familiar with both Aristotle's text and Saussure's to find something less than straightforward in this connexion.

Derrida's exegesis of the passage from Aristotle is just as dubious as his implied interpretation of the passage from the *CLG*. In Derrida's French translation of the Greek, Aristotle claims that written words ('mots écrits') are symbols of spoken words ('mots émis par la voix'). But Aristotle claimed nothing of the kind. In the Greek text there is nothing which corresponds to the linguistic unit 'word' (*mot*). Anyone who notices this interpolation will ask why Derrida introduces it. The answer is not far to seek. It facilitates the establishment of historical continuity between Aristotle and Saussure. For Saussure (*CLG*: 147 ff.; 158) takes the word (*mot*) as a convenient approximation to the sign unit (*signe*) of structural linguistics. If, however, we compare Aristotle's Greek with Saussure's French it becomes obvious that Aristotle is not talking about the *signe* (in Saussure's sense) at all. Derrida passes over in silence the fact that in this same passage from *De Interpretatione* Aristotle distinguishes between signs (*semeia*) and symbols (*symbola*), although in quite a different way from Saussure. For Saussure, the *symbole*, as opposed to the *signe*, is based on a non-arbitrary relationship of some kind:

> Le symbole a pour caractère de n'être jamais tout à fait arbitraire; il n'est pas vide, il y a un rudiment de lien naturel entre le signifiant et le signifié. (*CLG*: 101)

Aristotle's *symbolon* is quite a different case. *Symbolon*, in Aristotle's day, was the term applied to the token shared between two parties to a contract as proof of their agreement. Each kept one half of a deliberately broken potsherd, bone or other small object. Aristotle's use of this metaphor to express the relationship between sounds and 'affections of the soul' is striking, and corresponds to nothing in Saussurean technical vocabulary. Saussure's *symbole* has long since lost any of the associations with trading practice that would have been familiar to Aristotle's audience. Aristotle's *semeia*, on the other hand, seem to be the sounds uttered as, or at least when considered as, expressions of the speaker's current thoughts or mental state. Thus if one were rash enough to try to force Aristotle's terminology into a Saussurean framework, the most plausible interpretation would be to treat *semeia* as units of *parole* and *symbola* as units of *langue*. Even so, Saussure would still be entitled to object that both *semeia* and *symbola* are vocal items: there is no recognition by Aristotle of anything corresponding to the *image acoustique*. Without that, any assimilation of Aristotelian semiology to Saussure's collapses.

As regards Saussure's famous analogy of cutting the sheet of paper, Derrida fails to mention that the sheet is not the sign. The sheet itself is *la langue*, as the *CLG* text makes perfectly clear: 'La langue est encore comparable à une feuille de papier: la pensée est le recto et le son le verso' (*CLG*: 157). Contrary to Derrida's apparent assumption, which side is recto and which is verso is not unimportant. For this is a quite different image from that presented just previously, where the interface between thought and sound was likened to that between air and water (*CLG*: 156). There no human action intervened: the image was drawn from natural phenomena. Now we are being invited to regard *la langue* from the point of view of the user, who wishes to 'cut out' a shape corresponding to some particular thought. And Saussure's point is that this cannot be done – the recto cannot be cut – without at the same time cutting out a corresponding shape on the verso. (Cutting is a deliberate act: it corresponds in Saussure's analogy to the voluntary, intelligent intervention of the individual which is the domain of *parole*. Saussure does not, for obvious reasons, speak of cutting the verso; for it would not automatically produce a meaningful configuration on the recto. But this would doubtless be pressing the analogy beyond the limits of its usefulness.)

Derrida wedges his foot in the semiological door with the claim that 'la notion de signe implique toujours en elle-même la distinction du signifié et du signifiant'. But does it? And where does this 'notion de signe [. . .] en elle-même' come from? Saussure, for one, would have been among the first to contest its validity. If there is any such notion, it must belong –

Saussure would argue – to 'psychologie pure' (*CLG*: 157). And this is an abstraction. But such abstractions, according to Saussure, have no place in linguistic theory. Straight away Derrida himself falls into the pit which he is busy digging for Saussure. For while there are various grounds on which Saussurean semiology might be criticized, it is question-begging to attack it by invoking an *a priori* 'notion of the sign itself'. By this maladroit opening manoeuvre, Derrida also throws doubt on his own credentials as a historian. Casting Saussure as the linguistic heir of Aristotle is one thing: casting Aristotle as the linguistic forebear of Saussure is another. That dubious reversal is essential to Derrida's case. It is the foundation of the trumped-up historical charge which Saussure will be brought to answer.

Saussure is then left standing in the dock for a whole chapter, while the prosecutor embarks on a long preamble, in the course of which various accomplices of the accused are identified. Among these the most interesting case is that of Jakobson. He has evidently been summoned to appear as witness for the prosecution; for he is quoted *in extenso* as providing the damning evidence Derrida cannot find verbatim in the *CLG*:

«La pensée structuraliste moderne l'a clairement établi: le langage est un système de signes [. . .]. La définition médiévale – aliquid stat pro aliquo – que notre époque a ressuscitée, s'est montrée toujours valable et féconde. C'est ainsi que la marque constitutive de tout signe en général, du signe linguistique en particulier, réside dans son caractère double: chaque unité linguistique est bipartite et comporte deux aspects; l'un sensible et l'autre intelligible – d'une part le signans (le *signifiant* de Saussure), d'autre part le *signatum* (le signifié). Ces deux éléments constitutifs du signe linguistique (et du signe en générale) se supposent et s'appellent néféssairement l'un l'autre.» (Derrida 1967: 24–5; quoting Jakobson, *Essais de linguistique générale*, p. 162)

Jakobson's testimony, however, is suspect, to say the least. The *signans* of the medieval grammarians is not Saussure's *signifiant*, any more than their *significatum* is his *signifié*. Nor is, for Saussure, 'le langage [. . .] un système de signes'. On the contrary, as the *CLG* insists repeatedly, it is not 'le langage' but 'la langue' which is a system of signs. What Jakobson's crude equation leaves out of account is Saussure's conception of systematicity. Once this is suppressed, all that remains is indeed the rather vague and malleable notion of the sign as a bilateral entity. And one bilateral entity can then be made to look very much like another. The result is manifest oversimplification. It is disingenuous of Jakobson (or anyone else) to suggest that structuralism merely 'revived' the ancient bi-partite distinction, already familiar to the thinkers of the Middle Ages. On the contrary, structuralism of the Saussurean variety replaced that traditional distinction by another, which also happens to be bi-partite but is based on a quite untraditional principle of 'partition'.

How central is Jakobson's suspect testimony to Derrida's case? Its importance can perhaps be gauged from the fact that five years later in *Positions* Derrida not only repeated the same Jakobson quotation but summarized its central point in his own words, reiterating in particular the medieval terminology of *signans* and *signatum* (Derrida 1972b). The purpose was to establish that Saussure is guilty of contradiction by accepting what Derrida grandly calls a 'transcendental' *signifié*. The tortuousness of the procedure by which, having failed to find any evidence of this in the *CLG*, the prosecution must constantly refer to someone's else's interpretation of it, hardly needs to be emphasized. In a court of law it is known as 'hearsay evidence' and disallowed.

Quoting Jakobson's garbled account of the history of 'la pensée structuraliste' is bad enough. What makes it worse is that it is far from clear that a bi-planar model of the linguistic sign was the only kind of model on offer in the Middle Ages. By calling Jakobson to the witness stand, Derrida is responsible for a double misrepresentation. Jakobson, the latter-day champion of binarism, has no time for distinctions that cannot be reduced to binary oppositions. His idiosyncratic version of structuralism is one which the Saussure of the *CLG* would doubtless have had serious problems in endorsing. But Derrida says nothing about this. The upshot is that Saussure is not only arraigned as a theorist who revived a medieval account of signs, but faces charges for which his successors should rightly be called to account. Thus in this carefully contrived 'history' of logocentrism, both the past and the future already conspire against the luckless Saussure.

When eventually the accused himself is put in the witness box, some twenty pages of Heidegger-and-Hegel later, it is because he has been selected as an 'exemple privilégié' to throw light on the 'présupposition métaphysique' on the basis of which 'la linguistique s'est instituée comme science'. This 'metaphysical presupposition' concerns, precisely, the relationship between speech and writing. According to Derrida:

> La science linguistique détermine le langage – son champ d'objectivité – en dernière instance et dans la simplicité irréductible de son essence, comme l'unité de *phonè*, *glossa* et *logos*. (Derrida 1967: 45)

Whatever this jumble of Greek terms might be supposed to mean, readers of Saussure will not find it in the *CLG*, nor any similar pretentiousness about the 'irreducible simplicity' of the 'essence' of language. Saussurean linguistics, whatever its defects may be, is not a philosophical inquiry into the 'essence' of anything, but a set of proposals for dealing systematically with certain *aspects* of language. What then becomes 'essential' becomes so in virtue of the perspective adopted. Derrida, who glibly confuses *l'essence* with *l'essentiel*, never seems to have been able to grasp this.

Language itself (*le langage*), the *CLG* tells us, is in its totality unknowable (*inconnaissable*) (*CLG*: 38). Its protean heterogeneity thwarts all attempts to treat it within the confines of a single science (*CLG*: 25). Saussure's insistence on the exclusion of writing is not based on metaphysics but on methodology. The separate activities of speaking and writing are too diverse to be brought within the focus of a single inquiry. Given this, the only question is: to which of the two should linguists devote their efforts in the first instance? For Saussure, as for all other linguists of his generation, the answer was never in doubt: it was decided not by any 'metaphysical' preoccupation but by the simple fact that only a very small proportion of the world's languages had ever been written down. To have focussed on written languages would therefore have seemed to them as historically perverse and narrow-minded as insisting that musicology must give priority to those musical traditions with a system of notation.

Derrida also, quite gratuitously, blames Saussure for the concentration on phonology in the work of his successors:

> L'orientation délibérément et systématiquement phonologique de la linguistique (Troubetzkoy, Jakobson, Martinet) accomplissant une intention qui fut d'abord celle de Saussure, nous nous en tiendrons, pour l'essentiel et au moins provisoire-ment, à cette dernière. (Derrida 1967: 45)

The apologetic disclaimers ('pour l'essentiel' and 'au moins provisioire-ment') already betray a certain awareness of just how shifty this attribution to Saussure of the preoccupations of a later generation might seem to readers familiar in detail with the *CLG*. For the Saussure of the *CLG* shows remarkably little interest in developing anything that could reasonably be described as structural phonemics. It is here that Derrida's lack of familiarity with his subject matter shows up clearly: he evidently supposes that Saussure's *phonème* and *phonologie* are already those of the Prague school. He has perhaps been misled too by later commentators who retrospectively saw in Saussure's early *Mémoire* of 1879 an anticipation of the Prague school concept. But it is quite implausible that Saussure should have formulated anything like this and kept silent about it for thirty years. (For discussion, see Harris 1987: 49 ff.) In any case, the sole passage in the *CLG* which might perhaps be adduced as evidence to the contrary is no more than a passing remark to the effect that syntagmatic and associative relations apply also *below* the level of the sign, i.e. in the composition of the *signifiant*. Thus, hypothetically, *anma* may contrast with *anva*, *anda*, etc. But the point is never developed, nor even formulated clearly. (For discussion, see Harris 1987: 130 f. Saussure introduced the example of *anma* in the Second Course (Engler: 2087), but dropped it from the Third.)

The phonologically obsessed 'science linguistique', for which Saussure is held responsible, is described by Derrida as being committed to the thesis that 'l'unité immédiate et privilégiée qui fonde la signifiance et l'acte de langage est l'unité articulée du son et du sens dans la phonie' (Derrida 1967: 45). But this is not Saussure's position at all. What Derrida calls *la phonie* (a term used neither by Saussure nor by his successors, but presumably introduced here because it answers to Greek *phonè*) is not the site of any 'immediate' or 'privileged' kind of 'unit': on the contrary, what emerges as sound has no determinate division into units: 'en elle-même, elle n'est qu'une ligne, un ruban continu, où l'oreille ne perçoit aucune division suffisante et précise' (*CLG*: 145). Sound sequences do *not* correspond, for Saussure, to any *acte de langage* (another term never found in the *CLG*). That is why phonetics tells us nothing about the structure of *la langue*, nor even about the segmentation of *la parole*. Derrida, in short, seems quite oblivious of the extent to which Saussurean linguistic theory, far from perpetuating the emphasis placed in the nineteenth century on sound and sound change, marked a reaction against this trend in the history of linguistics. (But that, for obvious reasons, would not fit in with – let alone be explicable in terms of – Derrida's account of Saussure's role in promoting the pervasive 'logocentricity' of the Western tradition.)

Faced with explicit statements in the *CLG* which deny that sound plays any intrinsic role in *la langue* – statements of a kind that had never been made by Saussure's predecessors – Derrida attempts to present them as symptomatic of a conceptual muddle. This fanatically logocentric Saussure (fanatical to the point of setting up as protector of *la langue* against 'la contamination la plus grave, la plus perfide, la plus permanente' – the hyperbole is Derrida's, not Saussure's) has unwittingly tripped himself up. For on the one hand he insists that only speech is natural, but on the other hand he has to devote a whole section of the *CLG* to explaining how it is that writing can so easily take over from speech and 'usurper le rôle principal' (*CLG*: 45). Saussure's explanation, for Derrida, only makes matters worse. For the explanation appeals, *inter alia*, to the alleged superiority of visual images over auditory impressions (*CLG*: 46):

> Elle fait imprudemment de la visibilité l'élément sensible, simple et essentiel de l'écriture. Surtout, en considérant l'audible comme le milieu *naturel* dans lequel la langue doit *naturellement* découper et articuler ses signes institués, y exerçant ainsi son arbitraire, cette explication ôte toute possibilité à quelque rapport naturel entre parole et écriture au moment même où elle l'affirme. Elle brouille donc les notions de nature et d'institution dont elle se sert constamment, au lieu de les congédier délibérément, ce qu'il faudrait sans doute commencer par faire. Elle contredit enfin et surtout l'affirmation capitale selon laquelle «l'essentiel de la langue est étranger au caractère phonique du signe linguistique» (p. 21). (Derrida 1967: 63)

So, apparently, not only has Saussure implicitly 'affirmed' a natural connexion between speech and writing but, between pages 21 and 46 of the *CLG*, before any detailed exposition of his subject has begun – for here we are still in the 'Introduction' to the *Cours* – he has already managed to commit himself to a serious contradiction. How can one possibly have any confidence in a theorist who gets caught in such a web of incoherence? Or in a discipline which hails such a theorist as its founder? (Derrida does not spell out the questions, but his presentation of Saussure's alleged conflations and illogicalities certainly invites them.)

As regards the web, it unravels as soon as one begins to examine how Derrida has woven it. The *CLG*, as commentators have pointed out, proceeds – in the manner one might expect from an undergraduate course – from fairly broad general statements at the beginning to progressively more sophisticated formulations. In the course of this development, the terminology changes. Qualifications to earlier statements are added. By ignoring this well-crafted progression, Derrida finds it relatively easy to pick out and juxtapose observations that at first sight jar with one another.

In the statement from *CLG*: 21 cited above, there is a parenthetical 'as we shall see', which Derrida omits. The original text reads: 'l'essentiel de la langue, nous le verrons, est étranger au caractère phonique du signe linguistique'. The reader is here being promised a later demonstration which will – and can only – be presented when more rigorous linguistic concepts have been introduced. We have not even yet had the distinction between *langue* and *parole*. The section of the text from which this statement comes is an introductory discussion of the relationship between linguistics and physiology. We are still at the stage of identifying, in a preliminary survey, the place that linguistics (as Saussure conceives it) occupies in the array of existing disciplines that have some claim to deal with *langage*. By the time the promised demonstration is reached the lay concept of *langage* will have been replaced by something much more precise, as will the lay notion of *signe*. In fact, it will gradually become apparent that the 'caractère phonique' of the 'signe linguistique' is itself illusory; an illusion that persists only for as long the failure to draw the *langue/parole* distinction in the way that Saussure now proposes.

There is nothing on page 46 of the *CLG* that 'contradicts' (*contredit*) what was said earlier on page 21. In the mean time the distinction between *langue* and *parole* has been introduced (*CLG*: 23–32, 36–9) as well as that between 'internal' and 'external' linguistics (*CLG*: 40–3), and we have now proceeded to a further area of introductory clarification, concerning the relationship between spoken and written language. The rationale for this clarification is one which Derrida's approach conveniently allows him to ignore. The Saussure who gave the Geneva lectures of 1907–11 was well aware of addressing students whose prior acquaintance with the teaching of Greek, Latin and comparative philology made it only too likely that they would tend to confuse the study of languages with the study of texts. Especially since Bopp and other authorities had written of languages in terms which invited exactly that confusion (*CLG*: 46). Furthermore, at the time when Saussure was giving his lectures, spelling reform was a current topic of debate. There are two allusions to this in the *CLG*. Derrida comments on one and ignores the other. The one on which he comments is Saussure's observation that it would be a mistake to try to substitute a phonetic alphabet for the alphabet currently in use (*CLG*: 57). Derrida concedes, somewhat reluctantly, that 'les raisons de Saussure sont bonnes' but complains that what Saussure says does not amount to a 'critique' of the relationship between speech and writing (which it never claimed to be). At the same time it indicates, according to Derrida, that Saussure actually shares the same assumptions as those whom he criticizes:

> ce qu'il dénonce comme préjugé aveugle des linguistes classiques ou de l'expérience commune reste bien un préjugé aveugle, sur le fond d'une présupposition générale qui est sans doute commune aux accusés et au procureur. (Derrida 1967: 58)

How this alleged common ground between Saussure and the reformers is shown Derrida never explains. It shows even less in the other remark on spelling reform, that Derrida never mentions (*CLG*: 46). This is the topical reference to the recent statement by Gaston Deschamps at the Académie Française that Berthelot (who had opposed spelling reform) had 'saved the French language from ruin'. (The remark comes from the Second Course, and Deschamps had apparently said this 'il y a quelques semaines'; Engler: 474.) It is fairly clear why Derrida does not mention this: it reflects, as Saussure rightly implied, the strength of the conservative (i.e. anti-logocentric) view inculcated by the French education system. The omission indicates the extent to which the distortions in Derrida's picture of Saussure are dictated by his determination to play down any aspects of the Western tradition that do not bear out his own accusations of logocentricity.

Saussure's view as presented in the *CLG* is quite different from that which Derrida attributes to him as founder of modern linguistics. The position taken in the *CLG* is a perfectly consistent position. It recognizes that languages are basically maintained and handed down by the processes of oral tradition. Necessarily so where there is no writing anyway; but also in cases where a writing system is established. The 'dangers' which Saussure warns against are not based on any 'metaphysical' view about essences: they are the dangers (for students) of confusing certain forms of evidence (i.e. written texts) with the oral traditions underlying them. Or, as a remark reported in Riedlinger's notes for the Second Course puts it, mistakes concerning 'la situation du document vis-à-vis de l'objet à étudier' (*CLG2*: 86). That is to say, they are on a par with the admonitions a geographer might issue to students who might be tempted to confuse geography with the study of maps. (The theory and history of maps constitute a subject of interest in its own right: that in no way diminishes the potential seriousness of the confusion.)

Finding it hard to mount any more cogent case, Derrida is reduced to making a song and dance about the variety of metaphors to be found in the *CLG*. According to Derrida, Saussure sometimes wants to have it that writing is just an 'image' of speech; whereas at other times Saussure claims that writing is a 'veil' which obscures one's view of speech. 'Étrange «image»' is Derrida's ponderously sarcastic comment (Derrida 1967: 52). As such, one might let it pass. But Derrida harps on it with manic persistence, hoping thereby to convict Saussure of yet another contradiction:

> On doit donc récuser, au nom même de l'arbitraire du signe, la définition saussurienne de l'écriture comme «image» – donc comme symbole naturel – de la langue. Outre que le phonème est l'*inimaginable* lui-même, et qu'aucune visibilité ne peut lui *ressembler*, il suffit de tenir compte de ce que dit Saussure de la différence entre le symbole et le signe (p. 101) pour ne plus comprendre comment il peut à la fois dire de l'écriture qu'elle est «image» ou «figuration» de la langue et définir ailleurs la langue et l'écriture comme «deux systèmes de signes distincts» (p. 45). Car le propre du signe, c'est de n'être pas image. (Derrida 1967: 66–7)

What is 'strange' in all this is not Saussure's deployment of the term *image* but his critic's failure to accept that one varies one's metaphor according to the particular point to be made. If metaphorical muddles were a crime, *De la grammatologie* itself would be a prime candidate for prosecution.

When it suits him, patently, Derrida takes no notice of metaphor whatever (as in his discussion of Aristotle's *symbolon*). But here he wants to have it both ways at once: the term *image* suddenly becomes Saussure's 'definition' of writing. Plato is even brought on to hammer a further nail in Saussure's coffin. For although, we are told, Plato said 'basically the same thing' as Saussure on this topic, at least in Plato's case this was one part of a more general theory of mimesis.

> Saussure commence ainsi par poser que l'écriture est «en elle-même étrangère au système interne» de la langue (p. 44). Externe/interne, image/réalité, représentation/présence, telle est la vieille grille à laquelle est confié le soin de dessiner le champ d'une science. Et de quelle science. D'une science qui ne peut plus répondre au concept classique de l'*epistème* parce que son champ a pour originalité – une originalité qu'il inaugure – que l'ouverture en lui de l'«image» y apparaît comme la condition de la «réalité»: rapport qui ne se laisse donc plus penser dans la différence simple et l'extériorité sans compromis de l'«image» et de la «réalité», du «dehors» et du «dedans», de l'«apparence» et de l'«essence», avec tout le système des oppositions qui s'y enchaînent nécessairement. Platon, qui disait au fond la même chose des rapports entre l'écriture, la parole et l'être (ou l'idée), avait au moins de l'image, de la peinture et de l'imitation une théorie plus subtile, plus critique et plus inquiète que celle qui préside à la naissance de la linguistique saussurienne. (Derrida 1967: 50–1)

This travesty of the history of ideas is so gross that it is difficult to know where to begin commenting on it. The fact is that Plato never discusses writing at the level at which it enters into Saussure's concerns at all. Plato is indeed sceptical about writing; but for quite different reasons from Saussure's. Throughout the whole of the *Cratylus*, which is Plato's major contribution to debates about language in antiquity, the issue of how speech is related to writing is never raised. Words are discussed throughout in terms which have even suggested to some critics that the Greeks may have failed to distinguish between sounds and letters. In the *Phaedrus*, Plato recounts (presumably with approval) the legendary response of the Pharaoh to the invention of writing: the gist of which is that it is not a blessing to mankind, but will weaken men's memories if they come to rely too much on it. In *Letter VII* (if it is genuinely Plato's) the complaint is not about writing but about books. It is a mistake, so the argument goes, to suppose that a definitive or permanent account of any serious philosopher's views can be put down on record. Why? Because the text cannot answer questions. Once in written form, it becomes subject to any interpretation that readers care to put upon it. Finally, Plato's famous banishment of poets from his Republic has nothing to do with writing at all, although it has a great deal to do with the doctrine of mimesis in art. For Plato, the archetypal poet was Homer, who neither read nor wrote. The existence of Homeric texts in Plato's day is an irrelevance to Plato's argument.

These are interesting and significant views, particularly in the cultural context of Plato's Athens. But to claim that what Plato and Saussure were saying about writing was 'au fond la même chose' verges on the grotesque. 'La même chose' (Saussure might have suggested) is a panchronic mirage, conjured up in this instance by Derrida himself.

By quoting selected snippets from the *CLG* out of context, Derrida manages to make Saussure appear to say in the witness box exactly what Derrida wanted him to say. This technique of cross-examination may be illustrated by the following examples.

1. Saussure, according to Derrida, presents the history of writing as:

> une série d'accidents affectant la langue et lui survenant *du dehors*, au moment de la «notation» (p. 45), comme si l'écriture commençait et finissait avec la notation. (Derrida 1967: 51)

Looking up the reference to *CLG*: 45, one finds that the implication that 'writing begins and ends with notation' is Derrida's gratuitous expansion. It corresponds to nothing in the *CLG* text. Nor does the text say anything about 'accidents' occurring 'au moment de la «notation»'. What it does say is something Derrida fails to mention: that it would be a mistake to suppose that the rate of linguistic change in the spoken language depends on the presence or absence of a writing system. The observation from which Derrida abstracts the single word *notation* is actually: 'Certains faits linguistiques très ténus se sont conservés sans le secours d'aucune notation' (*CLG*: 45). This is the sole occurrence of the term *notation* in the chapter in question, and the example given is the absence in spelling of any indication of the palatalization of certain consonants in the history of Germanic. A quite different point from the one Derrida misrepresents it as being.

2. Saussure, according to Derrida, has only a very 'narrow' conception of the function of writing:

> Étroite parce qu'elle n'est, parmi d'autres, qu'une modalité des événements qui peuvent survenir à un langage dont l'essence, comme semblent l'enseigner les faits,

peut toujours rester pure de tout rapport à l'écriture. «La langue a une tradition orale indépendante de l'écriture» (*Cours de linguistique générale*, p. 46). (Derrida 1967: 46)

If one consults the text of the *CLG*, it immediately becomes apparent that in order to give the statement quoted the generality that would appear to confirm Derrida's claim, the word 'donc' has been silently omitted before 'une tradition orale'. In fact, the statement is not a generalization at all, but a comment on the specific example Saussure has just supplied in order to demonstrate that sound changes are not always registered in orthography.

3. According to Derrida, Saussure is committed to the assumption of a 'natural' bond between sound and meaning:

Selon les présuppositions historico-métaphysiques que nous évoquions plus haut, il y aurait d'abord un lien *naturel* du sens aux sens et c'est celui qui passe du sens au son: «Le lien naturel, dit Saussure, le seul véritable, celui du son» (p. 46) Ce lien naturel du signifié (concept ou sens) au signifiant phonique conditionnerait le rapport naturel subordonnant l'écriture (image visible, dit-on) à la parole. (Derrida 1967: 53)

Once again, if we trouble to look up the passage cited from the *CLG* we find not only that Derrida has truncated the quotation to suit his own purposes but that the point being made in the *CLG* does not even relate to the relationship Derrida is discussing, i.e. that between *sens* and *son*. What this passage is about, in fact, is our perception of linguistic continuity over time: 'l'unité de la langue à travers le temps'. According to the *CLG*, we are easily misled into seeing this unity as something reflected in the history of written texts; whereas actually the underlying connexions between one period and the next are based on speech – connexions which are consequently far more difficult to follow. It is in this sense that 'le lien naturel' (i.e. between one stage and its successor – not between *sens* and *son*, as Derrida's preposterous reading would have it) is 'celui du son'.

4. Among the contradictions of which Saussure is guilty, according to Derrida, is trying to maintain both (1) that *la langue* is independent of writing, but also (2) that *la langue* is affected by writing.

Tout se passe donc comme si Saussure voulait *à la fois* démontrer l'altération de la parole par l'écriture, dénoncer le mal que celle-ci fait à celle-là, et souligner l'indépendance inaltérable et naturelle de la langue. «La langue est indépendante de l'écriture» (p. 45), telle est la vérité de la nature. (Derrida 1967: 61)

The alleged contradiction hardly stands up to inspection. (It is in fact no contradiction at all: 'X is independent of Y' and 'X is affected by Y' are not incompatible propositions.) But the feature of interest once again is how Derrida has both decontextualized and truncated a quotation in order to make Saussure testify against himself. When we turn to *CLG*: 45 we find that this is not the generalization Derrida pretends it is. The sentence reads in full: 'Cela seul suffit pour montrer combien la langue est indépendante de l'écriture.' The reference here is to the immediately preceding example, which concerns the documentary evidence for Lithuanian, where the earliest texts date only from the sixteenth century. Nevertheless – and this is Saussure's point – the Lithuanian of that period is as close to primitive Indo-European as the Latin of the third century BC. In other words, the comparison shows that *the pace of linguistic change does not correlate directly with the presence or absence of a writing system*. Which is quite a different proposition from Derrida's version, according to which Saussure is claiming that the independence of *la langue* is a 'vérité de la nature'.

Thus in quoting from just two pages of text (*CLG* 45–6) Derrida manages to distort the interpretation of at least four key points. If it is deliberate, it is ingenious, although deplorable: if it is not deliberate, it is obtuse. In either case, to invoke a Saussurean term that Derrida makes great play with, it might reasonably be called 'monstrous'.

Derrida's comments on Saussure's use of the word *monstruosité* provide another revealing example of the methods of Derridean exegesis. In what verges on a parody of Saussure's view, Derrida writes:

> La perversion de l'artifice engendre des monstres. L'écriture comme toutes les langues artificielles qu'on voudrait fixer et soustraire à l'histoire vivante de la langue naturelle, participe de la monstruosité. C'est un écart de la nature. (Derrida 1967: 57)

And again:

> Ainsi, à l'intérieur de l'écriture phonétique commune, il faut se garder d'introduire l'exigence scientifique et le goût de l'exactitude. La rationalité serait ici porteuse de mort, de désolation et de monstruosité. (Derrida 1967: 57)

Nowhere in the *CLG* will the reader find anything corresponding to these theatrical exaggerations. Nowhere does Saussure condemn attempts to use language with precision or scientific accuracy: he merely thinks spelling reforms misguided. Nowhere are attempts to rationalize linguistic practices described as harbingers of death, desolation or monstrosity. The term *monstruosité* is never applied by Saussure to writing at all: the term occurs only once in the *CLG*. What Saussure describes thus is the (hypothetical) spelling-pronunciation of *vingt* envisaged by Darmesteter: 'Darmesteter prévoit le jour où l'on prononcera même les deux lettres finales de *vingt*, véritable monstruosité orthographique' (*CLG*: 54). What Derrida fails to see – or sees but chooses to ignore – is that such a pronunciation of *vingt* – if it were ever to become current, which seems improbable – would actually be 'unFrench' in the sense of actually reversing the trend – conspicuous throughout the history of French – to reduce consonant clusters in word-final position. Once this is realized, the appositeness of Saussure's term becomes apparent.

The word *monstruosité* is being used here in the technical sense borrowed from biology. This is clear if we read the rest of the paragraph in the *CLG*, which concludes with Saussure's proposal that spelling-pronunciations are to be seen as 'déformations phoniques' and treated as 'cas tératologiques'. They fall outside what can be accounted for in terms of established sound laws, to which they are, in fact, exceptions. Saussure was not the first linguist to use the term *monstruosité* in this sense. It belongs to the wide range of metaphors that linguistics appropriated from the sciences of nature during the nineteenth century. A 'monstrosity' in the vocabulary of science is a developmental abnormality: it becomes horrendous or frightening only in the popular imagination, where it acquires those connotations that Derrida deliberately – and misleadingly – plays on here.

Of all the artful misrepresentations displayed in Derrida's interpretation of Saussure, none is more insidious than the attempt to portray the *CLG* as the fire-and-brimstone tract of a puritanical doctrinaire. Here all Derrida's rhetorical tricks are brought into play. Saussure becomes 'the Genevan linguist' and his observations about writing an attempt to root out idolatry:

> La contamination par l'écriture, son fait ou sa menace, sont dénoncés avec des accents de moraliste et de prédicateur par le linguiste genevois. L'accent compte: tout se passe comme si, au moment où la science moderne du logos veut accéder à son autonomie et à sa scientificité, il fallait encore faire le procès d'une hérésie. [. . .] En s'emportant ainsi, la véhémente argumentation de Saussure vise plus qu'une erreur théorique, plus qu'une faute morale: une sorte de souillure et d'abord un péché. (Derrida 1967: 52)

Writing as sin. Saussure as the Calvin of linguistics. (For *Geneva*, read 'centre of reformed protestantism, hotbed of Calvinism'. It is on a par with implying that X is a Commmunist by alluding to the fact that X

comes from Moscow. The phrase 'le linguiste genevois' is another polished example of the Derridean smear.) Sin, heresy, redemption: Derrida, as self-appointed Grand Inquisitor of Western culture, is well qualified in the art of extracting self-condemnatory confessions.

*   *   *

Derrida's long tirade against 'logocentrism', both in Saussure and in the Western tradition in general, turns out to be conducted in order to promote and validate a new concept of Derrida's own invention. He has also invented a name for it: *archi-écriture*. For Derrida, it seems, both speech and writing are in some way subsumed under it. The main rhetorical purpose of this exercise in lexical engineering seems to be that it allows Derrida to construct arresting but shallow paradoxes to the effect that speech itself is a form of writing. What exactly the positive features of 'archi-écriture' are it is by no means easy to determine, since what Derrida says about 'archi-écriture' tends to be fenced round with disclaimers such as:

> C'est que l'archi-écriture, mouvement de la différance, archi-synthèse irréductible, ouvrant à la fois, dans une seule et même possibilité, la temporalisation, le rapport à l'autre et le langage, ne peut pas, en tant que condition de tout système linguistique, faire partie du système linguistique lui-même, être située comme un objet dans son champ. (Derrida 1967: 88)

Or:

> L'archi-écriture comme espacement ne peut pas se donner *comme telle*, dans l'expérience phénoménologique d'une *présence*. Elle marque le *temps mort* dans la présence du présent vivant, dans la forme générale de toute présence. (Derrida 1967: 99)

Readers who find it hard to interpret such sibylline pronouncements as these will find it difficult to determine exactly what relevance the concept of 'archi-écriture' might have to Derrida's interpretation of Saussure, or imagine what modern linguistics might have become if only Saussure had thought up 'archi-écriture' himself, instead of getting stuck in the old logocentric rut.

In a remarkable interview published four years after *De la grammatologie*, Derrida roundly denied that he had ever accused Saussure's 'project' of being logocentric or phonocentric, at least 'in its entirety' (Derrida 1972b: 30–1). This astonishing display of Humpty-Dumptyism doubtless, for some, bears witness to the invigorating flexibility of Derrida's thinking; while for others it points to the futility of arguing with a philosopher who reserves the right to call black white, or vice versa, even if only retrospectively.

Were it not for the prestige which Derrida currently enjoys in the sphere of 'cultural studies', and the number of students whose understanding of earlier figures in the Western tradition is coloured, if not entirely shaped, by what Derrida has written about them, it would hardly be worth the tedium of pointing out how and why Derrida's interpretation of Saussure is academically worthless. It is all the more necessary to question the perspective of teachers who claim that *De la grammatologie*, although a controversial text, nevertheless offers a 'close, sustained' reading of Saussure. There are indeed close, sustained readings of Saussure available to students (e.g. De Mauro, Sanders 1979, Gadet 1987, Holdcroft 1991), which differ from one another both in the interpretation of details and in overall assessment. But what Derrida offers is nothing remotely resembling a close, sustained reading. It is a caricature of Saussure, drawn in order to prop up a philosophical thesis of dubious worth.

CHAPTER ELEVEN

History's Saussure

J. R. Firth once divided all linguists of his generation into four classes: Saussureans, anti-Saussureans, post-Saussureans and non-Saussureans (Firth 1950: 179). As will be evident from the preceding chapters, what exactly it means to be a 'Saussurean' (or an 'anti-Saussurean', etc.) is by no means a cut-and-dried matter, for interpretations of Saussure's teaching have varied considerably. So Firth's pronouncement in the end tells us rather less than at first sight it might appear to. Even Firth, who regarded himself fairly unequivocally as a 'non-Saussurean', falls into that category only if we accept his interpretation of Saussure's position as 'mechanistic structuralism' (Firth 1950: 179–83). Nevertheless, the fact that this classification was suggested by a distinguished British linguist who had no connexions with the Geneva school not only confirms a perception of Saussure's pivotal position in the history of modern linguistics but raises the question of why, internationally, Saussure's ideas had come to be seen as so important.

It will perhaps seem to some readers that this book might more appropriately have been called *Saussure and his Misinterpreters* and is intended to teach a lesson about the difficulties of evaluating the materials he left to posterity. 'Misinterpretation' is, however, too prejudicial a term, for some of Saussure's interpreters were well aware that what they were doing was re-interpreting and modifying Saussure's insights rather than merely reformulating them. Or perhaps the book will be seen as implying that there is no 'right' way of reading Saussure. Personally, I would not wish to speak, as Godel finds it possible to do, of 'la vraie pensée de Saussure' (Godel 1961: 295); but that may reflect Godel's more intimate acquaintance with the available Saussurean sources and with the climate of thought that was Saussure's legacy to his colleagues and the Geneva school. On the other hand, avoiding expressions like 'la vraie pensée de Saussure' still leaves room for recognizing that there are interpretations of Saussure that are in various respects inaccurate or mistaken. If there is no 'right' way of reading Saussure there are nevertheless plenty of wrong ways.

Relativism has made such inroads into historical thinking that it is nowadays difficult to pass judgment on interpretations of Saussure (or any other important thinker) without immediately inviting a kind of criticism which relies on the assumption that all interpretations are equally valid (in their own terms, of course – an escape clause which reflects the academic paranoia that prompted it). It is possible to put forward accounts of particular scholars' interpretations of Saussure, accompanied by disclaimers to the effect that these must not be regarded as ' "true" in any kind of objective sense' (Joseph 1990: 75). But truth cannot be dismissed so easily. Unless there were *some* kind of objectivity attaching to one's account, objectivity of the kind which laid the account open, both in general and in detail, to judgments of being – or not being – well-founded, then publishing it would be of no more academic interest than publishing one's holiday plans or one's laundry list.

Saussure himself, in any case, did not belong to a generation accustomed to taking refuge behind relativist whitewash. It would never have occurred to him to qualify a statement about language or linguistics by a renunciation of any debt to objectivity. He might even have regarded that as a culpable evasion of intellectual responsibility. Intellectual responsibility, thus understood, implies historical accountability. Those inclined to contest this will doubtless suggest that it is illegitimate to appropriate such a loaded concept as 'intellectual responsibility' in this way. So let us rephrase it and say that Saussure did not belong to a generation who supposed that any old interpretation is as good as another. If he had indeed supposed that, then he would have had precious little to offer his own students as a new perspective on language. But that new perspective is exactly what seems to have inspired his teaching at Geneva. If this is right, Saussure would have had no qualms in 'correcting' some of his interpreters – perhaps even his students and his editors – by disagreeing with their formulation of his ideas, or even their (second-hand) account of his words.

The reason why it is worth taking some trouble to examine even highly questionable interpretations of Saussure is not that such investigations are essential prolegomena to producing *the* historically 'correct' interpretation. Nor is it even to show how negligent or fallible some prestigious interpreters were: or, more generally, how shaky are the theoretical foundations of modern linguistics. (That could be demonstrated with far less effort.) Rather, the point is that questionable or flawed interpretations, precisely because they are questionable or flawed, can be important as historical evidence. Particularly if, as in the cases that have been considered here, what emerges from studying and comparing them is that they were *not* the products of random error or personal idiosyncrasy, but are related in a coherent pattern. Once we see that pattern, we begin to understand not only how Saussure's proposals made it inevitable that he would always be fighting a posthumous intellectual battle on several fronts simultaneously, but also what is otherwise quite inexplicable: why his modest, faltering and inchoate attempt to set up a rational programme for his own discipline should have provided instead one of the central strands in twentieth-century thought.

Dubious interpretation alone explains little; for many thinkers have been construed in questionable ways, both in their day and by posterity, without thereby becoming catalysts for great intellectual movements. The question that needs to be addressed is why Saussure's teaching in particular came to fulfil this role. In order to address it, there is a broader historical context that needs to be taken into account – broader, that is to say, than is revealed by examining developments in Saussure's own academic discipline. As has often been observed, Saussure's influence was as important outside the domain of linguistics as within it. It has even been argued that, contrary to academic folk history, there never actually was a 'Saussurean revolution' within mainstream linguistics itself (Tobin 1990). That is doubtless overstating the case. What would be nearer the mark is to say that, except in the field of phonology, fewer linguists than one might have expected took up the challenge of working out any detailed application of Saussurean theory.

That observation, made with the benefit of historical hindsight, is as good a place as any to begin if we are interested in why Saussure's reputation took the form that has come down to us. That Saussurean theory should have borne its first fruits in (Prague school) phonology is perhaps surprising; but it is not a puzzle. Phonology deals with structures below the level of the linguistic sign, where the totality of what has to be accounted for is (relatively) easily surveyable and isolable. Once one tries to deal with the linguistic sign itself and the innumerable combinations in which it participates, there is a problem for the dedicated Saussurean. For Saussure's recommendation is that the linguist must start from the system as a whole and proceed by analysis to determine what the ultimate units actually are: 'c'est du tout solidaire qu'il faut partir pour obtenir par analyse les éléments qu'il renferme' (*CLG*: 157). These units, i.e. the signs, cannot simply be detected straight off by casual inspection (*CLG*: 149, 153); and they may turn out to be rather different from what might have been supposed initially. Readers of the *CLG* were never promised that it would be plain sailing (*CLG*: 139, 147). But the methodological problem is where to find and how to survey this 'tout solidaire' in the first place, before any analytic work on it can begin. By beginning with phonology, the problem can be sidestepped or at least deferred. For here (supposedly) the linguist is dealing with a limited number of phonic contrasts between meaningless phonic elements, i.e. with the organization of the *signifiant* alone, not the combination '*signifiant* plus *signifié*'. (A conflicting view would be that even this is a mistake; or at least cannot be justified without invoking a supplementary principle of 'double articulation' that Saussure himself never proposed. Such a principle certainly does not follow from his two established principles of arbitrariness and linearity.)

When it comes to the sign (as distinct from the *signifiant*) it is the holism of Saussure's conception of *langue* that is the analytic stumbling block. But that is the very feature of *langue* that fascinated non-linguists, who found it important and exciting. They could afford to, because it was not their professional job to work out the linguistic details. Furthermore, encouraged by reports of success in the new 'structuralist' phonology (where again the minutiae of the various consonants and vowels involved were of no particular interest to the non-linguist) they tended to assume that this success validated the whole Saussurean concept of the synchronic system.

Right from the start, therefore, the Saussurean synchronic system played an oddly ambivalent role. On the one hand, it was a central feature of the conceptual apparatus that made Saussurean thinking about language attractive to many who were not professional linguists. On the other hand, it set the linguists themselves a task which was methodologically quite problematic, to say the least. The problem, indeed, was never solved – other than below the level of the sign – either by the structuralists of the inter-war period or later by their generativist successors. (The latter fudged it by assuming that 'the sentence' was a well-defined unit and proceeding in effect to do old-fashioned sentence analysis dressed up in new algebra. This would doubtless have made Saussure throw up his hands in despair.) But many linguists who were not Saussureans nevertheless managed to convince themselves that the establishment of a theoretical distinction between the synchronic and the diachronic somehow justified once and for all the relegation of the study of linguistic change to a quite separate (and subordinate) compartment of their subject.

In America, in particular, it could be seen as underwriting in retrospect the work of Boas and other anthropologists who tried to record, on the basis of testimony from living speakers, the surviving Amerindian languages of that continent. It has even been claimed – with these anthropologists in mind – that 'the great majority of synchronic linguists have been Americans' (Sampson 1980: 57). But they could hardly have been thus baptized before the term 'synchronic linguistics' was imported from Europe and had a foundation in linguistic theory. Furthermore, the contents of the famous *Handbook of American Indian Languages* (1911) to which Boas and his collaborators contributed, although impressive, look far more like traditional grammarians' lists of forms and illustrative examples than like an account of any synchronic system in Saussure's sense. (If this is synchronic linguistics, then Horatio Hale was already a synchronic linguist when he brought back word lists and other 'philological' field notes from around the world on the United States expedition of exploration under Charles Wilkes in 1838–42.) Similarly, it is anachronistic to congratulate Sapir, as one of his admirers does (Hymes 1985: 600), on having produced a 'thoroughgoing synchronic analysis' of Takelma grammar in 1909 without any assistance from Saussure. The question is not whether Sapir was inspired by Saussure but simply: what were Sapir's options? Obviously, if no historical materials have survived, a linguist has no alternative but to rely on living informants. But if that counts as taking a 'synchronic' approach, it is synchrony by default. (Sapir's Takelma grammar seems in any case to have been based largely on the speech of a single informant, which makes it even odder to call it a synchronic account of a language. From a Saussurean point of view, that would be rather like confusing an analysis of the moves made by one player with an account of the rules of chess.)

The theoretical legitimation of synchronic linguistics after Saussure's introduction of the term soon meant in practice that students could become fully qualified academic linguists without bothering at all about the history of the language they were studying, even where historical materials were available. Description for description's sake – divorced from any pedagogic or normative purpose – became for linguists as influential and liberating a creed as art for art's sake had been for artists. Thus one of the main side effects of a focus on synchrony, particularly for linguists who had borrowed the term but not fully grasped the notion, was to make the analysis of some quite restricted corpus of contemporary linguistic 'data' a self-validating exercise. This was regarded as a legitimate 'synchronic' study, even though it was actually directly contrary to the holistic letter and spirit of Saussurean synchrony. Thus watered down, the doctrine of synchronic systems rapidly became accepted as a banal truism of modern linguistics.

One of the things that was frequently forgotten was Saussure's stipulation that the term *synchronique* be understood as an abbreviation for *idiosynchronique* (*CLG*: 128, 141). The latter term, which Saussure proposed in the Second Course, but found clumsy and subsequently dropped, had the prefix *idio-* to draw attention to the fact that 'il s'agit de l'ordre particulier, propre d'un idiome', as one of his students noted at the time (Engler: 1508 B35). In other words, *synchronie* and *langue* are not independently definable as technical terms. Once this is overlooked, as it often was, *synchronie* is open to misinterpretation, as Saussure feared (*CLG*: 128; Engler: 1508).

*   *   *

The question of why, outside the domain of linguistics, Saussure's synchronic system was such an attractive idea is more complex. It is often suggested that one reason was that it fitted in rather neatly with similar ideas that were becoming familiar in other disciplines in the late nineteenth and early twentieth centuries. Piaget argued that the first field in which structuralism made itself felt was mathematics, with the concept of the 'group', which in turn links up with the kind of formalization of logic associated with Russell and Whitehead's *Principia Mathematica* (Piaget 1968). Piaget is doubtless right in detecting conceptual parallels between mathematical structuralism and linguistic structuralism. It is also clear that, much later, generativists borrowed from mathematical logic such concepts as that of the 'well-formed formula' and tried to force English syntax into this Procrustean bed. It must be open to question, however, whether any of this comes very close to explaining something much more fundamental about the appeal of the synchronic system. For mathematics and mathematical logic have no social implications; or if they do, these are not obvious to the generality of educated people, or at least to those who would have regarded themselves as educated at the time when these ideas were being advanced. Similarly, although Cassirer is right to point out the parallels between structuralism in linguistics and the structuralism implied by theories of the electromagnetic field, as developed by Faraday and Maxwell (Cassirer 1944: 121), one must question whether these would have struck many people at the time.

What cannot be denied, however, is that not only in mathematics and physics but in philosophy, in art, in politics, in religion and in other areas, European culture was in a state of impending crisis in the early years of the twentieth century. Old assumptions and institutions were everywhere being challenged and found inadequate to meet the demands placed upon them. At international level this crisis culminated in what was rightly called 'the Great War', which destroyed not only lives in unprecedented numbers but beliefs and commitments that had been in place for generations. The Great War negated virtually every Enlightenment idea and ideal of human conduct. It demonstrated, on a massive scale and beyond any shadow of doubt, that the veneer of civilization in what purported to be the most civilized countries in the world was very thin, and that not far beneath its surface lay barbarity.

The trauma of this realization affected every corner of Western culture. Saussure did not live to witness it, but he seems in an uncanny way to have anticipated it; or at least to have seen what the consequences might be if the old assumptions about language and society were radically questioned or brusquely abandoned. Synchronic linguistics was eminently suited to be the 'new' linguistics for an era that wanted to forget the past. Its most conspicuous effect, evident to any lay person, was to place a strict limit on what the past could be held responsible for and, at the same time, to show that, when the debt to the past has been paid in full, we have not *even begun to explain* how language functions in the present. For the values built into and maintained by the synchronic system are invariably and necessarily current values: they are not, and *cannot be*, the values of earlier systems (in spite of what traditionalists may claim).

This is a very powerful idea. If it is valid in the case of language, might it not also be true over a much broader spectrum of human activities? This is the question which holds the key to understanding how and why Saussurean assumptions gradually infiltrate all kinds of discussion about the individual and society in the twentieth century. They begin to be taken as an implicit point of reference for such discussions, even when Saussure is not mentioned by name. Saussure himself, by invoking a future science of semiology, for which linguistics was to be a model, had suggested prophetically how the notion of synchronic systems could be extended beyond the domain of language.

In Saussurean synchronic linguistics, the irrelevance of prior systems is linked to and counterbalanced by the assumption that, whatever may have happened in the past, and however destructive the effects of change may apparently have been, the human *faculté de langage*, which for Saussure presides over signs in general (*CLG*: 27), has the internal resources to reorganize spontaneously and produce a new system no less coherent and effective than its predecessor. This optimistic message, which contrasted markedly with the dispiriting notions of decay and collapse so frequently invoked in nineteenth-century historical linguistics, was particularly welcome in the aftermath of the most disastrous war of recent times.

It could be read as underwriting not only a new departure in language but new departures in painting, in sculpture, in literature, in music and all other art forms employing sign systems of their own. It provided, in short, a *validation of modernity*.

So here straight away we have two attractive general ideas, (1) a moratorium on debts to the past, and (2) reliance on inherent regenerative powers, that are harmoniously associated in and by Saussure's concept of synchronic systems. At the same time, Saussure had managed to link this concept to some very traditional Western assumptions about language. One of these was the notion that linguistic communication involved the transference of ideas from the mind of the speaker to the mind of the hearer. This assumption concerning the telementational function of speech is the basis of the *CLG* account of the *circuit de la parole*. Another, closely linked to it, was the notion that a language provides a code, by means of which those who know the code can reliably exchange messages with one another (*CLG*: 31). These two assumptions dovetail, inasmuch as the latter provides the explanation of how the process postulated by the former would be possible (Harris 1981: 9 ff.). Their dovetailing goes back, via Locke, at least as far as Plato (Harris 1987: 205 ff.).

The first important point to note is that the novel notion of languages as synchronic systems does not begin to have much intellectual leverage until coupled with the far older notion of linguistic communication as a telementational process carried out on the basis of a public verbal code. Only then does its explanatory potential become apparent. That is why theorists who are not keen to link language with communication and who reject or play down the idea that communication was always the primary function of human speech (Chomsky and Hjelmslev would both be examples) tend also to be those who construe Saussure as advancing a thesis about what is present in the mind ('linguistic knowledge') rather than a thesis about what goes on in society ('speech activity').

Connected with this is the point already mentioned above: that synchrony is itself a more complicated notion than might appear on the surface. (That is one reason why reducing Saussure's ideas to a set of simple dichotomies like '*synchronic* versus *diachronic*', as the usual text-book accounts do, is the worst possible way to set about expounding them. The result is not to explain Saussure's teaching but to dismember it.) The *CLG* points out that linguistics is not the only discipline where a distinction between the synchronic and the diachronic is needed, and the example singled out for special mention, significantly, is that of economics (*CLG*: 115) *for this too is a science which has to deal with values*. It is this which necessitates the synchronic/diachronic distinction, not the mere fact that one must not confuse the present with the past. Thus, for example, a map drawn fifty years ago may now be out of date; but that does not require a fundamental separation between synchronic carto-graphy and diachronic cartography. Synchronic cartography, for Saus-sure, would be a nonsense; for cartography is not required to deal with values, just with information. (Which is not to deny that the cartographer needs a system of signs in order to represent the information that the map purports to give. But that is a quite different point. A map can give information about the past just as easily as information about the present, or even about changes over time, without requiring any drastic revision of the concept 'map'.)

Synchrony, to repeat, was never just a chronological notion. Synchrony entails grammar (in the Saussurean, not the traditional, sense of *gram-maire*), unlike diachrony: 'diachronique équivaut à non-grammatical, comme synchronique à grammatical' (*CLG*: 194). Saussure's editors grasped this, but some of his interpreters did not. And once that essential point is lost, it becomes very difficult to see why Saussure's ideas should have struck anyone as original or exciting. Bloomfield is an example of an interpreter who could not see that they were at all remarkable, because he misidentified 'synchronic' with 'descriptive' and 'diachronic' with 'his-torical'. Bloomfield is happy to concede that 'in order to describe a language one needs no historical knowledge whatever' (Bloomfield 1933: 19). Quite so. But it is equally true that in order to describe an armchair or an omelette one needs no knowledge of the history of furniture or the history of cookery. The point is trivial and entirely misses what is special about systems of values.

The same misunderstanding affects the reasons for regarding synchro-nic studies as taking priority over diachronic studies. It is not because the linguistic past is more difficult of access than the linguistic present (the reason given by Bloomfield in 1914). That is not Saussure's reason. Nor is Saussure's the argument given by Jespersen, who maintains that historical linguistics 'must always be based on the description of those stages of a language which are directly accessible to us' (Jespersen 1924: 31). (Which is fairly obviously false in any case.) The priority of the synchronic, for Saussure, rests squarely on the claim that the synchronic system is the only relevant psychological reality for current speakers of the language. What may or may not be known about the past counts for little or nothing.

It is essential, therefore, not to construe synchronic systems as systems which just happen to be synchronic (as opposed to other systems which are not). Divorced from the qualification 'synchronic', the notion of a 'system' in itself does not take us very far. A system is some kind of organized complex. As Mounin points out, it is very easy to suppose at first that Saussure was just continuing the traditional use of the term *système* as found in the work of the comparative grammarians and in earlier discussions of language going back to the eighteenth century (Mounin 1968: 59 ff.). This is the way elementary grammar books still use the term when they refer to the 'vowel system' or the 'system of tenses' in such-and-such a language. Such systems are easily described by listing a set of forms and explaining their usage, just as one might describe a tool kit by identifying the various shapes of the individual tools and explaining what each is for. A system of *values* is something quite different, whether in the sphere of language or any other. Simple machines are systems; but they are not systems of values. Furthermore, we do not need to know anything about the history of machines in order to analyse how they work. Being acquainted with the history of the bicycle, going back to the penny-farthing and even earlier models, is quite irrelevant to explaining how any given bicycle functions. It might even be argued that some such machines also exemplify holistic systems, insofar as interdependencies between the various working parts ensure that any internal alteration or adjustment will affect the functioning of the whole. None of this is in the least perplexing or intriguing to anyone brought up in a modern industrialized society. A child can explain such things with a simple diagram (and has no need to resort to technical terms in order to do so). But we enter a different conceptual world when the notion of a holistic working system is harnessed metaphorically to the traditional notions of telementation and code-based communication. And that is exactly what Saussure's *circuit de la parole* does. (Also with the help of a simple diagram.)

What has happened here to transform a rather humdrum idea into a very adventurous one? The gain comes from the metaphorical harnessing. For we are now looking in a new way not only at how our minds work but *at the same time* at how certain social processes work. And that is why those interpreters of Saussure who divorce the notion of synchrony from either its psychological or its social implications, or both, are not giving Saussure anything like his due.

This, then, is another part of the general pattern of 'interpreting Saussure' that falls into place. There are interpreters who fail, for one reason or another, to see how the Saussurean synchronic system provides a modern revision or up-dated version of a certain view of language(s) that is deeply entrenched in the Western tradition. Too deeply entrenched to be easily overthrown; and Saussure in any case had no wish to do that. For this view is, in a sense, the whole basis of Western education. If it is wrong, it becomes difficult to see how learning from teachers or from books would be possible in the first place. And if that is not possible, then there could be no linguistics (of the kind that Saussure and his colleagues were concerned with) anyway.

Saussure is in this respect a very conservative revolutionary (or revolutionary conservative). His distinctive contribution to the traditional account of language is two-fold. The part we have been dealing with first is the way in which he claims, via the concept of synchronic systems, that language is one of those areas of human experience in which it is not only possible but *necessary* to separate the past from the present *if we wish to understand either*. This was – and has hitherto remained – too iconoclastic a prescription for many people to swallow. So they have tended to dilute it by proposing that all this means is that linguists should not conflate, in linguistic studies, historical information with contemporary observation. It does mean that, to be sure; and the *CLG* gives some well-chosen examples of the conflation. But anyone who supposes that is *all* it means will never be able to understand the impact Saussure's ideas made on modern thought. Or why they appeared at just the right time.

Even if we take the most diluted version of Saussure's synchronic thesis, can anyone suppose that it raises no further questions concerning the human condition? Can it be *only* in the sphere of human speech that the past cannot explain the present and values are to be understood solely in terms of reciprocal relations? As mentioned above, Saussure himself pointed out that the same holds for economic systems. But if the notion of a synchronic system applies both to language and to economics, why should it not apply to *all* human activities where signs and values are involved? Does not every culture, including its language, beliefs, institutions and forms of organization, constitute a single synchronic mega-system? Is not this cultural whole the ultimate *objet* of a Saussurean semiology? Once we ask that, we are no longer dealing just with guidelines for linguists but with a philosophical thesis of far deeper import. We are in effect considering the synchronic system as a (possible) abstract model for understanding many different aspects of civilization. Adopting such a model entails taking what would have been regarded by many in Saussure's day as a very subversive view of the limits of historical explanation in general. For the nineteenth century, evolutionary processes in the end accounted for most things: for Saussure, they accounted for far less than was generally supposed, and for the most important things not at all.

The second aspect of the Saussurean synchronic system that needs to be considered is its bi-planarity. Synchronicity does not, in itself, entail a specifically bi-planar sign. But if that proviso is added, then everything depends on the two planes involved. For Saussure, the two planes were acoustic and conceptual. Once this restriction is granted, an important corollary follows: no appeal to anything else is needed in order to explain how languages can function as instruments of telementation. (In this respect, Saussure's theory differs radically from – is incommensurable with – those of Aristotle or Locke.) The implication is that however much the external world alters, however much is destroyed or replaced, however many lives are lost or cities devastated, however many Great Wars there are, it makes no difference. The synchronic system of correlations between acoustic images and concepts is an automatic product of the *faculté de langage*. That is also why an appeal to the past or to prior systems is irrelevant for an understanding of how any given system operates in the present. The language faculty systematizes – *makes* such systems – by imposing a certain structure of relations on the two otherwise undifferentiated continua of sounds on the one hand and thought on the other (*CLG*: 155–6). The completed systematization, to be sure, is highly complex; but nevertheless, logically and psychologically, that is the basic operation. Those interpreters who, like Chomsky, regard Saussure as proposing a simplistic and impoverished view of linguistic ('surface') structure are mistaking for an account of grammatical relations what is manifestly put forward as something quite different; namely, the basis on which the synchronic system articulates values.

It is not any one of the above features but their combination that makes the model of the Saussurean synchronic system seem so relevant to the problem of coping not just with linguistic change but with cultural upheavals in general. With the regeneration of languages thus assured, life can resume, communication can be re-established, education and all the other language-related processes can be reinstated, *whatever the disruption*. This was a message – social and psychological, rather than narrowly linguistic – that was desperately needed in Europe in the years after 1918, from whatever source it might come. It actually appeared in print – historical coincidence – in the year 1916. And it was a message far more important to the twentieth century than, say, messages about the curvature of space or the speed of light or human genetics, because it had very immediate practical implications.

*   *   *

For that very reason, some of the implications were not uncontentious. The collapse of the Austro-Hungarian empire and the Treaty of Versailles had altered the political map of Europe. National boundaries had been redrawn. The geographical relationship between the distribution of states and the distribution of languages had been changed (apparently overnight and by fiat). But that in a way confirmed the Saussurean assumption that the linguistic facts were more fundamental. It was up to politicians to see sense and respect the linguistic facts, not up to linguistics to conform to the decisions of politicians. This was not simply – or ever – a debating point. With Saussure's identification of the *masse parlante* as the indispensable social factor that stabilizes and maintains a given system of values, the study of language(s) staked a claim to carry some weight in discussing the 'realities' of modern Europe.

For the Saussurean synchronic system, whatever else it was taken to imply, certainly implied the existence of a single, internally coherent language. Two separate *langues* combined in the same synchronic system would have been a Saussurean contradiction in terms. Saussure had said – or his editors had made him say – that 'c'est dans une large mesure la langue qui fait la nation' (*CLG*: 40). It is not difficult to see how, in certain ethnic situations, such a message would be political dynamite. And still is.

That is not all. There are two other related points. First, a synchronic system might seem to imply a monolithic social order without internal divisions of any linguistic note; or at least a society in which such divisions can be ignored because of a single linguistic standard educationally established and available to all. Second, each synchronic system is a law unto itself: 'la langue est un système qui ne connaît que son ordre propre' (*CLG*: 43). It is strictly autonomous vis-à-vis not only all earlier systems but any co-existing systems. There is no hierarchy of dependencies relating one such system to another; no equivalent of the familiar family-tree model so frequently employed in historical linguistics.

Thus the notion of synchronic systems, although in some respects attractive, could hardly fail to bring in its wake a train of awkward sociopolitical questions about its actual implementation, particularly in a post-1918 Europe shaped by politicians who had sat round a table and drawn lines on a map. According to Newmeyer, it was because these implications were realized that structuralism was suppressed in some countries:

Both Nazi Germany and fascist Italy had officially condemned structuralism as incompatible with the ideology of the state. During the Nazi period, the pages of German linguistic journals were filled with vivid descriptions of how the German soul manifests itself in its people's masterful language. Likewise, in Italy in this era, many accounts of language consisted of a peculiar mixture of aesthetics and nation-worship, as scholars strove at one and the same time to identify the features of a particular language with the presumed spiritual characteristics of its speakers and to demonstrate the superiority of Italian as a medium of creative expression. The state sponsorship of such an approach to linguistic matters went along with official disapproval of structural linguistics. Indeed, practically no structural linguistics was done at all in German and Italy in this period. Structuralism, with its value-free analysis of individual languages and equal attention to all of them, regardless of the race or cultural level of their speakers, was anathema to official ideology in those countries. (Newmeyer 1986: 37–8)

As regards Germany, this account has been seriously questioned by Hutton, who writes in *Linguistics and the Third Reich*:

any notion that structuralism was repressed under National Socialism must be dismissed as a complete myth [. . .], as is the notion of a delayed reception of the *Cours* in Germany [. . .]. Nor is there any corollary between the holding of racist views and anti-structuralism: Eberhard Zwirner, the founder of a specific branch of structuralist linguistics (*Phonometrie*), is a case in point [. . .].

Saussure's significance as a linguistic theorist was recognized in Germany immediately on the publication of the *Cours*, as the perceptive review by Schuchardt (1917) shows. Saussure's *Cours* had been assimilated without too great difficulty into inter-war neo-Kantian 'organicist' linguistics, as Stroh [. . .] illustrates. In Weisgerber's writings of the late 1920s and early 1930s Saussure's *Cours* is taken for granted as part of the intellectual background. Mathesius (1935/6) used the term 'synchronisch' without direct reference to Saussure. [. . .] In an explicitly structuralist article, Funke, writing from Bern, recorded in a footnote [. . .] that he had presented the material in talks at the universities of Bonn and Marburg in 1942, i.e. in the heart of the German academic establishment at the height of the war. (Hutton 1999: 18)

Similar doubts must be raised concerning linguistics and fascism in Italy. There were, indeed, linguists who were keen supporters of Mussolini. Bertoni (according to Hall 1963: 70) even wore the black shirt in lectures and at examinations. But what Bertoni objected to, as an adherent of the 'idealist' school of linguistics, was not so much Saussure as the Neogrammarians and their blind 'sound laws'. His own distinction between *lingua* and *linguaggio* is quite reminiscent of Saussure's between *langue* and *parole*: he might even be seen as a theorist who championed the claims of a *linguistique de la parole* against those of *linguistique de la langue*. One critic speaks disapprovingly of Bertoni's 'inability to see beyond the level of the individual idiolect' (Hall 1963: 69). But that is a different matter from rejecting structuralism for reasons of political conviction or ideological principle.

What is even odder about the notion that Saussure would have been automatically repugnant to the followers of Hitler or Mussolini is that the synchronic system lends itself very readily to nationalistic ideological versions. The *langue* of a community provides all its members with a common stock of linguistically communicable ideas, and is to that extent the guarantor of a common mentality or identity of outlook. Any 'new' ideas have to be introduced via the processes of *parole* and provided with adequate linguistic expression. It is but a short step from this to drawing the twin conclusions that the ideal state will have a uniform language which does not tolerate deviations, and that state control of *langue* and *parole* is one of the most potent weapons an authoritarian government has at its disposal for inculcating its own views and suppressing opposition. Setting up ministries of propaganda à la Goebbels would be incomprehensible if this kind of thinking had been utterly discredited. Such regimes ought to have been erecting public statues of Saussure, not sacking structuralist professors for their structuralism (if they ever did).

In Russia, Voloshinov had disappeared during the Stalinist purges of the 1930s, and his disappearance did not exactly encourage any further attempt to discuss Saussurean theory from a Marxist perspective. But it is interesting that years later, when Stalin himself intervened publicly in a linguistic debate in 1950, what he said has a detectable Saussurean subtext, even though Saussure is not mentioned. The issue is the relationship between the linguistic community and its language. Stalin rejects the idea that revolution makes any difference to the language, even when accompanied by sweeping economic changes. This is because, although economic structure is indeed the basis of society, a society's language is not, in Marxist terms, part of the superstructure (Stalin 1954: 7 ff.). So even the most radical reforms affecting property, class relations, political institutions, etc. have no effect on the language, other than in the relatively superficial matter of introducing a few new words. It would be difficult to imagine a more direct (albeit veiled) endorsement of Saussure's claim that society 'est liée à la langue telle qu'elle est' (*CLG*: 104). Like Saussure, Stalin treats sociolectal variation within a language ('class dialects') as negligible and of no particular theoretical significance. A language is 'created as a single language for the society, common to all members of that society, as the common language of the whole people' (Stalin 1954: 10). Thus in Russia there is a single national language (Russian) which serves all classes and interest groups alike. Stalin chides those comrades who have convinced themselves that a 'national language is a fiction' (which, in effect, was Voloshinov's judgment on Saussure's *langue*). Stalin also believes, like Saussure, that thought is impossible without language: there are some who claim that thoughts arise in the mind of man in 'a naked form', without linguistic clothing, but that 'is absolutely wrong' (Stalin 1954: 51). Like Saussure, Stalin upholds the traditional Western doctrines of telementation and code-based communication. Language, he proclaims, is 'an instrument with the help of which people communicate with one another, exchange thoughts and understand each other' (Stalin 1954: 30). It 'makes possible the exchange of thoughts in human society'. It must be understood by all: indeed, 'without a language understood by a society and common to all its members, that society must cease to produce, must disintegrate and cease to exist as a society' (Stalin 1954: 30). Even Saussure had not gone so far as to claim that the alternative to maintaining the synchronic system was anarchy, Babel and social collapse. In this astonishing intervention, Stalin disavows any expertise as a linguist: however, 'as to Marxism in linguistics, as in other social sciences, this is something directly in my field' (Stalin 1954: 7). The claim to cathedratic authority is undisguised. These are the right answers, so all argument can now cease. As Calvet observes, what is remarkable is not only what Stalin says but his overt recognition, by this pronouncement, of the political implications of linguistic theory (Calvet 1975: 66–7); and, one might add, his tacit acceptance of the Saussurean framework of discussion.

It would be a mistake, however, to try to gauge the level of acceptance of Saussurean ideas by adding up nods of approval or frowns of disapproval from governments, their agencies or their political supporters. Nor do we learn very much from counting mentions of Saussure in learned publications. A much more difficult assessment is required. Structuralist ideas would have filtered down to many people whose acquaintance with the *CLG* was second- or third-hand, and who may not have realized what the precise textual source of those ideas was, or labelled them explicitly as 'Saussurean'. Even at this level some configuration of such ideas might have seemed to offer a sensible and relevant conceptual scaffolding for the discussion of language and language-related issues. That may sound altogether too vague and evasive for scholars who like precise bibliographical references and footnotes before they will pay any attention to anything. But history cannot be captured in references and footnotes. One should not suppose that history's Saussure can be, either; even in the narrowly academic domain. It is worth quoting in this connexion the observation of one editor, commenting on a collection of linguistic papers published in America between 1925 and 1956, who writes:

> The position of Saussure in linguistics today is very much like that of Ibsen in the drama. Only now and then is he spoken of, and then in a ritualistic way. The

innocent bystander or the neophyte gets the impression that this or that detail derives from him and that all else, for which he is customarily not cited, is independent of him. Actually, the inverse of this would be nearer the truth. His contribution is rather a whole mode of thought [. . .] (Joos 1957: 18)

The same writer goes on to note that, apart from linguists who had read the *CLG*, there were as many who had 'got it second-hand'. How? In 'an atmosphere saturated with those ideas [. . .]' (Joos 1957: 18). What is important is not so much separating the first-hand from the second-hand, but how and why the atmosphere – both inside and outside university departments of linguistics – came to be 'saturated with those ideas' at all. And the short answer to that is the aftermath of the First World War, which made Saussure's ideas about language, signs and values (whether one agreed with them or not) seem to be not just theoretical abstractions but thoughts both timely and pertinent to the anxieties of a socially, politically and economically unstable Western world.

*   *   *

It is at first sight surprising that after the Second World War Saussure's ideas achieved even wider diffusion and a higher profile than after the First. For we are now dealing with a generation that knew that 'the War to end all wars' had failed to do so. Here was another war with even more horrendous physical and moral consequences than its predecessor. (It saw the implementation of a racist policy of genocide on one side, and the deliberately indiscriminate bombing of civilian populations on the other. It saw the systematic propagation of official lies on both sides. Plus a premonition of global catastrophe in the 'scientific' development and use of atomic power for military purposes.) This was not just war as hitherto recognized by military historians, but 'total war'.

We consequently see, in the aftermath of that second conflict, a 'second look' at Saussure; inevitably so, for the optimism that could have been kindled by the perpetual synchronic promise – a new start and new values for the next generation – now seemed hollow. What might have been regarded in 1918 as an unfortunate one-off mistake never to be repeated (i.e. 'the Great War') now looked like being a recurrent phenomenon. What use was a new start for the world every twenty-five years?

It may or may not be coincidence that the theorist who had all along refused to accept the Saussurean concept of synchrony and denounced it as illusory, namely Jakobson, was a Russian Jewish emigré who had been uprooted as a political consequence of the 1914–18 war, was driven into exile again during the 1939–45 war, and ended up making a highly successful career in America. He spoke and wrote several languages, had an abiding interest in historical continuities, and was a cosmopolitan in every sense of the word. His whole life was, from a certain point of view, a pragmatic refutation of the synchronic system. He adapted. But without discontinuous leaps. Adaptation, and the possibility of adaptation, were for him far more cogent 'realities' than discrete systems. One might perhaps argue that this experience was possible only because he was always shifting at the same social level from one local version of a certain form of academic life to another local version, and because most of the languages he was familiar with were either phylogenetically related or typologically not dissimilar, and because Jewish communities in any case are not so different in different cities of the Western world. If he had been forced to emigrate alone to some totally different environment – say a village in New Guinea – that might have altered his linguistic perspective rather more dramatically.

Something very like that had happened to Firth's mentor Malinowski, who, as a result, began to look at language from a quite non-European point of view (Malinowski 1923). But it is interesting that Malinowski, who found Saussure's concept of *langue* 'totally useless for his empirical studies' (Szymura 1988: 108), nevertheless saw language as the key to a society's culture. In his posthumously published *Freedom and Civilization*, nowadays little read, Malinowski addressed what he saw as the moral evil of war. His conclusion, as an anthropologist, that 'language and value are [. . .] intrinsically related' (Malinowski 1947: 206) has an oddly Saussurean ring to it, coming from a 'non-Saussurean'.

Although cultural systems that can collapse or be blown away every quarter of a century are not very satisfactory for anyone concerned, it is not much consolation to turn instead to a belief in continuous (albeit 'structured') adaptation, which seems no less poorly equipped to deal with repeated cataclysms. The effect of not just one but two world wars was, predictably, to foster scepticism concerning structuralist explanations of culture in general. It was no less predictable that Saussure, seen in retrospect as one of the leading theorists of structuralism, should come under increasingly critical scrutiny from 'post-structuralists'. Where had Saussure gone wrong? This became the focus of post-structuralist discontent. As a false prophet, Saussure began to acquire an even bigger reputation than he had as a true one. Might not structuralism have been in part responsible for the intellectual and moral blindness that had allowed fascism to flourish unchecked?

The synchronic system, as applied to language and related cultural manifestations, now came to be regarded as a reflection of 'totalitarian' thinking. The rationale for this condemnation can already be seen, shorn of any theoretical trappings, in a widely discussed work whose author never mentions Saussure and would have been surprised to find himself classified as a 'post-structuralist'. Four years after the end of the Second World War, George Orwell published his novel *Nineteen Eighty-Four*, with its chilling vision of a future in which systematic mind-control would be exercised through systematic language-control. The acclaim that this book received and the controversy it aroused tell us more than any pronouncements by theorists or politicians about how the Saussurean 'mode of thought' about language was now viewed by many people. It represented a threat, not a promise.

The connexion between *Nineteen Eighty-Four* and the *CLG* did not go unnoticed, although no one supposed that Orwell had actually read the latter work. But what one commentator called the 'strange parallel between the Saussurean *langue* myth and the Orwellian Newspeak parable' was not strange at all. It provides an interesting example of that second- and third-hand diffusion of Saussurean ideas which had been in train ever since the *CLG* was published. The link between Orwell and Saussure was the Cambridge academic C. K. Ogden. Ogden had been one of Saussure's most trenchant critics (Ogden and Richards 1923) but in spite of that he seems to have seized on two of Saussure's ideas and made them the theoretical point of departure for a project of his own. (Whether he consciously thought of these ideas as 'Saussurean' is another question, but it seems more than a coincidence that they are so clearly expressed in the *CLG*.) The first idea was that a language (*langue*) both provides and interconnects all the concepts its users need for analytic thought, and the second was that, because of the structure of the system, if one word were removed from the vocabulary, the effect would be to 'redistribute' its meaning over neighbouring words (*CLG*: 160). It might seem to follow from this that it would in theory be possible to remove any number of 'unnecessary' words and still be left with a coherent system for expressing the same basic range of thought.

This is the foundational contention underlying Ogden's project, Basic English. Ogden believed that it would be possible 'to say almost everything we normally desire to say' with just 850 English words if these were 'scientifically selected' (Ogden 1944: 9). The intention was that this 'scientifically' reduced form of English should become an international auxiliary language. This proposal was supported politically by the British wartime premier, Winston Churchill. Although as a socialist Orwell welcomed in principle the idea of an international language, he also

found the notion of promoting one's own national language for this
purpose 'imperialistic' (Orwell 1944: 108). Whether Newspeak was
intended to be a parody of Basic English is debatable (Bolton 1984:
152). What is certain is that Orwell, like many others, saw the dystopian
possibilities of a single 'scientifically' reduced language and the potential
threat not just to freedom of speech but to freedom of thought. Insofar as
this can be seen as continuing an old theme about the deceptions of
language, going back at least as far as Bacon's 'idols of the market', there is
nothing very original in it; what is new is the idea that the whole
synchronic system might impose a deceptive view of the world on its
speakers. It is here that the Saussurean notion of systematicity bites: that
is to say, the system, being holistic, is closed and there is no way out of it.
It is structured in such a way that no internal contradiction is detectable:
the deceptive concepts and values are mutually self-supporting. In
Newspeak there are no words such as *honour*, *justice* or *democracy*, while
Big brother is ungood, although a grammatically possible sentence, expresses a self-evident absurdity. In short, a language – conceived in this
way – becomes a prison for the mind. It is ironic that Ogden saw Basic
English as being needed to counteract the psychological and cultural
consequences of two world wars. It would afford a means 'by which the
mind of man may be lifted out of its narrow prison house' (Ogden 1944:
171). Nor can he have been unconscious of echoing Saussure and
extending Saussure's argument when he wrote: 'What makes a nation
is a common language. What will make men international will be a
common language' (Ogden 1944: 171).

   The idea that uniformity of language determines uniformity of outlook
in turn links up with a theory that had become a focus of debate in post-
war American linguistics: the so-called 'Sapir–Whorf hypothesis' (Hoijer
1954). Although various versions of this theory were on offer, and none
was articulated with very great clarity or precision, they had in common
the notion that we analyse 'reality' in accordance with the mental
categories imposed upon it and us by our native language. Speakers of
different languages will thus see things differently. 'The worlds in which
different societies live are distinct worlds, not merely the same world with
different labels attached' (Sapir 1928: 162). Although neither Sapir nor
Whorf explicitly presented this as a Saussurean idea, and may not have
derived it consciously from Saussure, it is unlikely that as linguists they
were unaware that it fitted perfectly with Saussure's conception of each
langue as an independent synchronic system (as distinct, for instance,
from rival behaviourist accounts of language, according to which one
would expect the same stimuli from the same external environment to

give rise to correspondingly similar linguistic structures, i.e. 'the same world with different labels attached'). Nor is it likely that awareness of Saussurean theory played no role in influencing linguists' reception of the Sapir–Whorf hypothesis. There is a link between the two, however one looks at it; for exactly the kind of example that Saussure gives to show that different languages have different *valeurs* (the grammar of plurality in French and Sanskrit; *CLG*: 161) is used by Whorf to support his own version of linguistic relativity (the category of plural in Hopi compared with English, French and German; Whorf 1939: 138). To what extent Saussure would have approved the positions taken by Sapir or by Whorf is another question and one which cannot be pursued here.

Enfin Lévi-Strauss vint. In retrospect, Lévi-Strauss looks like the last of a generation prepared to give Saussure the benefit of the doubt. Introduced to Saussure's ideas at the height of a war inspired by nationalism and racial hatred (of which he himself was a victim), Lévi-Strauss sought desperately – even perversely – to derive from Saussurean structuralism an approach to cultural analysis that would in the end demonstrate the brotherhood of man. It would reveal hidden universal patterns underlying the superficial diversity of human customs and beliefs. Optimism of this order was not shared by many of Lévi-Strauss's younger contemporaries. In the end, in Lévi-Strauss's hands, structuralism became 'neither a theory nor a method but a "way of looking at things"' (Leach 1973: 37). The question in that case was whether it was a desirable or undistorted way of looking at things.

The climate of opinion in which structuralism came under suspicion as the product of, or as being associated with, a 'totalitarian' mode of thought was that of the Cold War. Many European left-wing intellectuals were disenchanted, to say the least, on finding that after the defeat of fascism there was no new dawn visible in Western culture. On the contrary, it was dominated by the same bourgeois values and capitalist economics that had presided over the emergence of fascism in the first place. Avant-garde critics began looking for ways of turning Saussurean ideas against Saussure. The most successful practitioner of this form of intellectual blood sport was Barthes, who claimed that Saussure had completely misunderstood the relationship between language and other sign systems. This was doubtless because Saussure's upper-middle-class view of society was quite untouched by the revelations of Marx. Saussure was a naive believer in 'democracy' who had taken this idealized social order as his model for a *linguistique de la langue* (Barthes 1973). He had consequently failed to see how simplistic it was in the modern world to regard the *masse parlante* as the custodian of *la langue* and 'collective ratification' as providing both its day-to-day maintenance and the criterion for accepting or rejecting change. The reality, as Barthes saw it, was quite different. The control of language, through the control of various forms of public discourse, was the way in which the ruling class imposed its values on the rest of society. Barthes's *Système de la mode*, published in 1967, but written between 1957 and 1963, is a *tour de force* in its demonstration of how, using Saussurean tools, one can reach a quasi-Marxist conclusion. Barthes's analysis of the language of fashion shows how a skilful manipulation of terminology can create the concepts that commerce requires to promote its own products. The *masse parlante* is not in control of this process, but the victim of it. 'La raison en est, on le sait, d'ordre économique. Calculatrice, la société industrielle est condamnée à former des consommateurs qui ne calculent pas [. . .] (Barthes 1967: 9).

Chomsky's ambiguous relationship with Saussure illustrates yet another post-war attempt to validate a 'science of language' in the wake of – but in spite of – what Saussure had already begun. For Chomsky, star pupil of an American generation brought up to regard the brain as a flesh-and-blood computer – for whom, therefore, language has to be reducible to 'rules' in a cerebral 'program' – Saussure is something of an embarrassment. After an awkward period of flirtation, and a temporary marriage of convenience, Chomsky resorts to the ancient strategy of cutting the Gordian knot. The 'social' and the 'cognitive' aspects of *langue* are henceforth to be treated as quite separate. One – universal – part (misleadingly called by the traditional term 'grammar') is accountable to the ineluctable processes of genetics and evolution: hence safe in the hands of the natural sciences, who nevertheless have yet to deliver on their share of the academic bargain. The other – endlessly diverse – part of language is shaped by the unpredictable dictates of social forces: thus abandoned to the vagaries of human whim, ignorance and turpitude. Either way, in Chomsky's doomsday scenario, Saussure as a theorist loses out for having supposed that *langue* was an internally coherent concept in the first place. He failed to distinguish (unlike Chomsky) between 'E-language' and 'I-language'.

An even more sweeping indictment of Saussure's view of language came from another quarter. Derrida's *De la grammatologie* (1967), although ostensibly presented as a philosophical inquiry into concepts of writing, is basically an attack on structuralism, in which Saussure is indicted as the main theoretical culprit and Lévi-Strauss as his chief acolyte. At the same time, a strained reading of Rousseau presents the author of the *Essai sur l'origine des langues* as an unwitting precursor with 'proto-structuralist leanings' (Howells 1998: 29). Arraigned alongside these three are various other structuralists, including Jakobson, Hjelmslev and Martinet. All this is part of a more inclusive condemnation of the alleged 'logocentrism' of the Western tradition. Unlike Barthes, Derrida is relatively indifferent to the shortcomings of Saussure's account of the relationship between *la langue* and *la masse parlante*. Why then, one must ask, does such a burden of guilt fall on Saussure and his followers if, as Derrida claims, the logocentrc point of view has been pervasive in Western thinking from at least the time of Plato onwards?

The answer is that Derrida's ultimate objective is to discredit certain philosophical lines of reasoning about the human condition. Here again one can hardly doubt that the cumulative disillusion left by two world wars has played a major role in forming what is basically a sceptical view of human self-understanding. Unlike Chomsky, who separates 'Orwell's problem' from 'Plato's problem' (Chomsky 1986), believes that 'the world is out of control' (Chomsky 1991), and seems to hold American governments and corporations collectively responsible for most of mankind's woes since 1945, Derrida offers a deeper diagnosis of what has gone wrong. Central to this diagnosis is the conviction that Western thinking has for centuries been based on a meretricious view of language. Rather than pursue the familiar linguistic arguments about how words relate to things and ideas, Derrida chooses a flanking attack, calculated to surprise the fortifications of traditional Western philosophy by exposing a hitherto unsuspected weakness. This weakness is the relationship between speech and writing, hitherto regarded as a marginal and uncontroversial issue of no particular philosophical importance. (Derrida's pursuit of this strategy is imaginative and original, although its inspiration almost certainly comes from Plato's *Letter VII* and other passages on writing in Plato.)

Derrida wishes to bring this issue to bear on the whole question of seeing man as the 'rational animal', i.e. the animal with *logos*, and hence on the way philosophers (and others) have reasoned about human actions and responsibilities throughout the Western tradition. If language is assumed to be the prime manifestation of *logos* in human affairs, then all human actions are presumably to be judged at the bar of reason itself. Hence the importance attached to the verbal mode of discussion so highly valued by Western teachers. Language is assumed to provide a neutral medium which makes available for its users a means of reasoning objectively about the world and their experience of it. The credibility of this 'rational' discourse will be undermined at a very basic level if it can be shown to rely on a question-begging view of the 'nature of language'. Hence Derrida's attack on the doctrine of the primacy of speech, which is presented in *De la grammatologie* as a 'metaphysical' assumption.

Inasmuch as Saussure unequivocally champions that doctrine, there is no mystery about why Derrida should have focussed on the *CLG* as a key text. But that does not quite explain why structuralism should be made to bear the brunt of the general assault on logocentrism, particularly when one considers that structuralism may be – and has been – seen as implying a profound critique of a more traditional view of the relationship between language and reality (that Derrida likewise rejects). Saussure explicitly refuses to endorse the old assumption that language presents a simple reflection of an external reality independently given. So does Derrida. So why is Derrida's condemnation of structuralism so emphatic? The reason is that Saussure's view of language is uncomfortably close to Derrida's own; far too close for comfort. Saussure therefore has to be exposed as a theorist enmeshed in contradiction, in order to reserve for Derrida the historical honours of introducing a radically modern philosophy of language. (Austin has to be denounced for a similar reason: Derrida 1972a: 382 ff.)

It is no coincidence, therefore, that what Derrida picks on for inter-rogation in the *CLG* is the one topic – writing – on which Saussure can be shown fairly clearly to be following in the well-worn footprints of many 'logocentric' precursors. Even on this, however, Derrida does not present the full picture. Had he done so, Saussure's semiology of writing would have emerged as significantly different from that perpetuated in the tradition which goes back to Aristotle (Harris 2000: 39 ff.). But that would not have suited Derrida's book at all. For then Saussure would steal the limelight as the revolutionary modern thinker, while Derrida would be one more victim of the endemic scriptism of Western academia (as in any case the much-quoted dictum 'Il n'y a pas de hors-texte' and the ungainly philosophical abstraction called *archi-écriture* strongly suggest).

The odd result is that in *De la grammatologie* the main linguistic charge – if there is one – against Saussure the structuralist is never pressed. Instead, Saussure is found guilty on a count of minor importance – his inadequate account of writing. It is rather like the conviction of Al Capone for failing to pay his taxes.

*   *   *

That a thinker's reputation should rise and fall, and perhaps rise again, in accordance with the preoccupations of later generations, is not surprising. But many of these ups and downs are as inscrutable as the whims of fashion. What is remarkable in Saussure's case is the fidelity with which changing interpretations of the *CLG* provide a barometer of the twentieth century's concerns with its own blemished record as custodian of civilization. And that is perhaps a mark of how close a writer comes to tapping the main intellectual arteries of the age. By bringing to public attention underlying worries which would otherwise have lacked an intellectual focus, such a writer risks running the whole gamut of praise and blame, from one extreme to the other, as Saussure has. At this level of the history of ideas, today's bold pioneer can so easily become tomorrow's culpable reactionary, only to be resurrected as a sage the day after tomorrow.

History has not done with Saussure yet. Of that one can be fairly confident. If language is central to our self-portrait of the human race, Saussure – whether he intended to or not – raised in a concise and debatable form most of the basic questions about this genre of portraiture that still need to be answered. In that sense, one might say of Saussure what Voltaire said of God: had he not existed, it would have been necessary to invent him. As in the case of God, mere existence has not deterred – and will not deter – those intent on reinventing him for their own purposes.

POSTSCRIPT

A New Saussure?

Since the first edition of this book appeared, a newly discovered cache of notes in Saussure's own hand, long hidden in a drawer of the Saussure family house in Geneva, has been published (*Écrits de linguistique générale par Ferdinand de Saussure*, ed. Simon Bouquet and Rudolf Engler, Paris, Gallimard, 2002. References to the new material in the text of this publication will be indicated by the abbreviation *ELG*, followed by the page and, where relevant, the editors' number of the item in question. Thus *ELG*: 82.29a refers to the note published on page 82 and numbered by Bouquet and Engler '29a'.) These notes, which run to some 90 printed pages in all, were unknown to Bally and Sechehaye when they compiled the original 1916 version of the *CLG*, and equally unknown to subsequent generations of commentators. The discovery adds substantially (in the order of 30 per cent) to the total corpus of surviving autograph documents. No detailed assessment of the new material had been published at the time this Postscript was written, and what follows can therefore be no more than a preliminary evaluation. It nevertheless raises a number of questions that cannot remain unaddressed.

The notes themselves are infuriatingly incomplete, unordered, and riddled with lacunae at crucial points. The sentences that tail off into thin air often project the picture of an absent-minded professor who had forgotten what he wanted to write down even before he had picked up the pen. Or else realized that what had seemed a moment ago like a great idea was not worth recording after all. One wonders whether there are any more discoveries of this nature waiting to see the light of day. For the moment, however, Saussurean scholars have to be content with what is currently available, and with asking themselves whether this discovery affects to a significant degree any view or views of Saussure's thought that were put forward in the twentieth century. Does it, for instance, confirm X's interpretation, or undermine Y's? Does it open up any new interpretations hitherto unsuspected?

In order to reach plausible answers, there is a preliminary matter which needs to be settled. It concerns the date of the new material, a question which Bouquet and Engler do not deal with in their editorial Preface. Are we dealing with premature notes that Saussure himself eventually rejected? Or with rough drafts of points for current lectures? Or do they contain ideas temporarily put on one side, but destined for later incorporation into a definitive exposition of Saussurean linguistics? It clearly makes a great difference.

The topics covered range overall from the very broadest – e.g. semiology (*ELG*: 43–5.8; *ELG*: 70–2.22b; *ELG*: 96–7.6; *ELG*: 288.4), etymology (*ELG*: 84–5.29e), analogy (*ELG*: 85–6.29g), the origin of language (*ELG*: 93–4.2) – to the most specific – e.g. cacuminal nasals in Sanskrit (*ELG*: 50.10b), Latin compounds of the *agricola* type (*ELG*: 133–4.4). Virtually the only clue throwing light on how Saussure might have classified them is that the majority were found in the same envelope with the label 'Science du langage' inside it. A number of these notes bear the words *De la double essence du langage*, *Double essence* or *Essence double (du langage)*. Accordingly, Bouquet and Engler have made this the main category in their presentation. The remaining notes they divide into three smaller groups, thus ending up with a fourfold classification, under the heads (I) *De l'essence double du langage*, (II) *Item et aphorismes*, (III) *Autres écrits de linguistique générale*, and (IV) *Notes préparatoires pour les cours de linguistique générale*.

Although such an arrangement points to certain interconnexions, as doubtless the editors intended, it will not be followed here. For purposes of determining the evidential status of the material, a thematic examination of the notes seems far more informative. It also promises to shed some light on the chronological question.

*   *   *

On first inspection it looks as though these notes were not drafted in connexion with any single project in Saussure's academic career but are spread out over a considerable period of time. Among the evidence which points to this, I single out two notes in particular.

Note *ELG*: 291–4.7, although classified by Bouquet and Engler under *De l'essence double du langage* and not *Notes préparatoires pour les cours de linguistique générale*, clearly belongs in the latter group, since it relates closely to the lecture Saussure gave on 15 November 1910. Here the wording often corresponds very closely to that which occurs in the students' lecture notes.

For instance, Constantin's notes on the Third Course include the following passage (Engler: 2950):

> La différence géographique appelle l'idée d'unité. Où se trouve cette unité? Elle se trouve dans le passé, à moins de la laisser toujours abstraite.

There follows a diagram showing five vertical arrows converging upwards towards a curve labelled *unité*. The text then continues:

> Par cela nous sommes transportés sur un domaine que nous ne prévoyions pas pour le moment. Au lieu de différences géographiques nous avons des différences évolutives. L'évolution de la langue est une des grandes parties de la linguistique.

In Dégallier's notes, the corresponding passages (Engler: 2950) read:

> Différence géographique appelle idée d'unité. Où se trouve cette unité? Dans le passé, à moins de la laisser toujours abstraite.

There follows a diagram of four vertical arrows converging upwards towards a curve labelled *unité*. The text continues:

> Par là, nous sommes transportés sur un domaine que nous ne prévoyions pas: au lieu de différences géographiques, nous avons différences évolutives. Évolution de la langue est une des grandes parties de la linguistique.

In the notes of Mme Sechehaye, there is a much briefer version, with no diagram, which reads (Engler: 2950):

> La différence géographique appelle l'idée d'unité, [unité] qui est dans le passé, c'est-à-dire dans le temps. Donc différences *évolutives*.

In the notes of Joseph, we find (Engler: 2950):

> La différence géographique appelle tout de suite une idée d'unité. Où se trouve-t-elle concrètement? Dans le passé, c'est-à-dire dans le temps.

> Par cela, nous sommes transportés dans un domaine que nous ne prévoyions pas. L'évolution de la langue est une des grandes parties de la linguistique.

Before 1996, the above passages were the only surviving evidence relating to what Saussure said in his lecture. We now have the following (*ELG*: 293) in Saussure's own hand:

> Différence géographique appelle l'idée d'*unité*. Où se trouve cette unité? Elle se trouve dans le passé, donc dans le temps.

Then comes a diagram comprising four vertical arrows converging upwards. The text continues:

sur un domaine que nous ne prévoyions pas immédiatement. Les différences géographiques donnent des différences évolutives. Toute l'évolution qui est une des grandes parties de la linguistique est évoquée.

It is difficult to compare these various passages and reach the conclusion that what appears in *ELG*: 293 is anything other than the source. Saussure may have elaborated it in *viva voce* presentation, but the order in which the ideas are presented, the diagram and the verbal correspondences leave no serious doubt. This is either the text Saussure had in front of him in the lecture room on 15 November 1910, or a rough draft of it. One can even make reasonable guesses about the lecturer's extemporizations. For example, *ELG*: 293 presents baldly, without hesitation or qualification, the idea that the unity suggested by geographical divergences is to be found in the past. But in the students' notes we find what sounds very much like an afterthought ('à moins de la laisser toujours abstraite') which is recorded by Dégallier and Constantin. Joseph registers the same reservation less directly when he uses the adverb *concrètement* to render more precise the question as to where this unity is to be found. We know from other sections in the *CLG* what importance Saussure attached to the distinction between *abstrait* and *concret*. So it is easy enough to imagine the lecturer hastily adding this rider, on realizing that the statement in his notes was insufficiently nuanced. This fits in convincingly with the picture of a Saussure always at pains to impress on his students that questions of general linguistics are not idle speculations but questions demanding empirical answers. It fits even more closely with the picture of a Saussure who has already criticized the comparative philologists for indulging in abstract comparisons remote from historical realities (*CLG*: 16–17).

If the above note in all probability dates from 1910, there are certainly others which belong to a much earlier period. For instance *ELG*: 134.5, in which a discussion of the etymology of the name *Favre* refers to the politician Félix Favre as the 'nouveau président de la République'. Since Favre was elected in 1895 and died in office in February 1899, after which he could hardly have been referred to thus, this note presumably antedates Saussure's succession to the chair of general linguistics by several years, and perhaps by as much as a decade.

Explicit indications of date are few and far between. *ELG*: 62–3.18 bears the date '6 Dec.91', although this does not appear in the text of the Bouquet and Engler edition. *ELG*: 40–3.7 is dated '15 déc', but no year is given. *ELG*: 37–40.6e is written on discarded sheets of a printed engagement announcement dated 'Octobre 1891', and other notes are scribbled on headed café stationery from the 1890s and 1900s.

Confirmation of a relatively early date for some of the new material is given by the frequency with which Saussure there insists on a distinction between *forme* and *figure vocale*. The latter term occurs repeatedly (*ELG*: 17, 21, 26, 29, 31, 37, 38, 41, 42, 44, 45, 50, 67, 73, 81). It is also found in Saussure's draft for the article on Whitney, dating from 1894, and in other previously known notes (Engler: 3295, 3295a, 3311.2) probably from about the same period or slightly later, but seems to have dropped out of Saussure's technical vocabulary by the time he gave the three Courses on general linguistics in 1907–11.

There is nothing which gives a definite indication that any of the new material postdates Saussure's Third Course.

*   *   *

It is possible to identify in the new notes a number of major themes with which Saussure is known to have been preoccupied for many years. Two of these are (1) the question of devising an appropriate terminology for a 'science of language' and (2) what might be called the fallacy of attempting to divide the indivisible. The two are linked, inasmuch as the latter lies at the root of Saussure's well-known dissatisfaction with the inadequacies of the traditional terminology of linguistics.

This dissatisfaction is reflected in *ELG*: 93.1, where Saussure toys with the idea of introducing the term *kénôme* in order to dispel a perceived ambiguity in the term *mot*. The choice of this neologism is revealing. It does not appear elsewhere in Saussure's writings. The word directly transliterates the Greek κένωμα meaning 'space, vacuum, empty container' and thus anticipates Hjelmslev's coinage *ceneme* (Siertsema 1965: 16). The ambiguity that *kénôme* is intended to deal with is, according to Saussure, the ambiguity which arises when one speaks of a word and its meaning (*signification*) as if dealing with an association between two distinct things – the word on the one hand and the meaning on the other. But the French word *voir* does not exist independently of its meaning.

> La meilleure preuve est que *vwar* dans une autre langue aurait un autre sens: n'est par conséquent rien en soi: et par conséquent n'est un *mot* que dans la mesure où il évoque un sens. *Mais, cela vu, il est donc bien clair que vous n'avez plus le droit de diviser*, et d'admettre d'un côté le *mot*, de l'autre sa *signification*. Cela fait tout un. (*ELG*: 93)

His proposal in this instance (to distinguish instead between the *kénôme* and the *sème*) ties in with previously known notes in which he proposes a distinction between *aposème* and *sème* or between *sôme* and *sème* (Engler:

3310–12, 3327.1–2). None of these tentative terminological innovations survived into the text of the *CLG*. But what is important is Saussure's worry that *metalanguage is a source of error*: hence his hesitations about the appropriate technical terminology for linguistics to adopt. These occur repeatedly in the *ELG* material, indicating that at the time most of these notes were written he had found no preferred solution.

Thus he writes in *ELG*: 17.1:

> Il est faux (et impraticable) d'opposer la *forme* et le *sens*. Ce qui est juste en revanche c'est d'opposer la *figure vocale*, d'une part, et la *forme-sens* de l'autre.

This is at least an improvement on the clumsy formulation tried out in Engler: 3295a, where the reference to 'le groupe son-idée' already sponsors the potential misconception that *son* and *idée* are two separate entities:

> Parmi les choses qui peuvent être *opposées* au son matériel, nous nions, essentielle-ment et sans aucune défaillance future dans le détail, qu'il soit possible d'*opposer* l'idée. Ce qui est opposable au son matériel, c'est *le groupe son-idée*, mais absolument pas *l'idée*.

One can hardly have a group consisting of a single unit with two complementary facets.

Nevertheless, *ELG*: 17.1 does not sit altogether happily with the categorical pronouncement in *ELG*: 47–50.10a that:

> La base saisissable qui est le premier et le dernier fondement de toute espèce de considération linguistique, historique, philosophique, psychologique, n'est
> – ni la forme, ni le sens,
> – ni en troisième lieu l'union indissoluble de la forme et du sens,
> – ni 4° la différence des sens,
> – mais c'est 5° la différence des formes. (*ELG*: 48)

The implications here of *saisissable* can be glossed by reference to the following statement in *ELG*: 17,1:

> Il y a lieu de distinguer dans la langue les phénomènes *internes* ou de conscience et les phénomènes *externes*, directement saisissables.

In other words, *saisissable* is what is available 'externally', i.e. to sense perception, as opposed to what is not. In the case of the spoken word, that can hardly be anything other than its sound. But this in turn seems to lead directly to the equation that Saussure is elsewhere at pains to deny, i.e. between *forme* and *figure vocale*.

Saussure's predicament, evidently, is that at this stage he has neither a settled terminology that meets his requirements nor an absolutely clear conception of the theoretical distinctions he wishes to emphasize, but is trying to juggle with both problems simultaneously. In *ELG* perhaps the most satisfactory – or rather least unsatisfactory – of the various attempts to state the basic duality that Saussure sees as essential to a rational study of linguistic phenomena is the following:

> Le dualisme profond qui partage le langage ne réside pas dans le dualisme du son et de l'idée, du phénomène vocal et du phénomène mental; c'est là la façon facile et pernicieuse de le concevoir. Ce dualisme réside dans la dualité du phénomène vocal COMME TEL, et du phénomène vocal COMME SIGNE – du fait physique (objectif) et du fait physico-mental (subjectif), nullement du fait «physique» du son par opposition au fait «mental» de la signification. Il y a un premier domaine, intérieur, psychique, où existe le signe autant que la signification, l'un indissolublement lié à l'autre; il y en a un second, extérieur, où n'existe plus que le «signe», mais à cet instant le signe réduit à une succession d'ondes sonores ne mérite pour nous que le nom de figure vocale. (*ELG*: 20–21.2d)

The snag is that the same troublesome ambiguity that plagues the term *mot* also, according to *ELG*: 96–7.6, affects the word *signe*:

> on dit «signe», en s'imaginant très faussement que cela pourra être ensuite séparé à volonté de «signification» et que cela ne désigne que la «partie matérielle» [. . .]

According to Saussure, it is

> entièrement illusoire d'opposer à aucun instant le signe à la signification. Ce sont deux formes du même concept de l'esprit, vu que la signification n'existerait pas sans un signe, et qu'elle n'est que l'expérience à rebours du signe, comme on ne peut pas découper une feuille de papier sans entamer l'envers et l'endroit de ce papier, du même coup de ciseaux. (*ELG*: 96)

Here we have a glimpse of the famous comparison between *la langue* and a sheet of paper that appears in the *CLG* (157), and which Saussure introduced in the Second Course in his lecture of 16 November 1908. This is the most striking and immediately plausible of Saussure's illustrations of the fallacy of divisibility. However, it does not seem that Saussure can take credit for it. Hans Aarsleff maintains, very plausibly, that Saussure borrowed the comparison from Taine (Aarsleff 1982: 357–8). Since it occurred in an article published by Taine in 1877 and also in the third edition of Taine's *De l'Intelligence* (1878), Saussure could have been acquainted with it for years before giving the Geneva lectures. There is no way of knowing when the idea entered his thinking. But the fact that it does not feature in the First Course and was dropped by the Third suggests that Saussure was only temporarily attracted to it. The reason why is not difficult to see. The sheet of paper is itself a physical object and cutting it is a physical process. Therefore the necessity involved in cutting both recto and verso *simultaneously* is itself a physical necessity, lending support to the notion that both sides of the sign and the correlation between them are somehow fixed and given in advance. Unfortunately, that is the very last conclusion that Saussure would have wished his audience to draw. As *ELG*: 96–7.6 makes clear, both *signe* and *signification* are to be envisaged as 'deux formes du même concept de l'esprit'. But that is not altogether perspicuous either, since it implies that what is basically a single concept can take two manifestly divergent forms; and the problem then arises for Saussure of explaining at what psychological level this originally unitary concept exists.

If we wish to reconstruct the development of Saussure's thinking, it is important to note that the terminological pairs *sôme* / *sème*, *aposème* / *sème* and *kénôme* / *sème* are not direct precursors of *signifiant* / *signifié*. As the etymology of the term *kénôme* indicates, Saussure is still at this stage envisaging sound functioning as an envelope or container of linguistic units, but contributing nothing to their identity. However, the curious expression *enveloppe du mot* survives in the students' notes for the Third Course (Engler: 1693), indicating that Saussure had not yet abandoned this way of conceptualizing the relationship between sounds and words. In Engler: 3320.1 we find him still trying hard to bring his terminology into line with his metaphors, but never in a totally convincing way:

> On ne peut vraiment maîtriser le signe, le suivre comme un ballon dans les airs, avec certitude de le rattraper, que lorsqu'on s'est rendu complètement compte de sa nature, – nature double, ne consistant nullement dans l'enveloppe et pas davantage dans l'esprit, dans l'air hydrogène qu'on y insuffle et < qui > ne vaudrait rien du tout sans l'enveloppe. – Le ballon, c'est le *sème*, et l'enveloppe le *sôme*, mais cela est loin de la conception qui dit que l'enveloppe est le *signe*, et l'hydrogène la *signification*, sans que le *ballon* soit rien pour sa part. Il est tout pour l'aérostatier, de même que le sème est tout pour le linguiste.

Clearly he would have done better to consign the whole muddle to the waste-paper basket and start over again; which, in effect, was what he did with the later introduction of the distinction between *signifiant* and *signifié*. By the Third Course, he has stopped talking about the combination he previously called *son-pensée* or *pensée-son* (Engler: 1830) and is insisting that:

> L'image acoustique < n'est pas le son matériel >, c'est l'empreinte psychique du son. (*CLG3*: 74)

This dispenses with the notion of a 'container' completely, and the resultant gain in clarity is immediately felt. But by that time, in spite of earlier misgivings, the word *signe* has been rehabilitated as Saussure's preferred term for the basic unit of *la langue*, and *signification* abandoned altogether. All this suggests to me that at least part of the material preserved in *ELG* reflects the intermediate stage in Saussure's thinking between the draft article on Whitney (1894) and the mature reflections of the Third Course (1910–11), and perhaps corresponds to his preparation of the Second Course, i.e. 1908.

He is still grappling with the whole question of the binary structure of the linguistic sign. How is the linguist to present this binarity without falling into the trap of conjuring up two potentially separable parts? Saussure is evidently well aware of the possible criticism that introducing a new terminological distinction between *kénôme* and *sème*, or *aposème* and *sème*, or *sôme* and *sème*, risks resurrecting the fallacy of divisibility at one remove. In fact, in Engler 3327.2 he seems on the point of giving up and accepting the impossibility of the terminological task:

> < Et > encore ne suis-je pas persuadé que, si *sôme* est accepté, on ne revoie *sôme* < bientôt > au double sens < de nouveau > de mot, avec tous les *vices indélébiles* attachés au premier. [. . .] Or cette raison est tellement puissante que c'est presque une entreprise impossible de chercher des termes établissant la séparation de ce qui est forme ou sens, j'entends des termes valant absolument et dont on ne soit pas exposé à être victime et dupe au premier détour du chemin.

In *ELG*: 95.4 he tries to pose the question in a visual form, in order to avoid the terminological trap. Representing the linguistic unit as a rectangle, he divides the rectangle into two triangles by drawing a line from the bottom left corner to the top right corner. Now the question can be put: 'Can we ever talk about [*y a-t-il jamais lieu de parler de*] one of these linguistic triangles in isolation from the other?' The point of the visual analogue seems to be that once the two triangles are considered in isolation we lose sight of the fact that they have a common base, i.e. the diagonal between two corners of the original rectangle. In fact, strictly speaking, *they cannot be separated*, because there are not two diagonals, one for each triangle: the hypotenuse of one is simultaneously the hypotenuse of the other.

It is worth drawing attention to the parallel with another item in the Saussurean corpus (Engler: 3310.7), where the binary nature of the linguistic sign is likewise shown as a rectangle divided into two triangles. There the conclusion drawn about the relationship between the two triangles is less ambivalent, and perhaps reflects a less mature consideration of the question: we are told that the triangle *sens* can only be defined as the *valeur* of the triangle *forme*. But in *ELG*: 95.4 the answer immediately given to the question about separating the triangles is, perhaps, surprising: 'Ce ne pourrait être qu'au point de vue diachronique.' What are we to make of this?

The thought appears to be that only in diachronic studies can there be any justification for treating form and meaning as separable. And this seems confirmed by the comment that follows: 'Mais cela ne constitue rien de linguistique' (*ELG*: 95.4), i.e. nothing linguistic in the sense of nothing to do with *la langue* as a system.

Why does the possibility of separation have to be conceded in diachrony? Light is thrown on this in *ELG*: 72–4.25:

Il existe dans la langue:

1° Si on la prend *à un moment donné*: non pas seulement des *signes*, mais aussi des *significations*, non séparables des signes, vu que ceux-ci ne mériteraient plus leur nom sans signification.

En revanche ce qui n'existe pas, ce sont

a) les significations, les idées, les catégories grammaticales hors des signes; elles existent peut-être extérieurement *au domaine linguistique*; c'est une question très douteuse, à examiner en tout cas par d'autres que le linguiste;

b) les figures vocales qui servent de signes n'existent pas davantage dans la langue instantanée. Elles existent à ce moment pour le physicien, pour le physiologiste, non pour le linguiste ni pour le sujet parlant. De même qu'il n'y a pas de signification hors du signe *a*, de même il n'y a pas de signe hors de la signification.

2° Si on prend la langue au contraire *à travers une période*:

Alors il n'existe plus ni signe ni signification mais seulement des *figures vocales*. C'est le domaine de la phonétique. (*ELG*: 72–3)

Basically the same explanation, although worded somewhat differently, is given in *ELG*: 53–5.12:

– Ou bien SIGNE et *suite de temps* mais alors point d'IDÉE dans le signe. C'est ce qu'on appelle la phonétique.

– Ou bien SIGNE et IDÉE: mais alors inversement point de *suite de temps*; nécessité de respecter complètement l'instant et uniquement *l'instant*. C'est le domaine de la morphologie, de la syntaxe, de la synonymie, etc.

L'existence qu'on peut accorder au signe n'est pas ailleurs, en principe, que dans l'association qui en est faite par l'esprit avec une idée: c'est pourquoi on peut et on doit s'étonner qu'il devienne cependant nécessaire de reconnaître au signe une seconde existence, non dépendante de l'idée à mesure qu'on marche dans le temps. Cette seconde existence, il est essentiel de le remarquer, ne se manifeste ou ne trouve de sanction tangible qu'à l'instant où il y a l'un en face de l'autre un *passé* et un *présent*, tandis que la première est immédiatement contenue dans le présent. Par compensation, l'existence deuxième du signe (*à travers le temps*) ne saurait être soutenue qu'en isolant le signe de sa signification, et de toute signification quelconque qui lui arrive. (*ELG*: 54)

If these passages had been written at the time of the Third Course, one would have expected the terminology to be different: in the first, *synchroniquement* would have replaced *à un moment donné* and *diachroniquement* would have replaced *à travers une période*. *Signifiant* and *signifié* would have been substituted for *signe* and *signification* or *signe* and *idée*. There would have been none of this vaguely metaphysical talk about 'a second existence' of the sign. But the reason that emerges for conceding that in diachrony separations are possible which would be inadmissible in synchrony becomes clear. Without that possibility, the study of linguistic change *would not be viable*. There would be no way of tracing sound changes in the traditional manner (i.e. without reference of any kind to meaning). That would have meant cutting off Saussurean linguistics *in toto* from its predecessors, and hence Saussure from most of his contemporaries.

In short, Saussure is looking for a compromise with Establishment linguistics. Whether that compromise can be justified is debatable. If we look carefully at the small print, it seems that the proposed *modus vivendi* is based on an equivocation: and, precisely, an equivocation about the key term *signe*. Diachronic linguistics is not after all being awarded separate triangles to use as a viable basis for its investigations, in spite of the conclusion of *ELG*: 95.4 quoted above. For once separated, the two triangles have no semiological status at all. The illusion that they do is maintained only by recourse to the notion of *signe* that Saussure has already rejected.

This conclusion brings us straight to an even more vital question about dividing the indivisible and thus to a keystone in the whole edifice of Saussurean linguistics: namely, does the alleged interlocking between synchrony and diachrony, so central to the *CLG*, hold up? There seem to be clear indications in the new *ELG* notes that Saussure, perhaps at various times, had serious doubts. *ELG*: 93–4. 2 elaborates an idea which appears in the *CLG* in a brief discussion of the origin of language. There we are told that no society has ever known its language as anything other than a historical inheritance which it cannot refuse to accept:

> En fait, aucune société ne connaît et n'a jamais connu la langue autrement que comme un produit hérité des générations précédentes et à prendre tel quel. C'est pourquoi la question de l'origine du langage n'a pas l'importance qu'on lui attribue généralement. Ce n'est pas même une question à poser; le seul objet réel de la linguistique, c'est la vie normale et régulière d'un idiome déjà constitué. (*CLG*: 105)

But *ELG*: 93–4.2 takes this much further by comparing a search for linguistic origins to attempting to discover the source of a stream. The search in both cases is vain.

Regarder la langue et se demander à quel moment précis une telle chose a «commencé» est aussi intelligent que de regarder le ruisseau de la montagne et de croire qu'en remontant on trouvera l'endroit précis où il a sa source. (*ELG*: 94)

To be sure, it may be possible to discover one point at which the stream first emerges *above ground*. But in what sense is that its source? The objection Saussure is making is not a *historical* objection. The question is conceptual or philosophical, not historical. The stream when it first appears above ground is already a stream; so we are none the wiser as to its *origin*. The *CLG* text contains no reference to streams in this connexion, but the students' notes show that in the Second Course there was a brief mention of the source of the Rhône. Gautier's notes are of particular interest here because they clarify the spatio-temporal ambiguity that hovers over such terms as *source* and *naissance*.

La question de l'origine du langage n'existe même pas.
Ce serait étudier où commence le Rhône, localement et temporellement. Question absolument puérile. (Gautier. Engler: 1191)

So the confusion Saussure condemns is not just that a *spatial* answer may sometimes be given misleadingly to a *chronological* question (e.g. 'French was born in the Île-de-France' as an answer to a question about the origin of the French language) but that neither the spatial nor the chronological questions themselves make sense. The spatial question involves a conflation between the notion of 'origin' and that of the location where the phenomenon is first observable, while the chronological question involves a conflation between the notion of 'origin' and that of the time when the phenomenon is first identified as such. But in both cases the existence of what was sought is already presupposed. We never catch it in an inchoate state, just coming into being. Hence the conclusion:

On peut discuter éternellement sur cette *naissance*, mais son plus grand caractère c'est d'être parfaitement le même que celui de la croissance. (*ELG*: 94)

In short, diachronic studies tell us *nothing* about languages or language, not even about how they may have originated.

* * *

ELG: 288–90.5 deals with the problematic relation between the linguistic system (*langue, système sémiologique*) and the linguistic community (*collectivité*). The *CLG* deals with the issue somewhat summarily (*CLG*: 112–13) as a matter of 'réalité sociale' and insists that no *langue* exists without a *masse parlante*:

il faut une *masse parlante* pour qu'il y ait une langue. A aucun moment, et contrairement à l'apparence, celle-ci n'existe en dehors du fait social, parce qu'elle est un phénomène sémiologique. Sa nature sociale est un de ses caractères internes. (*CLG*: 112)

This last pronouncement is worth noting because it appears at first to conflict with what we read in *ELG*: 288–9, where the following account is given of what happens to a linguistic system when it becomes the property of a linguistic community:

il cesse de pouvoir être apprécié selon ses caractères internes ou naturels: parce qu'en effet rien ne garantit plus depuis le moment où le système de signes appartient à la collectivité que ce soit une raison intérieure, une raison faite à l'image de notre raison individuelle, qui va continuer à gouverner le rapport du signe et de l'idée. (*ELG*: 289)

However, on reading further in the same note we find that a system of signs:

n'est fait que pour s'entendre entre plusieurs ou beaucoup et non pour s'entendre à soi seul. C'est pourquoi à aucun moment, contrairement à l'apparence, le phé-nomène sémiologique quel qu'il soit ne laisse hors de lui-même l'élément de la collectivité sociale: la collectivité sociale et ses lois est un de ses éléments *internes* et non *externes*, tel est notre point de vue. (*ELG*: 290)

Here the terms *interne* and *externe* are being used to draw a quite different distinction from that discussed earlier (*ELG*: 17.1). Throughout the note, the entire account of the relationship between system and collectivity is based on a curious analogy with ships and shipbuilding. According to Saussure, once a ship is built and leaves dry dock for the open sea, it is at the mercy of forces that cannot be controlled. The ship, in this metaphor, is the linguistic system, *la langue*.

La langue, ou le système sémiologique quel qu'il soit, n'est pas le vaisseau qui se trouve au chantier, mais le vaisseau qui est livré à la mer. Depuis l'instant qu'il a touché la mer, c'est vainement qu'on penserait pouvoir dire sa course sous prétexte qu'on saurait exactement les charpentes dont il se compose, sa construction intérieure selon un plan. (*ELG*: 289)

Nothing of this metaphor survived in the *CLG*, but there are clear traces of it in the students' notes, as we see from the following excerpts:

il n'y a que le vaisseau sur mer qui soit un objet à étudier dans l'espèce vaisseau, pas le vaisseau sur terre. [. . .] Le système de signes est fait pour la collectivité < et non pour un individu, > comme le vaisseau < est fait > pour la mer. (Riedlinger. Engler: 1286)

Le vaisseau ne mérite d'être étudié que comme il se comporte sur mer. Un système de signes tend toujours à trouver ce milieu où seulement il vit (comme le vaisseau à la mer). (Gautier. Engler: 1286)

Lequel est le vrai du vaisseau sur terre et sur mer? Comme vaisseau à étudier: n'est intéressant que le vaisseau en tant qu'allant sur mer. (Bouchardy. Engler: 1286)

What is immediately obvious, however, is that the point as understood by the students is no longer quite the point made in Saussure's own note. They take his analogy as stressing the need to study the system as a working system in its social context: that, for them, is like studying the ship at sea, as opposed to studying it in dock. But they fail to see (or perhaps Saussure failed to bring out) the other facet of the comparison, i.e. that the ship was originally made on dry land, although destined to put to sea. What is dry land here? It is human reason, presiding over the construction of the sign:

en effet rien ne garantit plus depuis le moment où le système de signes appartient à la collectivité que ce soit une raison intérieure, une raison faite à l'image de notre raison individuelle, qui va continuer à gouverner le rapport du signe et de l'idée. (*ELG*: 289)

Once the system is at the mercy of the collectivity, it is no longer subject to rational control. When we turn to the version that emerged in the *CLG*, it is evident that Bally and Sechehaye, although dropping the maritime analogy, saw Saussure as presenting a progression through three stages in ways of looking at the system. In ascending order of adequacy, these are: (1) the system as an 'ensemble des habitudes qui permettent à un sujet de comprendre et de se faire comprendre', (2) the system as a social fact, and (3) the system as a historically determined product (*CLG*: 112–13). Each of the three presents a certain linguistic picture, but only the third captures the whole truth.

However, all the passages in the students' notes which mention the ship relate to the Second Course. It seems, again, that by the time of the Third Course this was an analogy Saussure had decided to discard. Once more, the reason is not hard to find. It was always an awkward analogy in the first place. To begin with, ships are built from the outset to go to sea and to be navigable: it is little short of absurd to suggest that once a ship has left the dock it is no longer under control. In the second place, ships do not put to sea until shipwrights have finished building them; but it is hard to see in what sense a language is ever complete in the individual before being put to social use. Third, whatever the rationale of the ship's design, it is not somehow abandoned or revised once at sea: on the contrary, what happens at sea is a good test of whether the ship is well designed or not. On none of these counts does Saussure's comparison hold up.

The other strand of Saussure's thinking that gets entangled in the maritime analogy involves his attempts to distinguish between 'internal' and 'external' linguistics. He evidently wished to claim that the social nature of *la langue* is one of its internal characteristics. This claim, variously formulated, appears in *ELG*: 290, *CLG*: 112, and in the notes of Riedlinger, Gautier, Bouchardy and Constantin (Engler: 1287), so there is not much doubt about its authenticity. But it jars oddly with Saussure's attempts elsewhere to explain what internal characteristics are. Supposedly, internal characteristics include everything that affects the structure of the system, as opposed to features that are adventitious or contingent. The most lucid of Saussure's efforts to explain this invokes his favourite analogy of chess (*CLG*: 43, Engler: 418ff.). The fact that chess came to Europe from Persia is external to the game, as is also the material of which the chessmen happen to be made. We can substitute wooden pieces for ivory pieces without changing the rules. But they would be changed automatically if the *number* of pieces were increased or diminished, and this is therefore an internal fact of chess.

So far so good. But this is difficult to square with the notion that when a ship leaves dry dock something will happen to its internal structure, which is presumably the expected corollary of equating the collectivity with the sea. There seems to be a collision here between the commonsense idea that a ship is built for sailing and the more questionable idea that a ship on dry land is not really a ship. Nor is it easy to extricate Saussure from this muddle by just dropping the ship analogy in favour of the chess analogy. For there we run into a parallel problem, which hinges on the fact that the 'social reality' of chess (i.e. that it is or is not played in certain communities, serves this or that cultural function, is played or not played by people of a certain standing, including professional players, etc.) does not in any straightforward sense constitute a rule or rules of the game. On the contrary, these circumstances are exactly those Saussure seems to reject as external to the game itself. What Saussure is groping for – but never quite finding – is a vivid, concrete way of expressing a very abstruse metatheoretical point: namely, that when he talks about a semiological *system* this is not to be understood as something existing at a different level from the communicational practices in which it is manifest. In other words, communication is not to be envisaged as being just a practical *application* of the system (as, for instance, calculating the area of a field may be regarded as a practical application of a system of measurement).

Unfortunately, he chooses to put this point about application in terms of a distinction between 'internal' and 'external', which is quite misleading. Translated into the chess analogy, what he is trying to say goes something like this: that the interpersonal dimension is an essential part of the game. In other words, one normally plays *against* one's opponent, and this is something more than merely being able to apply one's knowledge of the correct rules for moving the pieces. A player who did not understand that chess is a competitive activity, but thought it was just an exercise in moving the pieces on the board in accordance with certain patterns, alternately with your partner, would have failed to grasp the reality of chess as a game. That would be like an individual who thought that speaking English or French was just a matter of producing strings of words in conformity with fixed phonological, grammatical and semantic rules, but usually taking it in turns with someone else to do so.

The point is one of capital importance, not least because, as Saussure clearly saw, the linguistic model implicitly adopted by traditional grammarians was precisely the flawed model of a system of rules existing *at one remove from* any practical application in human intercourse. There is more to be said (see below) about this notion of communication as an 'internal' feature of semiological systems, but for the moment it suffices to draw attention to the fact that the *ELG* material throws interesting light on Saussure's hesitations about how to develop it (at least in a way that would be comprehensible to his students). The ship analogy is an unsuccessful attempt, but a revealing one.

*   *   *

The cases examined above confirm that the new *ELG* notes do include preparatory lecture material, although probably relating to different Courses. But since we know that Saussure did not usually keep his lecture notes (*CLG*: 7–8), the question arises of why he kept these. The null hypothesis is that he did not keep them, but that they survived by accident. On the other hand, perhaps he put some of them aside intentionally because they dealt with points to which he intended to give further consideration. (This is suggested by the fact that so many of the pages that have survived were folded neatly into four and tucked away in small labelled envelopes.) It seems possible to make out a case for saying that Saussure kept (most of) these notes precisely because they bore on certain *arrière-pensées* that he was having and which, when fully worked out, would have entailed a radical revision of the thinking presented in the Third Course. Some of them include linguistic observations which go far beyond the scope of anything contained in the Third

Course and one may see in them the embryo of that *linguistique de la parole* which was promised to his last students but never delivered.

For this purpose, Saussure would seem to have been contemplating a fundamental revision of the celebrated but crude dichotomy between *langue* and *parole* (on which posterity's version of structuralism is based) and working towards its replacement by the subtler notion of undivided *langage* conceived simultaneously from various perspectives.

The key phrase here, as Bouquet and Engler rightly identify it, is *l'essence double du langage* and not, it should be noted, *l'essence double de la langue*. In fact the notion of *essence double* goes back in Saussure's thinking at least as far as the draft article on Whitney of 1894, where he explores the analogy between language and chess and uses this phrase ('la nature de cette chose, en tout cas double, de son essence': Engler: 1489) to emphasize that in order to grasp the reality of the phenomenon we need to recognize that it has both 'historical' and 'abstract' features, which must not be conflated. From this it follows, according to the logic of the Whitney article, that linguistics itself must be a 'science double':

> Nous nourrissons depuis bien des années cette conviction que la linguistique est une science *double*, et si < profondément, irrémédiablement > double, qu'on peut < à vrai dire > se demander s'il y a une raison suffisante pour maintenir sous ce nom de *linguistique* une unité < factice >, génératrice < précisément > de toutes les erreurs, de tous les inextricables pièges contre lesquels nous nous débattons chaque jour [. . .]. (Engler: 3297 [14a])

In *ELG* this duality of *langage*, Saussure is at pains to stress, is not to be confused with the usual distinctions, for instance, form versus meaning, or physical versus mental. Saussure is inviting us to see language (not languages) as having a dual structure, which itself underlies the various viewpoints from which linguistic phenomena may be considered. In coming to terms with these various perspectives, we need to recognize that our linguistic experience is constantly subject to a process of analysis through which a specious determinacy is foisted upon linguistic units.

Thus certain of these passages reflect a philosophy of language which is very close to what one would nowadays call not 'structuralism' but 'integrationism'. The Saussurean notion of holistic structure is pressed beyond the point of linguistic closure. The alleged 'system' (the term verges on self-contradiction) is never complete or determinate, but exists only in the actual praxis of verbal communication, which is seen as presupposing and dependent upon contextual factors of all kinds. The most radical of these new integrationist pronouncements concern the existence of words and meanings.

Here Saussure criticizes, first, the static 'dictionary' notion of what a word is, which is foisted upon us by lexicographers. This he sees as based upon a false externalization of both form and meaning. It involves making the word into:

> un être existant complètement en dehors de nous, ce qui peut être figuré par le mot couché dans le dictionnaire, au moins par l'écriture; dans ce cas le sens du mot devient un attribut, mais une chose distincte du mot; et les deux choses sont dotées artificiellement d'une existence, par cela même à la fois indépendantes l'une de l'autre et indépendantes chacune de notre conception; elles deviennent l'une et l'autre *objectives* et semblent en outre constituer deux entités. (*ELG*: 82–83.29b)

Then he attacks the notion that words are items belonging to the external, physical world, while their meanings exist only in the mind. This too is a mistake. How, then, do words have an existence? Or any other supposed linguistic facts?

According to *ELG*: 19.2b:

> On n'est pas dans le vrai, en disant: un fait de langage veut être considéré à plusieurs points de vue; ni même en disant: ce fait de langage sera réellement deux choses différentes selon le point de vue. Car on commence par supposer que le fait de langage est donné hors du point de vue.
>
> Il faut dire: primordialement il existe des points de vue; sinon il est simplement impossible de saisir un fait de langage.

This may be compared with the remark in Engler: 3295a (possibly dating from before the Whitney article) where we are told:

> il nous est interdit en linguistique, quoique nous ne cessions de le faire, de parler «*d'une chose*» à différents points de vue, ou d'une chose en général, parce que c'est le point de vue qui seul FAIT la chose.

Readers of the *CLG* will recognize here a thought that is reflected in a much more cautious form at the beginning of Chapter 3 of the Introduction:

> D'autres sciences opèrent sur des objets donnés d'avance et qu'on peut considérer ensuite à différents points de vue; dans notre domaine, rien de semblable.[. . .] Bien loin que l'objet précède le point de vue, on dirait que c'est le point de vue qui crée l'objet [. . .]. (*CLG*: 23)

If either of the two more radical formulations in Saussure's notes is accepted, it would seem to follow either that there are *no* linguistic facts (in which case some entrenched academic versions of linguistic inquiry are on a hiding to nothing), or that there are *as many different classes of linguistic fact as there are points of view*. Earlier in Engler: 3295a Saussure seems to draw back from the former conclusion and suggests that the facts created will indeed correspond 'à des réalités' if the perspective is a correct one ('quand le point de départ est juste'), but not otherwise. However, he insists, in either case:

> aucune chose, aucun *objet* n'est donné un seul instant en soi. Non pas même quand il s'agit du fait le plus matériel, le plus évidemment défini en soi en apparence, comme serait une suite de sons vocaux. (Engler: 3295a)

This is a very remarkable affirmation and is made so emphatically that it cannot lightly be brushed aside. Saussure is making it clear beyond any doubt that this applies not only to the identification of items within the system, but to *all manifestations of language*. He then goes on to conclude as quoted above: that 'c'est le point de vue qui seul FAIT la chose'. The word *seul* is crucial here. That is to say, it is not any set of objectively observable data which, when analysed from a certain point of view, yields facts for the linguist, but *the viewpoint alone and of itself.*

Here, in short, we have the key to opening up a linguistic epistemology which finally and utterly breaks with the positivism that dominated language studies throughout the nineteenth century (and, we may add in retrospect, continued to do so long after Saussure's death). What are the consequences of this break? How did Saussure envisage them? In the light of these questions, it is tempting to see the *ELG* notes as a repository of all his earlier formulations that Saussure realized needed careful revision, plus a few indications of how that revision might proceed.

In the first place, he must have realized that the old positivist programme for linguistics, still preserved in the first lecture of the Third Course (28 October 1910), was no longer viable. This was the programme based on the dictionary definition of linguistics (by Hatzfeld, Darmesteter and Thomas) as «*étude scientifique des langues*». Unfortunately, that was to be precisely the positivist agenda that survived under Saussure's name in the *CLG*, which envisages such utopian 'scientific' goals as eventually producing descriptions of all known languages and recording their history. It likewise, in the same scientific spirit, envisages the linguist as seeking to establish 'general laws' under which all known linguistic facts can be subsumed and by which they are explained (*CLG*: 20). Little of this can survive once it is realized that the rejection of positivist science is tantamount to conceding that there is no such thing as a 'panchronic' point of view. The possibility of panchronic knowledge is the epistemological fetish of positivism.

Saussure's incipient doubts about this fetish had already begun to surface in the Second Course. An attentive reading of Riedlinger's notes shows Saussure hesitating between outright rejection of the notion and a compromise which allows it to survive at one remove from genuine knowledge.

> N'y a-t-il pas un point de vue panchronique dans la langue? On est obligé de faire une distinction dès le début. S'il ne s'agit que de généralisations, elles peuvent être panchroniques, < mais ce ne sont que des généralisations: par exemple > les changements < phonétiques > en eux-mêmes sont diachroniques; mais comme ils se passent < et se passeront > toujours on peut les appeler panchroniques. Mais si l'on parle de faits concrets il n'y a pas de point de vue panchronique. (*CLG2*: 35)

Then he tries to find an example of what it would be like to consider a linguistic fact 'panchronically'. For example, the word *chose*.

> Si j'essaie le point de vue panchronique je vois que ce qui est panchronique dans ce mot c'est les sons: |šoz|: dans tous les temps on a pu prononcer *šoz*. Mais cette matérialité des sons n'a qu'une valeur acoustique, pas linguistique. La suite de sons *šoz* n'est pas une unité linguistique. (*CLG2*: 35)

But then he realizes, on second thoughts, that even this is too great a concession to the old way of thinking:

> < J'ai encore trop accordé: > même au point de vue panchronique, |šoz| n'est pas une unité, < n'est qu'une dépouille matérielle; > c'est un morceau < phonique > découpé dans autre chose, c'est une masse informe délimitée par rien [. . .]. (*CLG2*: 35)

It is but a short step from this to realizing that the so-called '*point de vue panchronique*' is not actually a *point de vue* at all; at least, not in the sense in which there is a synchronic *point de vue* and a diachronic *point de vue*. It is at best a level at which one can try to summarize – crudely and unsystematically – some of the knowledge gained by applying a genuine *point de vue*. But even when this is possible, it does not mean that there are actually panchronic *facts*.

When we look at the *CLG* version of this passage (*CLG*: 134–5) and compare it with the students' notes, it becomes evident that at this point Bally and Sechehaye tried to make the best of a bad job by interpolating a reference of their own to the game of chess. They evidently thought that the search for panchronic laws should be retained as one of the goals of linguistics, and tried to validate this concept by comparing it to the existence in chess of 'des règles qui survivent à tous les événements'. But here they leap from the frying pan into the fire. For what 'survive' the events of any particular game are nothing other than the rules of chess, and they 'survive' the events simply in the sense that the game was played throughout according to those rules. *But that is exactly what is lacking to validate the linguistic comparison.* There may be indeed synchronic rules governing the word *chose*, and possibly diachronic rules (accounting for its phonetic and semantic history), but no *panchronic* rules. The notion does not even make sense. There are no panchronic features of the word *chose*. There are only extrapolations from the synchronic and diachronic facts already known.

*   *   *

If the positivist agenda were to be rejected, along with the suspect notions of panchronic knowledge, 'objective' facts, linguistic universals, etc., what would be required as the alternative basis for a rational programme of linguistic inquiry? Clearly, a theory of *points de vue*. Saussure evidently came to realize this, and *ELG*: 21–2.2e gives us the first outline of such a theory. There four general points of view are distinguished and defined, the first two being described as 'necessary' and the latter two as dependent on the first two.

1. The point of view of 'l'état de langue en lui-même'.
2. The point of view of 'identités transversales'.
3. The anachronic point of view ('point de vue anachronique').
   3a. The etymological point of view.
4. The historical point of view ('point de vue historique').

There are a number of ways in which this schema of perspectives already marks an advance over the old framework for linguistics outlined at the beginning of the Third Course.

First, an important distinction is drawn here between the *point de vue historique* (4) and the old diachronic perspective, which is now renamed and appears as the point of view based on *identités transversales* (2). These *identités* which provide the basis for (2) are said to be:

> *données* d'abord nécessairement par celles du précédent [i.e. (1)]; mais après cela deviennent *le deuxième ordre d'identités* linguistiques, irréductibles avec le précédent. (*ELG*: 21)

The *point de vue historique*, on the the other hand, is described as being based on:

> la fixation de deux états de langue successifs pris chacun en lui-même, d'abord, et sans subordination de l'un à l'autre [. . .]. (*ELG*: 22)

As opposed to the others, the *point de vue anacronique* (3) is 'artificiel, voulu et purement didactique'. It involves projecting from one morphology on to another. This projection is said to rely on a combination of viewpoints (1) and (2).

(3a), the *point de vue étymologique*, is characterized in oxymoronic terms as the 'point de vue anachronique retrospective' and is said to include more than is normally considered as falling under *étymologie*. One of the features that distinguishes it from (4) is that it takes no account of 'l'époque B en elle-même'.

Of these four 'legitimate' points of view, Saussure writes, only (2) and (3) are currently adopted in linguistics.

> Ce qui est en revanche vivement cultivé, c'est la confusion lamentable de ces différents points de vue, jusque dans les ouvrages élevant les plus hautes préten-tions scientifiques. Il y a là certainement, très souvent, une véritable absence de réflexion de la part des auteurs. Mais ajoutons tout de suite une profession de foi: autant nous sommes convaincu à tort ou à raison qu'il faudra finalement en venir à tout réduire théoriquement à nos quatre points de vue légitimes reposant sur deux points de vue nécessaires, autant nous doutons qu'il devienne jamais possible d'établir avec pureté la quadruple ou seulement la double terminologie qu'il faudrait. (*ELG*: 22)

All this is clearly an agenda rather than a fully worked-out programme, and as such it perhaps poses more questions than it answers. For instance, in what sense are the *identités transversales* of (2) not only *given* but initially given *necessarily* ('*données* d'abord nécessairement') by those of (1)? Saussure, we know, was already puzzling over the question of diachronic identities in his Second Course. The problem he recognized was acknowledged by Bally and Sechehaye, but evaded rather than solved – on Saussure's behalf – in their text of the *CLG*. There we are told that:

> l'identité diachronique de deux mots aussi différents que *calidum* et *chaud* signifie simplement que l'on a passé de l'un à l'autre à travers une série d'identités synchroniques dans la parole, sans que jamais le lien qui les unit ait été rompu par les transformations phonétiques successives. (*CLG*: 250)

But this is a fudge; in fact a double fudge. For in the first place it corresponds to nothing in the students' notes for the Second Course; and in the second place, even if it did, the 'explanation' offered is circular.

When Saussure discussed this in his lecture of 7 December 1908, what he said, according to Riedlinger (confirmed by Patois; *CLG2*: 125–6) left the question unresolved:

A tout moment nous nous trouvons placés devant une sorte d'identité que M. de Saussure définit: identité à travers le temps. < On peut même proposer un terme > – diachronique (traversant le temps); c'est celle par laquelle nous disons < que > *sevrer* c'est *separare*! Sur quoi repose exactement cette identité? C'est de quoi doit s'occuper une partie de la linguistique. Mais nous ne dirons pas par exemple que *fleurir* soit la même chose que *florere*: quelque chose a changé, ce n'est pas la même forme en ligne directe (il faudrait en tout cas *florire*). Donc d'un côté on pose identité et de l'autre on ne la pose pas. Dans son type (pas absolument) le plus signalé l'identité diachronique c'est ce qu'on appelle l'identité phonétique. < Qu'on ne se fie pas à ce terme, le mot n'explique rien. > Mais parce qu'on a fait intervenir l'idée de son < il ne faut pas croire qu' > on ait rendu compte du phénomène. Si on se demande en quoi il consiste on voit qu'il faut sortir de l'idée du son! L'idée qu'il s'agit du son est précaire de beaucoup de façons: par exemple dans tout changement phonétique, dans toute loi phonétique est-ce le son qui change? Non: < *a* ne devient pas *e*, > on n'a fait que reproduire une forme en s'écartant; le lien d'identité est en dehors du son. C'est comme un air de musique que vous reproduisez mal; ce n'est qu'au nom de l'unité que vous pouvez juger s'il y a eu changement: elle est plus importante que le changement phonétique. Il est mystérieux < le lien de > cette identité diachronique qui fait que deux mots ont changé complètement (*calidus* : *śo*, *aiwa* : *je*) et qu'on en affirme cependant l'identité. En quoi consiste-t-il? Précisément! Il y aura donc dans la linguistique toute une série de questions < à résoudre ou plutôt à scruter > qui se rapportent aux identités, unités diachroniques. (*CLG2*: 30–1)

In the second place, if the passage just cited is taken at face value, then the explanation offered by Bally and Sechehaye in *CLG*: 250 cannot be right. In other words, diachronic identities cannot be explained just as summarizing a chain of phonetic changes at successive points in time (linking e.g. Latin *calidum* to French *chaud*) because in order to identify any such intermediate change we already need criteria by which to judge whether one sequence of sounds is or is not 'the same' as a subsequent sequence of sounds. The recourse to phonetics here has no explanatory value, but merely restates the identity already postulated.

In Engler's critical edition of the *CLG*, presumably in order to support Bally and Sechehaye's interpretation of the explanation of diachronic identity in the Second Course, reference is made to another passage in Saussure's own notes (Engler: 2750 [3295a]). But this passage turns out to be making a point which leads us back to exactly the same unanswered question that Riedlinger's account leaves pending. The example discussed is the postulated 'change' over time of the sound sequence *alka* to *ôk*.

Au fond, où est le LIEN entre *alka* et *ôk*? Si nous entrons dans cette voie, *et il est inflexiblement nécessaire d'y entrer*, nous verrons bientôt qu'il faudra se demander où est le LIEN entre *alka* et *alka* < lui-même >, et à ce moment, nous comprendrons qu'il n'y a nulle part < comme fait primordial > une *chose* qui soit *alka*, < ni aucune chose > ; mais qu'il y a d'abord un *genre de rapports* que nous établissons,

par exemple le rapport entre *alka* et *ôk*, qui nous suggère l'idée d'une certaine
< espèce d'> unité, encore très difficile à définir. (Engler: 3295a)

It follows that to say that the diachronic identity of *calidum* with *chaud*
reduces to an uninterrupted series of phonetic changes linking the former
to the latter is vacuous *unless* we can propose general criteria for defining
'uninterrupted' phonetic change. But specifying these criteria *is*, precisely, the problem of diachronic identities. We have not solved the
problem but merely redescribed it, and it is exactly the same problem that
resurfaces in *ELG*: 21–2.2e under the rubric *identités transversales*. But
the step forward that has been taken with the introduction of the term
identités transversales is that any attempt at a 'phonetic' explanation is
abandoned, since these identities are now treated as *given* ('données') by
reference to a certain *état de langue*. That is to say, it is conceded that we
first have to specify linguistic signs in semiological or synchronic terms
before any question of diachronic evolution arises.

The answer to the question of what makes *alka* the same as *alka* (or
calidum the same as *calidum*, or *chaud* the same as *chaud*) is, at this phase in
Saussure's thinking, that the sameness consists in the fact that these pairs
of phonetic items ($alka_1$, $alka_2$, etc.) are recognized as instantiating one
particular sign belonging to a particular *état de langue*, and, as such,
distinguishable from any other sign belonging to that *état de langue*. So it
is in virtue of the existence of the sign – and that alone – that we are able
to say when a sound sequence counts as *alka* and when it does not.

However, as Saussure doubtless came to see, that does not quite solve the
problem either. It bobs up again when someone asks about a sequence
which does not sound *quite* like the familiar *alka*, but does not sound *quite*
like any other previously known sign either. Has a change taken place? And
if so, are we now in a new *état de langue*? Here the appeal to defining sound
sequences by reference to signs gets its comeuppance, because it emerges
that distinguishing a new sound sequence and distinguishing a new *état de
langue* are head and tail of the same coin. That is to say, given a stable *état
de langue* it makes sense to dismiss the slightly odd sound sequence as a
mispronunciation of *alka* (cf. the analogy of the old tune badly sung,
reported by Riedlinger in *CLG2*: 30); but once that reassuring premiss of
stability is dropped, and we have to contemplate the possibility of a
continuous succession of *états de langue*, the answer is by no means clear.
Except, self-evidently, that the answer cannot come from continually
invoking whatever sign was originally assumed to provide the basis for
identifying a sound sequence as *alka*. On that basis, *ôk* could still be *alka*.

This is where the problem of *langue* and *parole* comes in. Saussure always assumed that linguistic innovations originate in *parole*. Innovations do not enter *la langue* until accepted by the collectivity. But this must mean that for the individual there are *identités* other than those of *la langue* that enter the picture. Otherwise permanent stasis would be the abiding condition of linguistic communication between human beings. Where do these other relevant *identités* come from and how do they impinge on *la langue*? These are the major problems that Saussure would have had to address in any *linguistique de la parole*.

He had had them in view ever since the unpublished draft of the article on Whitney, which begins with the observation that:

> L'objet qui sert de signe n'est jamais 'le même' deux fois: il faut dès le premier moment un examen < ou une convention initiale > pour savoir au nom de quoi, < dans quelles limites > nous avons le droit de l'appeler le même; là est la fondamentale différence avec un objet quelconque, et la première source très simple. (Engler: 3297)

It is exactly the problem he returns to in Engler: 3295a, cited above. What makes the sound sequence *alka* the sound sequence *alka*, as distinct from being any *other* sound sequence?

The answer given in the Whitney text is annoyingly incomplete:

> Par exemple, la table que j'ai devant moi est matériellement la même aujourd'hui et demain, et la lettre *b* que j'écris est tout aussi matérielle que la table, mais elle n'est pas [ ].

How would the sentence have concluded? And why was it left unconcluded? Perhaps because the writer already saw that the anticipated conclusion was going to leave him in deep trouble with respect to that postulated autonomy of *la langue* which underlay all his thinking hitherto. So he stopped abruptly and started again with a quite different *entrée en matière* to discussing Whitney's achievement as a linguist.

But the abandoned question would not go away. It crops up again in Engler: 126 [3295] in the guise of whether there is a sound ('figure vocale') *nü* which exists independently of any language in which it might occur (e.g. as a pronunciation of the French word *nu*). The answer given is that it does exist:

> Elle existe parce que nous la déclarons identique à elle-même.
> Mais nous ne pouvons pas la déclarer identique à elle-même sans invocation < tacite > d'un *point de vue*.

So there is, it would seem, a language-neutral *point de vue* that allows the identification of such items. But this is a postponement of the question rather than a full answer. Furthermore, the question itself is badly posed. For what is at issue is not why we 'declare' one particular item to be self-identical (what else could it be?) but why we count two different examples as examples of the same thing.

Saussure returns to the problem in *ELG*: 31–2.5b and there formulates it less clumsily with a different illustration:

> Quand j'ouvre deux fois, trois fois, cinq cents fois la bouche pour prononcer *aka*, la question de savoir si ce que je prononce peut être déclaré identique ou non dépend d'un examen.[. . .]
>
> Le fait par exemple que *aka* est prononcé par telle personne à un certain endroit et à un certain moment, ou le fait que mille personnes à mille endroits et à mille moments émettent la succession de sons *aka*, est absolument le seul fait donné: mais il n'en est pas moins vrai que seul le fait ABSTRAIT, l'*identité acoustique de ces aka*, forment seul l'*entité acoustique aka*: et qu'il n'y a pas a chercher un objet premier plus tangible que ce premier objet abstrait. (*ELG*: 31–2)

In the next section of the same note, Saussure proceeds to address the question: 'Les entités de l'ordre vocal sont-elles des entités linguistiques?' and supplies the categorical answer:

> Non. Hors de tout langage humain, *aka* est égal à *aka*, et, étant donné le langage humain, *aka* pris dans une langue est égal à *aka* pris dans une autre. S'il y a différence, c'est qu'on a trop grossièrement séparé les entités vocales, et qu'il y a lieu d'en établir deux où on n'en voyait qu'une. (*ELG*: 32)

This corresponds in obvious respects to a similar passage in previously published notes (Engler: 132 [3295]) dating probably from about 1893:

> En prenant ce qu'il peut y avoir dans le langage < à la fois > de plus matériel, de plus simple et de plus indépendant du temps, par exemple 'le groupe *aka*' ou '*la voyelle a*', préalablement dégagés de toute signification, de toute idée d'emploi, cela ne représente rien qu'une série d'*actions* < physiologi[co]-acoustiques > que nous jugeons concordantes. A l'instant où nous les jugeons concordantes, nous faisons de *aka* ou *a* une *substance*. Or < il est impossible de se rendre compte de ce que vaut cette substance, sans s'être rendu compte du point de vue au nom duquel nous la créons >. (Engler: 132)

Philosophers will doubtless claim that, as regards debate about language in the Western tradition, these replies place Saussure squarely in the front rank of diehard nominalists. Do they?

If so, then Saussure has created serious theoretical problems for himself as a linguist. For, in effect, any insistence on the priority of *point de vue* over linguistic facts then translates into a priority of metalanguage over language. And that in turn leads to a regress where grammarians hold the whip hand. *Their* metalinguistic distinctions and categories will determine the limits within which a 'science of language' can be set up. And that is the last conclusion that Saussure ever wanted to reach, being a self-declared dissident from the traditional orthodoxy.

Is there an escape route? If there is, it must lie in recognizing that the *point de vue* of the individual is, after all, very different from the *point de vue* of the collectivity: in other words, that *parole* is not just determined by *langue*, nor *langue* by the totality of *parole*. Recent research in an integrationist framework seems to show that 'if one takes the language-user's own perspective seriously, it soon becomes apparent that it yields no determinate view of what belongs to *la langue* and what does not. It will vary from speaker to speaker and from occasion to occasion' (Davis 2003: 13).

If such are the realities of *parole*, as an integrationist would claim, did Saussure recognize them? And, if so, how did he propose to accommodate them theoretically? In the *ELG* notes there are indications that Saussure was beginning to realize the perils of insisting on the pre-eminence of the collectivity. One can detect a developing tension between three key ideas, all asserted in various places with equal conviction:

> 1. that the form and meaning of a sign are inseparable and mutually defining;
> 2. that a semiological system is constituted by its own internal oppositions, operating quite independently of the external world;
> 3. that meaning is not only indeterminate but constantly varying.

In *ELG*: 83.29b he admits that words and their meanings exist only in the awareness we have of them, or bring to bear on them, in any given instance. In short, the linguist must come to terms with the fact that

> le mot pas plus que son sens n'existe hors de la conscience que nous en avons, ou que nous voulons bien en prendre à chaque moment. (*ELG*: 83)

The quantum leap is captured in the second half of that sentence. As if to make sure that what we thought was a leap was not just a verbal illusion, he then spells it out in unmistakable terms:

> Un mot n'existe véritablement, et à quelque point de vue qu'on se place, que par la sanction qu'il reçoit de moment en moment de ceux qui l'emploient. (*ELG*: 83)

This seems to anticipate a *linguistique de la parole* which is based not on the holistic priority of *la langue* but rather on the integrationist premise that 'communication proceeds by means of signs which are created at and for the moment of communicational exchange' (Wolf and Love 1993: 313). For an orthodox linguistics which has put its faith for the past century in setting up an autonomous and stable domain of linguistic inquiry (largely on allegedly Saussurean principles), in which languages are so many separate 'codes' tied to linguistic collectivities, and held to be objectively describable by the rigorous application of tried methods and empirical procedures, it is a deeply subversive idea. The implications are revolutionary, roughly comparable to the supersession of Newtonian cosmology by Einsteinian cosmology. They bring Saussure in one stride from the nineteenth century into the postmodern world. Words no longer have meanings with a stability guaranteed by their relations to physical reality. Nor do words have meanings whose stability is guaranteed by the internal organization of the system of signs to which they belong culturally (which is usually the position attributed to 'Saussure the structuralist'). Worse still, words have no guaranteed meanings on either basis, since their interpretation is subject to contextual factors that cannot be identified in advance and, in retrospect, are not replicable. If this is so, one must conclude that any attempt to write a 'grammar' or a 'dictionary' is a self-defeating enterprise. Or rather, any such work would be a forlorn attempt to fossilize words rather than to describe them.

Saussure presses this point by insisting on the impossibility of listing the meanings of common words such as *fer* ('iron') and *chêne* ('oak'). He says that the task would take longer than a human life span; would be endless. But its futility, if rightly understood, can teach us an important lesson. The task is futile not because life is too short, but because it rests on a misconception of meaning. Words are meaningful not because each is associated with a specific set of positive concepts, but because in discourse each has an ongoing potential for communicational deployment.

> C'est pourquoi vouloir épuiser les idées contenues dans un mot est une entreprise parfaitement chimérique, à moins peut-être de se borner à des noms d'objets matériels et d'objets tout à fait rares, par exemple l'*aluminium*, l'*eucalyptus*, etc. Déjà si l'on prend le *fer* et le *chêne*, on n'arrivera pas au bout de la somme de significations (ou d'emplois, ce qui est la même chose) que nous donnons à ces mots [. . .]. (*ELG*: 77)

The potential is open-ended, conditioned solely by the availability of other words for the communicational purpose in hand, which varies from one moment to the next. This, again, is integrationism, not structuralism. According to one integrationist:

> an integrationist's approach to the problem of linguistic units pursues to their logical conclusion the implications of the Saussurean dictum that in linguistics it is the viewpoint adopted which creates the object. (Davis 2001: 195)

Elsewhere the same writer spells out those implications as far as *parole* is concerned: 'The context of the linguistic act, which includes the assumptions the speaker may hold about the hearer's intentions, creates the sign' (Davis 2003: 13). That formulation, and the interpretation on which it was based, now finds ample support in a number of the *ELG* texts. The sign of *parole* is the product of an integration of many factors, which may – and often do – vary from one moment to the next.

The term *intégration* is in fact used by Saussure in this connexion. In *ELG*: 87–8.29j he describes *intégration* (or *postméditation-réflexion*) as 'the dual phenomenon which subsumes all the active life of language (*langage*)'. Linguistic communication, according to this view, is a human activity involving signs, but an activity in which nothing is determinate except by reference to whatever signs are present or absent concurrently:

> et, comme le nombre et l'aspect réciproque et relatif de ces signes changent de moment en moment d'une manière infinie, le résultat de cette activité, pour chaque signe, et pour l'ensemble, change aussi de moment en moment dans une mesure non calculable. (*ELG*: 88)

This is an important statement about human communication: perhaps the most important on record in the annals of modern linguistics. It will take linguistics (not to mention literary studies, psychology, anthropology and political theory) at least half a century to take on board its full implications. It outflanks in one sentence not only the classic versions of structuralism (including Chomsky's various generativist versions) but the anti-structuralist criticisms of Derrida and his cohorts. It opens up new applications of Saussurean integrationism that have yet to be seen.

If this was to be the message of Saussure's *linguistique de la parole*, it presages not only a fundamental revision of his earlier priorities but the impossibility of getting *outside* the activities involved. It means, in short, that where language is concerned there is ultimately only one *point de vue*.

That was, as doubtless Saussure realized, not a thesis well suited for the purpose of undergraduate teaching, which was better served by a clear distinction between synchronic and diachronic statements, and by abstracting from all the complications involved when the particular context of a linguistic act is taken into account. At the pedagogic level, it may even be essential to erect some classroom totality identified as *la langue*. But Saussure must have realized that this would not do when it came, outside the classroom, to accounting for *faits de parole* in the world of everyday communication.

It is here that the question of 'réalité sociale' resurfaces, and here that one can at last make sense of Saussure's contention that in semiological terms a system:

> n'est fait que pour s'entendre entre plusieurs ou beaucoup et non pas pour s'entendre à soi seul. C'est pourquoi à aucun moment, contrairement à l'apparence, le phénomène sémiologique quel qu'il soit ne laisse hors de lui-même l'élément de la collectivité sociale: la collectivité sociale et ses lois est un des éléments *internes* et non *externes*, tel est notre point de vue. (*ELG*: 290)

Insisting on the 'internality' of social factors is perhaps not the most lucid way of making the integrationist point about communication. But if it is to be given its full due, as the above statement indicates that it must be, what is involved is a revision of the glib formula that found its way in to the text of the *CLG* and has been quoted endlessly ever since: 'la langue est pour nous le langage moins la parole' (*CLG*: 112). If we are to judge by the evidence of the students' notes, it is a formula that is the handiwork of Saussure's editors rather than a direct reflection of Saussure's words in his lecture of 19 May 1911. Where the formula is misleading is in its suggestion that there is a given whole (*langage*) which can be neatly divided into two quite separate parts (*langue* on the one hand and *parole* on the other). But as far as the individual is concerned this can never be the case. And if a *linguistique de la parole* focuses on the *point de vue* of the individual, as presumably it must, then it must likewise reject that crude separation.

In *ELG* we find Saussure constantly returning to the notion that in practice the speaker must give physical embodiment to the sign. That being so, what exactly is the relationship between the sign itself and the many ephemeral manifestations it receives in acts of speech? That, for Saussure, is the basic problem of a theory of *parole*, and he explores various ways of tackling it, none of them completely satisfactory.

At first he identifies the sound of a word as the *figure vocale* (a term which occurs repeatedly in the new *ELG* notes) and tries out various permutations of the idea that the *figure vocale* is what is left over when the *signification* is removed. To this approach belong his tentative termino-logical experiments (*kénôme*, *sôme*, etc.), all of which seem to hinge to some extent on the metaphor of sound as being a shell or container. But these are abandoned when he sees that this leads nowhere, because the sound produced in *parole* does not contain anything else 'inside' it. In any case, he wants to reject any suggestion that the sign itself is composed of separable parts.

He also sees that it will not do to say that the sound uttered simply *is* the physical or physiological rendering of some ideal sound in the speaker's head. For, apart from the explanatory vacuity of such a conception, it fails to account for the variability of the renderings themselves. In *ELG*: 36–7.6d he considers the different ways of pronouncing French *r* in the word *courage*, and concludes that these quite distinct 'fluctuations' (as he calls them) point to the fact that the consonant in question is defined not by any positive features but by the differences that distinguish it internally from other consonants in the language. While this may be a valid point at the level of *langue*, however, it still does not explain what determines the occurrence of any particular fluctuation in *parole*, nor why certain theoretically possible fluctuations seldom or never occur.

In *ELG*: 31–3.5b a different comparison is invoked in order to throw light on what happens in *parole*. A sound, we are told, exists for a certain length of time, after which it ceases to exist. This is true of the sounds of music just as much as of the sounds of speech. But where is the piece of music to be located? (This is like inquiring into the whereabouts of the sound sequence *aka*.) The answer given is:

> Réellement cette composition n'existe que quand on l'exécute; mais considérer cette exécution comme son existence est faux. Son existence, c'est l'*identité* des exécutions. (*ELG*: 32)

Again, the answer is not completely convincing. For the performances (*exécutions*) are by no means identical, as musicians are well aware. But this in any case is a quite different answer from saying that the composition exists only by contrast with other pieces simultaneously available in the repertoire; or saying that it is identified by reference to something other than the performances, e.g. the written score.

In *ELG*: 37–40.6e yet another analogy is introduced to explain how the *figure vocale* can 'become' *une forme*:

> Une figure vocale devient une forme depuis l'instant crucial où on l'introduit dans le jeu de signes appelé langue, de la même façon qu'un *morceau d'étoffe* dormant à fond de cale devient un *signal* à l'instant où il est hissé 1° parmi d'autres signes hissés au même moment et concourant à une signification; 2° entre cent autres qui *auraient pu* être hissés [. . .] (*ELG*: 38)

Particularly significant here is the importance implicitly assigned to the act of *parole* in creating the sign. The piece of cloth is not a signal until the very moment of being hoisted, and even then it has to be hoisted in the right place in relation to other flags. It is their co-presence *as well as* the absence of other flags that *might* have appeared – but did not – which is crucial. What this brings to the theory of *parole* is the notion that the speaker is not just the performer of some pre-arranged programme (as the analogy of the musician unfortunately suggests) but the organizer of the activity that brings the sign into being as a sign. The flag lying in the ship's hold is not a *signal* at all but just a *morceau d'étoffe*. Here Saussure comes a step closer to Wittgenstein's view of *use* as a more fundamental semiological notion than either form or meaning, and at the same time to the integrationist axiom that 'what constitutes a sign is not given independently of the situation in which it occurs or of its material manifestation in that situation' (Harris 1996: 154).

An exactly parallel range of questions to those about the relationship between *figure vocale* and *forme* also arises in respect of meaning in *parole*. But here Saussure shows less inclination to grasp the nettle. In *ELG*: 74–5.25 he discusses the question of the meaning of the word *soleil* and claims that when Diogenes said to Alexander on one particular occasion 'Ôte-toi de mon soleil' (an acte of *parole*):

> il n'y a plus dans *soleil* rien de *soleil* si ce n'est l'opposition avec l'idée d'*ombre*; et cette idée d'*ombre* elle-même n'est que la négation combinée de celle de *lumière*, de *nuit parfaite*, de *pénombre*, etc., jointe à la négation de la chose illuminée par rapport à l'espace obscurci, etc. (*ELG*: 74)

To follow the point we have to accept the fiction that Diogenes spoke French: but, assuming this, we are invited to conclude that what a word means depends not on any positive idea associated with it, but, negatively, on its opposition with other words.

In this analysis there seems to be no semantic counterpart to the *figure vocale*, although logically there should be, given Saussure's binary conception of the linguistic sign. What emerges, however, is once again the integrationist idea that the speaker (Diogenes in this instance) makes the word *soleil* mean what it does by using it in a particular way in a particular context. Its value as a linguistic sign depends on its contrasting in this case with *ombre*, and owes nothing to the fact that in other contexts it can be used to designate the star at the centre of the solar system (as distinct from the planet Venus, etc.). If we carry over the flag analogy to the same example, it would seem that we are invited to see the word *soleil* itself as having no meaning until it is brought into use. The question that then arises for a theorist of *parole* is the following: *how* did the action of Diogenes in using the word as he did bring into play the opposition *soleil* / *ombre*, as distinct from any of the hundreds of other oppositions into which *soleil* might enter?

Saussure supplies no clear answer to this question; but it is clear what kind of answer he does *not* want to give, i.e. one in which the speaker associates the word positively with some feature or features of the actual situation. And yet it is clearly a feature of the situation (i.e. Alexander standing where he does) that makes the particular opposition *soleil* / *ombre* (as opposed to, say, *soleil* / *terre*) communicationally relevant. Saussure's vehement anti-nomenclaturism leads him to deny theoretically that the resources of *la langue* reflect in any way the structure of the external world. But in the case of Diogenes his own example speaks against him.

In *ELG*: 75–6.26 he points out that one and the same building may be called *maison*, *construction*, *bâtiment*, *immeuble*, etc. This proves, according to Saussure, that:

> l'existence des faits matériels est, aussi bien que l'existence des faits d'un autre ordre, indifférente à la langue. Tout le temps elle s'avance et se meut à l'aide de la formidable machine de ses catégories négatives, véritablement dégagées de tout fait concret, et par là même immédiatement prêtes à emmagasiner une idée quelconque qui vient s'ajouter aux précédentes. (*ELG*: 76)

But this reluctance to admit the relevance of *faits matériels* leads occasionally to Saussure tying himself in knots when it comes to explaining how words have meanings. The same note in which Saussure introduces the example of the flag (which does not become a *signal* until hoisted) begins with the observation that a linguistic form (*forme*) does not necessarily have a precise meaning (*sens*):

> Une forme est une figure vocale qui est pour la conscience des sujets parlants *déterminée*, c'est-à-dire à la fois existante et délimitée. Elle n'est rien de plus; comme elle n'est rien de moins. Elle n'a pas nécessairement «un sens» précis; mais elle est ressentie comme quelque chose qui *est*; qui de plus ne serait plus, ou ne serait plus la même chose, si on changeait quoi que ce soit à son exacte configuration. (*ELG*: 37)

It is not at all clear how this is to be reconciled with the emphasis Saussure places elsewhere on the indissoluble complementarity of both sides of the linguistic sign; in other words, it is not obvious why the form has to have an 'exact configuration' but not the meaning. It even conflicts with the statement later in the same note that in *la langue* 'il n'y a d'autre détermination que celle de l'idée par la forme et celle de la forme par l'idée' (*ELG*: 39). Nevertheless, Saussure reaffirms the indeterminacy of meaning when he goes on to discuss the meanings of moral terms such as *crime, passion, vertu, vice*, etc. These words presumably have well-defined forms, but Saussure denies the possibility of giving them precise definitions:

> il n'y a pas un seul objet matériel, nous l'avons vu, auquel s'applique exactement et exclusivement un mot; cela ne supprime pas l'existence de ces objets matériels. De même, il n'y a pas un seul fait moral, qu'on puisse exactement et exclusivement enfermer dans un certain terme; mais cela n'atteint pas un seul instant l'existence de ces faits moraux. (*ELG*: 37–8)

So 'moral facts' do exist, it would seem, independently of language, just as physical objects do. Furthermore, according to Saussure, it is perfectly possible to investigate the connexions between words and 'moral facts', just as between words and physical objects:

> Ce qui peut être proposé comme une question digne d'examen, c'est jusqu'où le mot correspond à un fait moral déterminé, de même qu'on est obligé de rechercher jusqu'où l'idée d'*ombre* par exemple correspond à un fait matériel déterminé. (*ELG*: 38)

But then comes the disclaimer:

> Les deux séries d'investigations ne relèvent plus de la linguistique. (*ELG*: 38)

This may be true if linguistics is envisaged in the narrowest sense as confined solely to the study of *la langue* qua system. That, however, is hardly the *point de vue* of the individual speaker. In everyday *parole* words have to be used in accordance with the dictates of the particular circumstances in which they are used, whatever the theorist of *langue* may say. One of the constant demands in *parole* requires reference to objects, persons, events, relations and classes in that external world, and reference to these as actually existing *realia* present here and now. Language is thus called upon to go beyond the level of generality that may easily satisfy the lexicographer or the grammarian. It must focus on the specifics of particular situations. In those situations, speakers 'know what they are talking about' because what they are talking about can be seen, or touched, or pointed to, or picked up, or tasted and subjected to all kinds of practical examination which go far beyond the limits of verbal description. When the stall-holder in the market shouts his wares, he may well use such common words as *grapes*, *carrots*, and so on. And in so doing he is doubtless relying to some extent on potential buyers' general concept of what a grape is and what a carrot is. Nevertheless, he is not talking about grapes and carrots in general, nor even the grapes and carrots on the next stall, but the grapes and carrots he is selling on *his* stall: and these you have to inspect for yourself. In short, it is the anchorage of words to the evidence of the senses that makes them mean what they do in such cases. So at the level of *parole* a theory of language has to come to terms with important retractions concerning Saussure's rasher claims for linguistics in general (e.g. 'elle est placée à l'extrême opposite des sciences qui peuvent partir de la donnée des sens', *ELG*: 19–20). In *parole*, on the contrary, what the senses deliver is basic, and words have to latch on to it as best they can.

By the same token, it is very relevant to any discussion of moral issues to determine how such words as *crime*, *passion*, *vertu*, *vice*, etc. are being used by the discussants, for this is directly pertinent to the arguments that are brought to bear on the subject. Nor would it be regarded as other than evasion if any of the parties stoutly refused to clarify the issue and claimed that since these words had a determinate form there was no need to supply any elucidation of their meaning. An investigation of *parole*, presumably, would have to include some account of how, in practice, words can be – and commonly are – employed metalinguistically to define other words. One might add that an even more basic requirement for a theory of *parole* making contact with 'the real world' is, at the very least, some account of the difference between a true statement and a false statement, since truth is an everyday concept. Without it the commonplace business of verbal intercourse between one individual and another, even in the most linguistically restricted of communities, could hardly proceed. No such account is hinted at in the three Courses that Saussure delivered in Geneva in the years 1907 to 1911. There the question of truth is not even mentioned. But we find an initial recognition of the problem in Engler: 3312.1, where there is a brief mention of a 'third' element in the semiological complex (i.e. additional to the *forme* and the *sens*), belonging to the outside world:

> le cas où il y a un *troisième* élément incontestable dans l'association psychologique du sème, la conscience qu'il s'applique à un être extérieur [. . .] assez défini en lui-même pour *échapper* à la loi générale du signe.

So there is, after all, a question about how the internal composition of the linguistic sign relates to what lies outside *la langue*.

Furthermore, even when what is spoken of is not actually present, it presumably falls within the province of a *linguistique de la parole* to recognize that the background to linguistic communication in most communities is provided by a taken-for-granted body of knowledge about what the 'real world' is like and what 'really happened' in the past. The notion that words may have no actual connexion to such realities is countenanced only in special cases where doubt arises for some reason about the facts of the case. Thus while it may be questioned whether any god called *Zeus* ever existed, or even any poet called *Homer*, no one seriously questions the existence of Julius Caesar, let alone Adolf Hitler. And if an argument should arise about whether the bird perched on the fence is a robin, few would dream of dismissing the question as no more than an argument about words. Looking up the word *robin* in the *Concise Oxford Dictionary* would in any case be a curious way of trying to settle the matter: the illustrations in *The Observer's Book of Birds* are likely to be much more helpful. In short, from the *point de vue* of the individual engaged in the social praxis of communication, the need to establish correlations between words and the external world is not merely constant but pressing. But those are precisely the correlations which find no place in the conception of *la langue* as an organized system of internal oppositions residing in what Saussure liked to call 'the collective soul' (Engler: 1285).

At the level of *parole*, the theorist will also need to take account of the fact that Bill Smith's English is never exactly the same as his neighbour Fred Jones's, even though Smith and Jones usually have no communicational difficulty at all in carrying on a conversation, and think of themselves as carrying it on 'in English'. In other words, whereas idiolectal variation – as distinct from geographical variation – can be, and is, ignored in the linguist's correlation between *langue* and collectivity, it cannot be suppressed in the analysis of *parole*.

This in turn is only one aspect of the greater complexity of *parole*. The communication situation – except in certain quasi-ritualized cases – is not a ready-made framework obligingly constructed to accommodate the shape of the verbal resources available, in the way the pieces of a child's puzzle fit together to make just the pattern or picture they were always designed to make when correctly assembled. On the contrary, the variety of actual communication situations is infinitely open-ended, and the communicational task of the participants requires a constantly creative effort in which linguistic signs must always be stretched, modified, supplemented and adapted to meet the requirements of the circumstances. Those efforts will depend to some extent on how well the speakers know one another; for we do not talk to acquaintances in the same way we talk to strangers. All these things are part of the 'social reality' of *langage*.

Given that social reality, there is no question of operating in *parole* with units that are already perfectly delimited by reciprocal contrast with others (as in the idealized static picture of *la langue* conjured up by the modern dictionary). For the circumstances of *parole* are such as to restrict, in ways unstated and perhaps unstatable, the contrasts that are relevant to interpretation. That is why speech and writing are so fraught with potential misunderstandings at every turn. The *imperfections* of a community's linguistic equipment are as much the concern of the theoretical linguist as its successes. Saussure recognizes this implicitly when he observes in *ELG*: 77 how 'perfectly chimerical' is any enterprise attempting to give a definitive list of the meanings of a single word. Recognition of that fundamental indeterminacy and its implications would have had to be the cornerstone of Saussure's *linguistique de la parole*. For only thus is it theoretically possible to accommodate the pragmatic give-and-take required of language in the tough and rumble of everyday communication. That in turn would have involved Saussure in a radical recasting of the relationship between *langue* and *parole*. For if Saussure took seriously his own affirmed conviction that:

> primordialement il existe des points de vue; sinon il est simplement impossible de saisir un fait de langage (*ELG*: 19.2b)

then he must also have realized the need to rethink the connexions between the *point de vue* of the individual and the *point de vue* of the collectivity.

That there is indeed a *point de vue* of the individual is scarcely open to doubt, even if it varies from individual to individual; for few of us doubt our own ability to communicate linguistically with (some) others. But whether there is any one collective *point de vue* embracing that of many individuals can certainly be doubted for all kinds of reasons – at least, assuming we dismiss without further ado such obfuscations as the *âme collective*. Once these are thrown out, it becomes incumbent on the linguistic theorist to rethink the dependencies involved. Instead of *parole* being a somewhat hit-or-miss implementation of the individual's knowledge of *langue*, *langue* re-emerges as a somewhat hit-or-miss extrapolation from the manifold complexities of *langage*.

*   *   *

It is notoriously difficult to establish any smooth progression in the development of Saussure's ideas. Engler once observed that on comparing the Third Course with the aphorisms that survive in notes from about 1897 to 1900, one might conclude that 'Saussure was further advanced before 1900 than he was in 1911' – 'which,' he added, 'would be an absurd conclusion' (Engler 1975: 837). But not quite as absurd as Engler appears to think. There are thinkers who take a long time to systematize into a coherent whole ideas which they may have had in an unsystematized or only partially systematized form for many years. This seems to have been the case with Saussure who, according to his own account, had been reflecting on problems of general linguistics for many years before ever having to lecture on the subject. It is consequently not surprising that, especially given the fragmentary nature of the documentary evidence available, a 'more advanced' idea may appear to antedate a 'less advanced' attempt at systematic statement. This is neither absurd nor inexplicable. In fact, the *CLG* recognizes exactly that point in connexion with the arbitrariness of the linguistic sign:

> il est souvent plus aisé de découvrir une vérité que de lui assigner la place qui lui revient. (*CLG*: 100)

In their preface to the 1916 edition of the *CLG*, Bally and Sechehaye hit the nail on the head when they described Saussure as one of those thinkers 'qui se renouvellent sans cesse'. What has been presented above is a manifestly hypothetical and incomplete sketch of how that renewal might have worked out in Saussure's attempt to deal with a *linguistique de la parole*. But although hypothetical, it is based on specific clues contained in the surviving manuscript material, and confronts problems already hinted at in the Third Course and elsewhere. The interesting question is whether Saussure had, before he died, worked out a solution to the problem of relating two apparently irreconcilable aspects of everyday linguistic experience.

On the one hand, every act of speech seems to the individual speaker unique, a specific expression of his or her intentions in a particular situation (and hence not to be decontextualized). On the other, what is said always seems to presuppose by its very mode of expression a potential decontextualization, the possibility of its being reported or written down, and hence its delivery to an indefinitely large collectivity of individuals not present on the original occasion. So words both do and do not belong to their speakers. Unless this Gordian knot can be tied in the first place it can never be cut; and there can be no *science du langage*.

Let us leave the last word to Saussure (much as he might in the end have repudiated the notion that in matters of *langage* there can be any 'last word'):

> Celui qui se place devant l'objet complexe qu'est le langage pour en faire son étude abordera nécessairement cet objet par tel ou tel côté, qui ne sera jamais tout le langage en le supposant très bien choisi, et qui peut s'il est moins bien choisi n'être plus même de l'ordre linguistique ou représenter une confusion de points de vue inadmissible par la suite.
>
> Or il y a ceci de primordial et d'inhérent à la nature du langage que, par quelque côté qu'on essaie de l'attaquer – justifiable ou non –, on ne pourra jamais y découvrir d'*individus*, c'est-à-dire d'êtres (ou de quantités) déterminés en eux-mêmes sur lesquels s'opère *ensuite* une généralisation. Mais il y a D'ABORD la généralisation, et il n'y a rien en dehors d'elle: or, comme la généralisation suppose un *point de vue* qui sert de critère, les premières et les plus irréductibles entités dont peut s'occuper le linguiste sont déjà le produit d'une opération latente de l'esprit. Il en résulte immédiatement que toute la linguistique revient non pas [ ] mais matériellement à la discussion des points de vue légitimes: sans quoi il n'y a pas d'objet. (*ELG*: 22–3.3a)

This is scarcely the *profession de foi* of a nominalist; at least, not a nominalist of the traditional ilk. Nor is it that of a structuralist; at least, not a typical structuralist of the kind often so praised or pilloried in the twentieth century. For here what takes priority is the claim that *points de vue* are themselves realities of everyday existence, not philosophical abstractions conjured up by clever processes of verbal manipulation. Moreover, *necessary* realities: necessary as such for any kind of linguistic activity, whether by linguists or by those whose linguistic activities – including their own – linguists set out to investigate.

Prior to 1996, without access to the newly discovered additions to the Saussurean manuscript corpus, none of Saussure's interpreters could have had much of an inkling of the extent to which doubts about the determinacy of the linguistic sign – and hence the theoretical viability of the hypothesized system which houses it – had already entered Saussure's thinking. For nowhere else do we find such trenchant formulations of a recognition that the linguistic continuum in which participants are obliged to engage varies from one moment to the next. This Heraclitan view of language stands in sharp contrast to many of the rigid theses frequently attributed to Saussure throughout the course of the twentieth century. It opens up links with more recent and more flexible approaches to developing a fuller understanding of human linguistic activities.

References

Aarsleff, H. (1970), 'The history of linguistics and Professor Chomsky', *Language*, 46, pp. 570–85.

Aarsleff, H. (1982), *From Locke to Saussure. Essays on the Study of Language and Intellectual History*, London: Athlone.

Ambrose-Grillet, J. (ed.) (1978), *Glossary of Transformational Grammar*, Rowley, MA: Newbury.

Bally, Ch. (1937), 'Synchronie et diachronie', *Vox Romanica*, 2, pp. 345–52.

Bally, Ch. (1940), 'L'arbitraire du signe: valeur et signification', *Le Français Moderne*, 3, pp. 193–206.

Bally, Ch. (1965), *Linguistique générale et linguistique française*, 4th edn, Berne: Francke.

Barthes, R. (1964a), 'Présentation', *Communications*, 4, pp. 1–3.

Barthes, R. (1964b), *Éléments de sémiologie*, Paris: Seuil.

Barthes, R. (1967), *Système de la mode*, Paris: Seuil.

Barthes, R. (1973), 'Saussure, le signe, la démocratie', in Barthes 1994, pp. 1584–7.

Barthes, R. (1993), *Œuvres complètes*, Vol. I, ed. E. Marty, Paris: Seuil.

Barthes, R. (1994), *Œuvres complètes*, Vol. II, ed. E. Marty, Paris: Seuil.

Barthes, R. (1995), *Œuvres complètes*, Vol. III, ed. E. Marty, Paris: Seuil.

Baskin, W. (1959), *F. de Saussure, Course in General Linguistics*, New York: Philosophical Library.

Bateson, F. W. (1968), 'Linguistics and literary criticism'. Reprinted in *Essays in Critical Dissent*, London: Longman, 1972. Page references are to the reprint.

Benveniste, E. (1939), 'Nature du signe linguistique', *Acta Linguistica*, 1, 1939, pp. 23–9. Reprinted in Benveniste 1966, pp. 49–55. Page references are to the latter.

Benveniste, E. (1966), *Problèmes de linguistique générale I*, Paris: Gallimard.

Benveniste, E. (1974), *Problèmes de linguistique générale II*, Paris: Gallimard.

Bloomfield, L. (1914), *An Introduction to the Study of Language*, New York: Holt and London: Bell.

Bloomfield, L. (1922), Review of Sapir, *The Classical Weekly*, 15, pp. 142–3. Reprinted in Hockett 1987, B13. Pages references are to the latter.

Bloomfield, L. (1923), Review of Saussure, *Modern Language Journal*, 8, pp. 317–19. Reprinted in Hockett 1987, B17. Page references are to the latter.

Bloomfield, L. (1927a), Review of Jespersen's *Philosophy of Grammar*, *Journal of English and Germanic Philology*, 26, pp. 444–6. Reprinted in Hockett 1987, B23. Page references are to the latter.

Bloomfield, L. (1927b), 'On recent work in general linguistics', *Modern Philology*, 25, pp. 211–30. Reprinted in Hockett 1987, B28. Page references are to the latter.

Bloomfield, L. (1933), *Language*, New York: Holt. British edition, London: Allen & Unwin, 1935. Page references are to the latter.

Boas, F. (1911), *Handbook of American Indian Languages, Part 1*, Washington, DC: Government Printing Office.

Bolton, W. F. (1984), *The Language of 1984*, Oxford: Blackwell.

Bourciez, E. (1937), *Précis de phonétique française*, 8th edn, Paris: Klincksieck. References are to paragraph numbers.

Burger, A. (1961), 'Significations et valeur du suffixe verbale français -*e*', *Cahiers F. de Saussure*, 18, pp. 5–15.

Calvet, L.-J. (1975), *Pour et contre Saussure*, Paris: Payot.

Cassirer, E. (1944), *An Essay on Man*, New Haven: Yale University Press.

Chomsky, A. N. (1957), *Syntactic Structures*, The Hague: Mouton.

Chomsky, A. N. (1959), 'A review of B. F. Skinner's *Verbal Behavior*', *Language*, 35, pp. 26–58.

Chomsky, A. N. (1961), 'Some methodological remarks on generative grammar', *Word*, 17, pp. 219–39. Reprinted as 'Degrees of grammaticalness' in J. A Fodor and J. J. Katz (eds), *The Structure of Language. Readings in the Philosophy of Language*, Englewood Cliffs: Prentice-Hall, 1964, pp. 384–99. Page references are to the latter.

Chomsky, A. N. (1963), 'Formal properties of grammars', in R. D. Luce, R. R. Bush and E. Galanter (eds), *Handbook of Mathematical Psychology*, New York: Wiley, pp. 322–418.

Chomsky, A. N. (1964), 'Current issues in linguistic theory', in J. A. Fodor and J. J. Katz (eds), *The Structure of Language. Readings in the Philosophy of Language*, Englewood Cliffs: Prentice-Hall, pp. 50–118.

Chomsky, A. N. (1965), *Aspects of the Theory of Syntax*, Cambridge, MA: MIT Press.

Chomsky, A. N. (1966), *Cartesian Linguistics*, New York: Harper & Row.

Chomsky, A. N. (1968), *Language and Mind*, New York: Harcourt, Brace & World.

Chomsky, A. N. (1986), *Knowledge of Language*, New York: Praeger.

Chomsky, A. N. (1991), *Deterring Democracy*, London: Verso.

Culler, J. (1986), *Saussure*, 2nd edn, London: Fontana.

Davis, H. G. (2001), *Words. An Integrational Approach*, London: Curzon.

Davis, H. G. (2003), 'Why rethink linguistics?', in H. G. Davis and T. J. Taylor (eds), *Rethinking Linguistics*, London: RoutledgeCurzon, pp. 1–15.

Derrida, J. (1967), *De la grammatologie*, Paris: Minuit.

Derrida, J. (1972a), *Marges: de la philosophie*, Paris: Minuit.

Derrida, J. (1972b), *Positions*, Paris: Minuit.

Dewey, J. (1938), *Logic. The Theory of Inquiry*, New York: Holt.

Dinneen, F. P. (1967), *An Introduction to General Linguistics*, Washington, DC: Georgetown University Press.

Ducrot, O. (1968), *Le structuralisme en linguistique*, Paris: Seuil.

Eco, U. (1976), *A Theory of Semiotics*, Bloomington: Indiana University Press.

Engler, R. (1975) 'European structuralism: Saussure', in T. A. Sebeok, (ed.), *Current Trends in Linguistics*, vol. 13, *History of Linguistics*, The Hague / Paris: Mouton, pp. 829–86.

Firth, J. R. (1950), 'Personality and language in society', *The Sociological Review*, 62. Reprinted in J. R. Firth, *Papers in Linguistics 1934–1951*, London: Oxford University Press, 1957, pp. 177–89. Page references are to the latter.

Fischer-Jørgensen, E. (1966), 'Form and substance in glossematics', *Acta Linguistica Hafniensia*, 10, pp. 1–33.

Gadet, F. (1987), *Saussure. Une science de la langue*, Paris: Presses Universitaires de France.

Gleason, H. A., Jr. (1955), *An Introduction to Descriptive Linguistics*, New York: Holt, Rinehart & Winston.

Godel, R. (1961), 'L'école saussurienne de Genève', in C. Mohrmann, A. Sommerfelt and J. Whatmough (eds), *Trends in European and American Linguistics 1930–1960*, Utrecht: Spectrum, pp. 294–9.

Godel, R. (1966), 'De la théorie du signe aux termes du système', *Cahiers F. de Saussure*, 22, pp. 53–68.

Guillaume, G. (1948), *Leçons de linguistique 1947–1948 Série C*, Québec: Presses de l'Université Laval.

Hall, R. A., Jr. (1963), *Idealism in Romance Linguistics*, Ithaca: Cornell University Press.

Hamp, E. P. (ed.) (1957), *A Glossary of American Technical Linguistic Usage 1925–1950*, Utrecht: Spectrum.

Harris, R. (1981), *The Language Myth*, London: Duckworth.

Harris, R. (1987), *Reading Saussure*, London: Duckworth.

Harris, R. (1996), *Signs, Language and Communication*, London: Routledge.

Harris, R. (2000), *Rethinking Writing*, London: Athlone.

Hatzfeld, A., A. Darmesteter and A. Thomas (eds) (1892–1900), *Dictionnaire général de la langue française*, Paris: Delagrave.

Hill, A. A. (1958), *Introduction to Linguistic Structures*, New York: Harcourt, Brace.

Hjelmslev, L. T. (1942), 'Langue et parole', *Cahiers Ferdinand de Saussure*, 2, pp. 29–44.

Hjelmslev, L. T. (1961), *Prolegomena to a Theory of Language*, tr. F. J. Whitfield, rev. edn, Madison: University of Wisconsin Press.

Hockett, C. F. (1958), *A Course in Modern Linguistics*, New York: Macmillan.

Hockett, C. F. (ed.) (1987), *A Leonard Bloomfield Anthology*, abridged edn, Chicago: University of Chicago Press.

Hodge, R. and G. Kress (1988), *Social Semiotics*, Oxford: Polity.

Hoijer, H. (ed.) (1954), *Language in Culture*, Chicago: University of Chicago Press.

Holdcroft, D. (1991), *Saussure. Signs, System and Arbitrariness*, Cambridge: Cambridge University Press.

Howells, C. (1998), *Derrida. Deconstruction from Phenomenology to Ethics*, Cambridge: Polity.

Hutton, C. M. (1999), *Linguistics and the Third Reich*, London: Routledge.

Hymes, D. H. (1985), 'Epilogue', in D. G. Mandelbaum (ed.), *Selected Writings of Edward Sapir in Language, Culture and Personality*, Berkeley, CA: University of California Press, pp. 598–600.

Iordan, I. and J. Orr (1970), *An Introduction to Romance Linguistics, its Schools and Scholars*, 2nd rev. edn, Oxford: Blackwell.

Jakobson, R. O. (1939), 'Signe zéro', in *Mélanges de linguistique offerts à Charles Bally*, Genève: Georg, pp.143–52.

Jakobson, R. O. (1942a), 'Six leçons sur le son et le sens', in *Selected Writings Vol. VIII*, Berlin: Mouton de Gruyter, 1988, pp. 317–90.

Jakobson, R. O. (1942b), 'La théorie saussurienne en rétrospection', in *Selected Writings Vol. VIII*, Berlin: Mouton de Gruyter, 1988, pp. 391–435.

Jakobson, R. O. (1956), 'Two aspects of language and two types of aphasic disturbances', in R. Jakobson and M. Halle, *Fundamentals of Language*, The Hague: Mouton, pp. 52–82.

Jakobson, R. O. (1959), 'Zeichen und System der Sprache', in *Selected Writings Vol. II*, Berlin: Mouton de Gruyter, 1971, pp. 272–9.

Jakobson, R. O. (1962), 'Retrospect', in *Selected Writings Vol. I*, Berlin: Mouton de Gruyter, 2nd edn, 1971, pp. 631–58.

Jakobson, R. O. (1971), 'Retrospect', in *Selected Writings Vol. II*, Berlin: Mouton de Gruyter, pp. 711–22.

Jameson, F. (1972), *The Prison-House of Language. A Critical Account of Structuralism and Russian Formalism*, Princeton: Princeton University Press.

Jespersen, O. (1916), 'Compte rendu du *Cours de linguistique générale* de F. de Saussure' (French translation of the review originally published in *Nordisk tidsskrift for filologi*, series 4, vol. 6, pp. 37– 41), in O. Jespersen, *Linguistica*, Copenhagen: Levin & Munksgaard, 1933, pp. 109–15. Page references are to the latter.

Jespersen, O. (1924), *The Philosophy of Grammar*, London: Allen & Unwin.

Johnson, C. (1997), *Derrida. The Scene of Writing*, London: Phoenix.

Joos, M. (ed.) (1957), *Readings in Linguistics I*, Washington, DC: American Council of Learned Societies.

Joseph, J. E. (1990), 'Ideologizing Saussure: Bloomfield's and Chomsky's readings of the *Cours de linguistique générale*', in J. E. Joseph and T. J. Taylor (eds), *Ideologies of Language*, London: Routledge, pp. 51–78.

Koerner, E. F. K. (1999), 'An hour with Noam Chomsky', in *Linguistic Historiography. Projects and Prospects*, Amsterdam: Benjamins, pp. 210–16.

Lacan, J. (1953), 'Fonction et champ de la parole et du langage en psychanalyse', in *Écrits I*, Paris: Seuil, 1966, pp. 110–208.

Lacan, J. (1957), 'L'instance de la lettre dans l'inconscient ou la raison depuis Freud', in *Écrits I*, Paris: Seuil, 1966, pp. 249–89.

Lacan, J. (1974), *Télévision*, Paris: Seuil.

Leach, E. (1973), 'Structuralism in social anthropology', in Robey (ed.) 1973, pp. 37–56.

Lemaire, A. (1977), *Jacques Lacan*, tr. D. Macey, London: Routledge & Kegan Paul.

Leroy, M. (1963), *Les grands courants de la linguistique moderne*, Bruxelles: Presses Universitaires de Bruxelles.

Lévi-Strauss, C. (1945), 'L'analyse structurale en linguistique et en anthropologie', *Word*, 1, no. 2, pp. 1–21. Reprinted in *Anthropologie structurale*, Paris: Plon, 1958, pp. 37–62. Quotations are from and page references to the latter.

Lévi-Strauss, C. (1949), 'Histoire et ethnologie', *Revue de Métaphysique et de Morale*, 54, no. 3–4, pp. 363–91. Reprinted in *Anthropologie structurale*, Paris: Plon, 1958, pp. 3–33. Quotations are from and page references to the latter.

Lévi-Strauss, C. (1951), 'Language and the analysis of social laws', *American Anthropologist*, n.s. 53, no. 2, pp. 155–63. Reprinted as Ch. 3 of *Structural Anthropology*, Harmondsworth: Penguin, 1968. Quotations are from and page references to the latter.

Lévi-Strauss, C. (1953), 'Social structure', in A. L. Kroeber (ed.), *Anthropology Today*, Chicago: University of Chicago Press, pp. 524–53. Reprinted as Ch. 15 of *Structural Anthropology*, Harmondsworth: Penguin, 1968. Quotations are from and page references to the latter.

Lévi-Strauss, C. (1955), 'The structural study of myth', *Journal of American Folklore*, 78, pp. 428–44. Reprinted as Ch. 11 of *Structural Anthropology*, Harmondsworth: Penguin, 1968. Quotations are from and page references to the latter.

Lévi-Strauss, C. (1956), 'Postface au chapitres III et IV', in *Anthropologie structurale*, Paris: Plon, 1958, pp. 93–110.

Lévi-Strauss, C. (1960), 'Le champ de l'anthropologie', in *Anthropologie structurale II*, Paris: Plon, 1973, pp. 11–44.

Lévi-Strauss, C. (1976), 'Les leçons de la linguistique', in R. Jakobson, *Six leçons sur le son et le sens*, Paris: Minuit. Reprinted in *Le regard éloigné*, Paris: Plon, 1983, pp. 191–201. Page references are to the latter.

Lyons, J. (1977), *Chomsky*, 2nd edn, Hassocks: Harvester.

Malinowski, B. (1923), 'The problem of meaning in primitive languages', in Ogden and Richards 1923, pp. 296–336.

Malinowski, B. (1947), *Freedom and Civilization*, London: Allen & Unwin.

Martinet, A. (1960), *Éléments de linguistique générale*, Paris: Colin.

Matejka, L. (1986), 'On the first Russian prolegomena to semiotics', Appendix I in Voloshinov 1929, pp. 161–74.

Meillet, A. (1916), 'Compte rendu du *Cours de linguistique générale* de F. de Saussure', *Bulletin de la Société de Linguistique de Paris*, 20, no. 65, pp. 32–6.

Mel'chuk, I. A. (1985), 'Three main features, seven basic principles, and eleven most important results of Roman Jakobson's morphological research', in K. Pomorska and S. Rudy (eds), *Verbal Art, Verbal Sign, Verbal Time*, Oxford: Blackwell, pp. 178–200.

Merleau-Ponty, M. (1953), 'Le problème de la parole', in *Résumés de cours, Collège de France, 1952–1960*, Paris: Gallimard, 1968, pp. 32–42.

Miller, G. A. (1962), *Psychology. The Science of Mental Life*. Page references are to the British edition, Harmondsworth: Penguin, 1966.

Mounin, G. (1968), *Saussure, ou le structuraliste sans le savoir*, Paris: Seghers.

Newmeyer, F. J. (1986), *The Politics of Linguistics*, Chicago: University of Chicago Press.

Ogden, C. K. (1930), *Basic English*, London: Kegan Paul, Trench, Trubner. Page references are to the 9th edn, 1944.

Ogden, C. K. and I. A. Richards (1923), *The Meaning of Meaning*, London: Routledge & Kegan Paul. Page references are to the 10th edn, 1949.

Orwell, G. (1944), 'As I please', in *The Collected Essays, Journalism and Letters of George Orwell*, vol. III, London: Penguin, 1970, pp. 105–8.

Orwell, G. (1949), *Nineteen Eighty-Four*, London: Secker & Warburg.

Paul, H. (1886), *Principien der Sprachgeschichte*, 2nd edn, Halle: Niemeyer. Tr. H. A. Strong, *Principles of the History of Language*, London: Longmans, Green, 1891.

Pettit, P. (1975), *The Concept of Structuralism: A Critical Analysis*, Berkeley, CA: University of California Press.

Piaget, J. (1968), *Le structuralisme*, Paris: Presses Universitaires de France.

Pinker, S. (1994), *The Language Instinct*, New York: Morrow.

Quine, W. V. O. (1953), *From a Logical Point of View*, Cambridge, MA: Harvard University Press.

Robey, D. (ed.) (1973), *Structuralism: An Introduction*, Oxford: Clarendon.

Sampson, G. (1979), *Liberty and Language*, Oxford: Oxford University Press.

Sampson, G. (1980), *Schools of Linguistics*, London: Hutchinson.

Sanders, C. (1979), *Cours de linguistique générale de Saussure*, Paris: Hachette.

Sapir, E. (1921), *Language*, New York: Harcourt, Brace.

Sapir, E. (1928), 'The status of linguistics as a science', in D. G. Mandelbaum (ed.), *Selected Writings of Edward Sapir in Language, Culture and Personality*, Berkeley, CA: University of California Press, pp. 160–6.

Sartre, J.-P. (1966), *L'existentialisme est un humanisme*, Paris: Gallimard.

Sechehaye, A. (1908), *Programmes et méthodes de la linguistique théorique. Psychologie du langage*, Paris: Champion.

Sechehaye, A. (1939), 'Évolution organique et évolution contingentielle', in *Mélanges de linguistique offerts à Charles Bally*, Genève: Georg, pp. 19–29.

Sechehaye, A. (1940), 'Les trois linguistiques saussuriennes', *Vox Romanica*, 5, pp. 1–48.

Siertsema, B. (1965), *A Study of Glossematics*, 2nd edn, The Hague: Nijhoff.

Sperber, D. (1979), 'Claude Lévi-Strauss', in Sturrock (ed.) 1979, pp. 19–51.

Stalin, J. (1954), *Marxism and Problems of Linguistics*, Moscow: Foreign Languages Publishing House.

Sturrock, J. (ed.) (1979), *Structuralism and Since. From Lévi-Strauss to Derrida*, Oxford: Oxford University Press.

Szymura, J. (1988), 'Bronislaw Malinowski's "Ethnographic theory of language" ', in R. Harris (ed.), *Linguistic Thought in England 1914–1945*, London: Duckworth, pp. 106–31.

Tallis, R. (1988), *Not Saussure. A Critique of Post-Saussurean Literary Theory*, London: Macmillan.

Tobin, Y. (1990), *Semiotics and Linguistics*, London: Longman.

Tynjanov, J. and R. O. Jakobson (1928), 'Problems in the study of language and literature', in K. Pomorska and S. Rudy (eds), *Verbal Art, Verbal Sign, Verbal Time*, Oxford: Blackwell, 1985, pp. 25–7.

Trubetzkoy, N. S. (1939), *Grundzüge der Phonologie*, Prague: Travaux du Cercle Linguistique de Prague. 4th edn, Göttingen: Vandenhoeck & Ruprecht, 1967.

Uldall, H. J. (1944), 'Speech and writing', *Acta Linguistica*, 4, pp. 11–16.

Voloshinov, V. N. (1929), *Marxism and the Philosophy of Language*, tr. L. Matejka and I. R. Titunik, Cambridge, MA: Harvard University Press, 1986.

Wartburg, W. von (1939), 'Betrachtungen über das Verhältnis von historischer und deskriptiver Sprachwissenschaft', in *Mélanges de linguistique offerts à Charles Bally*, Genève: Georg, pp. 3–18.

Wellek, R. and A. Warren (1962), *Theory of Literature*, 3rd edn, New York: Harcourt, Brace & World.

Wells, R. S. (1947), 'De Saussure's system of linguistics', *Word*, 3, pp. 1–31.

White, R. W. (1959), 'Motivation reconsidered: the concept of competence', *Psychological Review*, 66, pp. 297–333.

Whitney, W. D. (1867), *Language and the Study of Language*, New York: Scribner.

Whitney, W. D. (1875), *The Life and Growth of Language*, New York: Appleton.

Whorf, B. L. (1939), 'The relation of habitual thought and behavior to language', in J. B. Carroll (ed.), *Language, Thought and Reality. Selected Writings of Benjamin Lee Whorf*, Cambridge, MA: MIT Press, 1956, pp. 134–59.

Wolf, G. and N. Love (1993), 'Integrational linguistics: an introductory survey'. In *Actes du XVe Congrès International des Linguistes*, Quebec: Presses de l'Université Laval, vol. 1, pp. 313–20.

Index